POLICE-COMMUNITY RELATIONS

THIRD EDITION

POLICE-COMMUNITY RELATIONS

CRISIS IN OUR TIME

By

HOWARD H. EARLE, D.P.A.

Visiting Professor
California State University
Los Angeles, California
Assistant Sheriff (rtd)
Los Angeles County Sheriff's Department

Foreword by

William M. Conroy

Inspector (rtd)
Los Angeles County Sheriff's Department

CHARLES C THOMAS • PUBLISHER
Springfield • Illinois • U.S.A.

Published and Distributed Throughout the World by

CHARLES C THOMAS • PUBLISHER

Bannerstone House

301-327 East Lawrence Avenue, Springfield, Illinois, U.S.A.

1967, 1970, and 1980, by CHARLES C THOMAS • PUBLISHER

ISBN 0-398-03900-3

Library of Congress Catalog Card Number: 79-10696

First Edition, 1967
Second Edition, First Printing, 1970
Second Edition, Second Printing, 1970
Second Edition, Third Printing, 1970
Second Edition, Fourth Printing, 1972
Second Edition, Fifth Printing, 1972
Second Edition, Sixth Printing, 1973
Second Edition, Seventh Printing, 1974
Second Edition, Eighth Printing, 1976
Third Edition, 1980

With THOMAS BOOKS careful attention is given to all details of manufacturing and design. It is the Publisher's desire to present books that are satisfactory as to their physical qualities and artistic possibilities and appropriate for their particular use. THOMAS BOOKS will be true to those laws of quality that assure a good name and good will.

Library of Congress Cataloging in Publication Data

    Earle, Howard H
        Police-community relations

        Bibliography: p.
        Includes index.
        1. Public relations — Police.   I.   Title.
    HV7936.P8E2   1979   363.2   79-10696
    ISBN 0-398-03900-3

Printed in the United States of America

WM-6

FOREWORD

In this chaotic age, marked by fear, uncertainty, and discontent, coupled with continuing public disorder and violent attacks against constituted authority, the acute need for establishing, maintaining, and expanding a meaningful relationship between law enforcement and the community has never before been more urgently apparent. It must, however, be based on mutual respect, patience, and understanding if we are to overcome the attitudes and conditions which continue to create, influence, and inflame a "crisis in our time."

Police-community relations (PCR) is an ever-expanding, ever-changing, extremely complex subject. This penetrating and authoritative analysis, while comprehensive and concise, is captivating and intriguing, yet practical. It provides a wealth of new information that will prove invaluable to students and practitioners alike in evaluating the past, guiding the action of the present, and planning for the future. It is hard-core PCR—at its best. For example, chapters covering Community Crime Prevention, Diversion, and the provocative concept of the Z-Cop illustrate some of the innovation and imagination taking place today in the field of professional law enforcement.

To present this study as a practical art, the publisher selected the one author who, professionally and academically, is preeminently qualified—Dr. Howard Earle. He is both a theorist and a practitioner who has always been "ahead of his time."

Dr. Earle has received, from the University of Southern California, his bachelor of science, master of science, and doctoral degrees in public administration. He is on the teaching staff at the University of Southern California, California State University, Long Beach, and East Los Angeles College and is presently a Visiting Professor at California State University, Los Angeles.

A veteran of the Los Angeles County Sheriff's Department, he began his career in 1951 as a deputy. His rapid advancement up through the ranks reached a pinnacle when, in 1972, following a competitive Civil Service examination, he was appointed Assistant Sheriff of this 7,000 man department—the largest sheriff's department in the world, and the fifth largest law enforcement agency in the United States. The innovative techniques and systems which he has developed in many different areas for his department have attracted nationwide attention and acclaim. Many of these new methods have been adopted by numerous law enforcement agencies throughout the country. His historical work on consolidation of police services serves as a model for agencies throughout the world.

For a period of eight years he was Coordinator of Community and Human Relations for his department. In addition, he was Chairman of the Police-Community Relations Committee of the California Peace Officers Association and served as the first President of the Southern California Police-Community Relations Officers Association.

During the past several years he has personally examined the PCR and training programs of thirty-seven foreign countries on six continents. His taped interviews are in constant demand and are being reproduced commercially.

Dr. Earle recently completed an in-depth analysis of President Carter's proposals on criminal justice, and he has been personally commended for this work.

His dedication to crime prevention and new approaches has brought occasional criticism from traditionalists, but also widespread acclaim from public and private sectors deeply committed to finding "a better way to go."

His findings about the *true* effect of high stress police recruit training ("Police Recruit Training — A Revolution"), while steeped in controversy, electrified the criminal justice community — and the country. While nonbelievers, still clinging to nineteenth century theories and "ankle-level" feelings, continue on the road of self-proclaimed rationality and mysticism, Dr. Earle prefers to follow the path of research, which leads to truth.

Typifying the many honors he has received throughout his distinguished career, Dr. Earle was selected to attend the eighty-second class of the Federal Bureau of Investigation Academy and was elected class president by his colleagues.

Dr. Earle recently concluded his law enforcement career to devote his full time and talent to writing, teaching, and consulting.

For all those who share a mutual interest and concern in the continuing successful role of police-community relations, this preceptive account, based on competent research and covering twelve years of personal experience and knowledge, provides an intelligent approach to this vital issue of our time.

As a citizen of the community, I am extremely grateful to Dr. Earle for his brilliant contributions. As a personal friend, I am extremely proud of his achievements, and I cherish our friendship.

WILLIAM MICHAEL CONROY

PREFACE

POLICE-COMMUNITY relations remains the subject of widespread views regarding its precise definition, its role, and its parameters. As we evolve toward more budgetary austerity, many program approaches to police-community relations that were instituted without prior attention to their substantive impact and evaluation are "in trouble." This is coupled with a growing desire to have PCR programs that are, in the final analysis, truly aimed at community crime prevention and crime reduction and are in need of constant attention and review by the police administrator. This is the subject of one of the new chapters in this text, even though the concept is still emerging—but then, so is PCR.

In addition to a variety of other changes, the Student-Instructor Guide, which was designed to accompany the Second Edition of this text, has been incorporated into this edition.

Another factor worthy of note centers around public confidence in their police: If PCR programs gain this end to a greater degree, will it possibly result in a greater willingness to report crime and "be involved?"

If so, we may achieve what will appear statistically to be a disproportionate increase (or lessened rate of reduction, in some instances) in crime. To the ill-informed, this could be a confusing and bewildering factor—reported crime rates are up, and so is public confidence in their police.

Finally, as police-community relations courses become mandatory requirements in progressive law enforcement agencies and universities, it is essential that emphasis be placed on the relevancy of information imparted. There is a broad base of knowledge that is fundamental to any PCR program, which this text is meant to provide; but it is also important to use local illustrative data as well, and the utilization of this text will assist in this.

ACKNOWLEDGMENTS

A LTHOUGH MANY persons assisted in preparing this book, particular appreciation is extended to the University of Southern California and the staff and student body of their Delinquency Control Institute's forty-fourth, forty-fifth, and forty-sixth classes. Their constructive analysis of the First Edition, plus their enthusiastic pursuit of additional information, helped considerably in evaluating the status of police-community relations and alternative proposals to more fully actualize its objectives.

H.H.E.

CONTENTS

Page

Foreword— William Michael Conroy v

Preface ix

Acknowledgments xi

PART I

THE GENERAL PROBLEM

Chapter

1. INTRODUCTION 5
2. THE POLICE IMAGE........................... 19
3. CRISIS AREAS................................ 37

PART II

ORGANIZATIONAL ASPECTS

4. ORGANIZATION FOR POLICE-COMMUNITY
   RELATIONS ACTIVITIES: A MODEL 57
5. GROUPS AND LAW ENFORCEMENT 76
6. THE PRESS 95
7. TRAINING AND EDUCATION IN
   POLICE-COMMUNITY RELATIONS............. 107
8. LAW ENFORCEMENT AND THE EDUCATOR 121

PART III

SOCIOLOGICAL DILEMMA OF
POLICE-COMMUNITY RELATIONS

9. SOCIOLOGICAL ASPECTS OF POLICE-COMMUNITY
   RELATIONS 135
10. CIVIL DISOBEDIENCE: CONCEPT AND
    PRACTICE 153
11. RIOTS: A TWENTIETH CENTURY PLAGUE...... 165

PART IV
POLICE-COMMUNITY RELATIONS TODAY
AND TOMORROW

12. DIVERSION 181
13. COMMUNITY CRIME PREVENTION 193
14. POLICE-COMMUNITY RELATIONS
    PROGRAMMING 209
15. ROLE OF THE INDIVIDUAL OFFICER 229
16. ROLE OF THE FIRST-LINE PEACE OFFICER 239
17. THE Z-COP: EMERGING MODEL FOR THE
    YEAR 2000 255
18. POLICE-COMMUNITY RELATIONS IN
    AMERICAN SOCIETY TOMORROW 267

Bibliography 279
Index 283

POLICE-COMMUNITY
RELATIONS

PART I

THE GENERAL PROBLEM

it is the basic premise of this text that law enforcement must do a far better and more realistic job . . . (rendering of author by rene podant, paris, 1976)

Chapter 1

INTRODUCTION

Objective: *To define the importance and benefits of good police-community relations to the first-line officer.*

- What is police-community relations?
- The 1 to 4 percent theory
- Benefits of good PCR for each officer
- Benefits of good PCR for the community
- *Mala in se* and *Mala prohibita*
- More law enforcement or more community involvement?
- Civil strife and the police
- Mission of law enforcement

THE IMPACT of unpropitious governmental matters has a dramatic impact on law enforcement activities. It will require government in toto to strive to overcome public concern with activities that have shocked us.

To this end, renewed dedication and effort are mandatory. Without overt action, every branch of government — federal, state, and local — faces the awesome spectre of a public that distrusts its activities.

Within this text's purview, there are countless other factors that have bearing on our law enforcement institutions. It is grossly unfair to "type-cast" *all*, because of the acts of a few; yet, it simply and clearly becomes a growing requirement for police and public alike to get to know one another better, have more and favorable personal contact, and, perhaps most importantly, for each law enforcement officer, in word and deed, to prove his/her merit, and thus earn the confidence of the public he or she serves.

Realistically, trauma in the police profession is a continuing reality; one need only to pick up a newspaper, listen to the radio, or watch television to gather an almost unbelievably broad array of data about police-related activities. The number of law enforcement related programs obtained simply by a brief survey of a weekly television log is surprising.

The ways in which the public learns about law enforcement is relatively new in comparison to law enforcement itself, but most of the problems are not. Historically, law enforcement has been one of the most critical and frustrating problem areas facing any society. It is that peculiar function of government that regulates, controls, and sometimes summarily disrupts the lives and activities of the people, especially those who violate the law. Inherent in this complex and delicate responsibility rests the potential for meritorious or mediocre service, depending upon the particular police agency — and police officer. Also depending upon this officer — or upon his/her individual community relationships — is much of the sum and substance of police-community rapport.

This text analyzes police-community relations, that traditionally downgraded and understaffed stepchild of law enforcement, which suddenly ascended to a position of foremost priority in the operations and objectives of progressive policing agencies. Whether this thrust will last remains for realists to *demand;* history reveals the need for PCR on a continuing basis. The compelling urgency and explosive nature of community relations to twentieth century enforcement has created a new awareness of the acute necessity to examine the community relations function and see where we have been, where we are, and where we are going.

What is Police-Community Relations?

One question often raised, and as yet unanswered relative to police-community relations, is how, precisely, do we define it? We hear the terms public relations, human relations, press relations, and person-to-person relations, but community relations per se is so broad as to defy a precise definition. When linked with the term "police," another rather vague concept, the matter of precise definition is further submerged in somewhat unidentifiable jargon.

The one most salient development involves the theme of *crime prevention and/or crime reduction*. Programs that afford no promise of either should be discontinued; scrutiny of the most intense nature should precede this, however, as there is still a "feeling of insecurity" that pervades many dedicated law enforcement officers if a program fails to produce instant results. As indicated in the introductory data to this edition, statistical crime rates must be viewed in light of reports that reflect unreported events.

Before attempting a definition of PCR, the reader is directed to two questions: Why do some people now attempt to disguise PCR? Does "CRP," "CPR," or "Community Services" (as names to describe the function) further aid in identifying the problem or providing a solution?

This text takes the position that devious rhetoric is not functional; it uses PCR definitions that come from the most descriptive authorities, as well as those that describe and do not attempt to bury the theme in "new" terminology, which can only confuse and not contain or solve the problem.

This should in no way be confused with the concept that is emerging as the cornerstone of effective PCR: *Community Crime Prevention*. Discussed at length later in this text, it still must be noted that future PCR approaches must encompass the more passionate involvement of every person in the community. Without such a development, crime rates — both statistical and real — offer no "safe streets."

The basic problem of survival in a nation plagued with criminality is of grave concern to all who look with open-mindedness on the reality of today. Change, that ever-present phenomenon, especially in today's world, can obviously have both negative and positive aspects, but it has not been conducive to the reduction of crime.

The reduction of illegal acts to an "acceptable level" drives *theorists* to cry "foul" and *realists* to say "right on:" Accepting the premise that *crime will be*, would not the *lowering* of the rate of increase be significant?

This text accepts the dismal reality of a crime problem that will continue to be the major social issue of the next decade, with a need for community involvement to provide hope for a crime rate that we can *live with* — or more importantly, a rate that allows us to *live*.

There are signs of hope, even with a crime rise; Ostrow paraphrases data from the FBI and the United States Attorney General: "Serious crime in the nation increased *8% in the second quarter of 1975, the first time* that the increase has *dropped from a double-digit place in 21 months*, the FBI reported. Former Attorney General Edward H. Levi *offered no explanation* for the reduced rate of increase and *expressed no pleasure* in the latest figures. 'Crime remains an enormous national problem and current levels are — and must be — seen as unacceptable.' " [1]

We may, however, provide a useful conceptual approach and say that police-community relations is an *art;* it is concerned with the ability of the police within a given jurisdiction to understand and deal appropriately with that community's problems; it involves the idea of community awareness of the role and difficulties faced by the police; and it involves the honest effort of both the police and the community to share the common goal of understanding the problems of both, with conscientious effort for harmony and cooperation.

Perhaps a few other "definitions" at the outset will clarify this concept and provide a better frame of reference for the material to follow.

The International City Managers Association describes police-community relations as:

---

[1] Ronald J. Ostrow: "Increase in National Serious Crime Rate Slows to 8%." *Los Angeles Times.* October, 1975.

A police department-initiated program designed to offer an opportunity for police and other public and private agencies and individuals in the community to discover their common problems, ambitions, and responsibilities and to work together toward the solution of community problems and the formulation of positive community programs . . . it is not merely a problem-solving device. It is a problem-avoidance methodology which, when correctly organized, can create healthy community attitudes.[2]

The President's Commission on Law Enforcement and Administration of Justice defines what police-community relations is not:

It is not a public-relations program to 'sell the police image' to the people. It is not a set of expedients whose purpose is to tranquilize for a time an angry neighborhood by, for example, suddenly promoting a few black officers in the wake of a racial disturbance. It is a long-range, full-scale effort to acquaint the police and the community with each other's problems and to stimulate action aimed at solving those problems.[3]

Momboisse emphasizes the importance of the individual officer to any explanation of the concept:

Police-Community Relations means exactly what the term implies—the relationship between members of the police force and the community as a whole. This includes human, race, public, and press relations. This relationship can be bad, indifferent, or good, depending upon the attitude, action, and demeanor of every member of the force both individually and collectively.[4]

Finally, the concept can be better understood when viewed in light of the various facets of the term that are reviewed in general throughout this text.

The One-to-Four Percent Theory

The number of "hard-core criminals" within the country remains debatable. Statisticians purport that between 1 to 4 percent of the population—over age fourteen and under age fifty—are responsible for a major portion of our crime. Police-community relations obviously cannot impact this habitually criminal element of the community. Unfortunately, too many people then accept the belief

---

[2] International City Managers Association: *Police-Community Relations Programs.* Washington, D.C., Management Information Service Report No. 286, 1967, p. 3.

[3] President's Commission on Law Enforcement and Administration of Justice: *The Challenge of Crime in a Free Society.* Washington, D.C., U.S. Government Printing Office, 1967, p. 100.

[4] Raymond M. Momboisse: *Community Relations and Riot Prevention.* Springfield, Thomas, 1974, p. 97.

that 96 to 99 percent of the people are inherently "good." However, why not accept the premise that if 1 to 4 percent of our populace is "bad," then, logically, only 1 to 4 percent could be termed "good"? Using mathematical formulae, the obvious need is to change the "norm" of the bellshaped curve of *human* behavior. Viewing the unaffected populace, from the standpoint of a proneness to—or away from—criminal activity, it is logical to assume an unimpacted curve similar to Figure 1.

RELATIONS *CURVE OF GOODNESS (COG)*

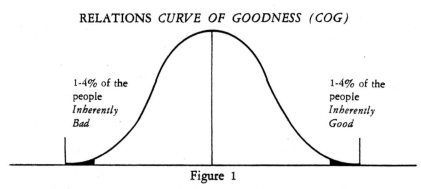

Figure 1

Figure 1 shows that the majority of people can "go either way." PCR has as a central theme the *skewing* of behavioral patterns, toward a willingness to obey the law and supportiveness of a system of justice that makes a better life for all of us.

The obvious need is to change the "norm" of the bell-shaped curve. Police-community relations is designed to bring citizen support to criminal justice, to remove *apathy,* and cause *total community involvement.*

Should this be accomplished, the change is a dramatic and

RELATIONS *CURVE OF GOODNESS (COG)*

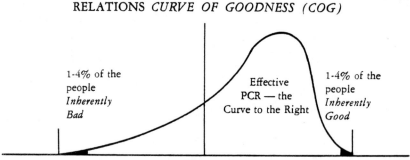

Figure 2

impactful curb on crime, and this normative bell-curve might change to that shown in Figure 2.

The Individual Law Enforcement Officer

A central theme permeating this entire text is the importance, or rather, the absolute indispensability, of the individual officer's daily commitment to the preservation of good police-community relations. He or she is the fundamental ingredient, the chief corner-stone, of any effective, on-going program.

Without each officer's support and dedication to the principles and philosophy of good police-community relations at the line level, the most carefully planned, fully supported, and adequately funded program will fail. The next question is, How do you get the line officer committed to appropriate police-community relations? Various ways to achieve such commitment include careful selection, training, supervision, retraining, and authoritative directive — all of which are necessary factors and basic building blocks of good police-community relations. But is not the human element that cements the whole framework together in a lasting fashion *enlightened self-interest?* Is not enlightened self-interest the prime persuader and motivator of most human pursuits?

We need to awaken and stimulate the line officer's awareness of his/her own personal stake in good police-community relations. We need to prove to each officer how practicing good PCR can be profited from personally, and also how the reverse can cost him or her personally.

The National Commission on Civil Disorders reported that the conduct of police officers was the "triggering" device in many major riots. Negative United States Supreme Court decisions that have redefined or limited important and universal police procedures, such as search and seizure, interrogation of suspects, and the use of informants, resulted from the manner in which a specific or small group of policemen handled, or mishandled, a situation.

Police work, with all of its awesome power and responsibilities, is not performed in a vacuum. Inherent in every citizen encounter is the potential for a multitude of repercussions, from individual personnel complaints to the raging inferno of a race riot. There are no winners in police-citizen repercussions — both sides lose.

In short, whether or not a police officer believes in the principles of good police-community relations, each acts in his/her own best interest by observing these principles. Consequences of rejection can be extremely costly to each officer, the department and the community. Police officers have a vested interest in preserving good police-community relations; to do so is not "coddling," it is good common sense!

It is not an easy task for the traditionalist in law enforcement to accept as fact that in addition to enforcement of laws and ordinances of the particular jurisdiction he or she must recognize the urgency for community contacts that go far beyond the concept of traditional law enforcement. Police must do more than simply mouth the theory that police-community relations is important.

In law enforcement, and, indeed, in any true (or near) profession, the "belief system" of the members becomes the key. A truly effective police agency of today and tomorrow must set aside the tradition of functioning solely as an automaton, merely arresting and citing law violators. The new approach demands the finest in individual person-to-person contacts, coupled with vastly expanded acceptance of participation with the community, in a broad array of group enterprises.

It is the basic premise of this text that law enforcement must do a far better and more realistic job in educating the public to the role of their police, as well as making our policing agencies and law enforcement officers as responsive as is humanly possible to the individualistic needs of each person contacted.

The cry of police brutality—whether fact or fiction, physical or verbal, a look or an attitude—can be utilized to portray the seriousness of the situation. Over a decade ago, the McCone Commission observed:

> An examination of seven riots in northern cities of the United States in 1964 reveals that each one was started over a police incident, just as the Los Angeles riot started with the arrest of Marquette Frye. In each of the 1964 riots "police brutality" was an issue, as it was here, and indeed, as it has been in riots and insurrections elsewhere in the world. The fact that this charge is repeatedly made must not go unnoticed, for there is a real danger that persistent criticism will reduce and perhaps destroy the effectiveness of law enforcement.[5]

---

[5] Governor's Commission on the Los Angeles Riot: *Violence in the City—An End or a Beginning?* Los Angeles, California, Jeffries Banknote Company, December 2, 1965, p. 28.

A Legalistic Dilemma

The peace officer has and will continue to be placed in a position where he or she must deal with violations of the law that are necessarily bad or evil — *mala in se* — of themselves, as well as acts that are criminal solely because society has found it necessary to regulate the conduct of the individual for the betterment of the masses — acts which are *mala prohibita*, bad because society says they are.

It is within this latter classification, covering such a vast collection of traffic offenses, so-called "victimless crimes," and other typical minor infractions, that we usually find an involvement with the normally law-abiding elements of society; thus, their only personal association with the law is of a punitive and negative nature on the infrequent occasions they have contact.

Since it becomes obvious from the outset that we cannot obviate the necessity for enforcing regulations dealing with these acts which are *mala prohibita*, two factors are of critical importance: (1) the highly personalized ability of each peace officer to deal appropriately with each human-to-human contact, and (2) far more must be done in the field of educating the general public as to both the role of law enforcement, and public acceptance and positive support for the men and women whom they have assigned to act as their governmental conscience.

The Police-Community Relations Function

For several decades we have continually accepted as desirable the removal of law enforcement officers from all functions not falling within the absolute purview of the basic law enforcement mission; the protection of life and property. It is equally apparent, even to the novice, that peripheral services to be performed have been, in fact, added in abundance.

The National League of Cities, Department of Urban Studies, believes that peace officers should be relieved of all duties not directly relevant to enforcing the law. Subsequent to their survey of 284 police departments, they reported, "Many police departments still waste manpower by assigning uniformed officers to tasks not directly related to crime fighting. Some activities could be stopped or transferred to other municipal departments." [6]

---

[6] Raymond L. Bancroft: "Municipal Law Enforcement." *Nation's Cities*, February, 1966, p. 26.

After studying both sides of this controversy, the President's Commission on Law Enforcement and the Administration of Justice concluded, "In the absence of conclusive proof to the contrary, the Commission believes that the performance of many of the non-enforcement duties by the police helps them to control crime and that radically changing the traditional police role would create more problems than it would solve." [7]

It is the belief of the author that law enforcement has exceeded the bounds of propriety in accepting removal of many functions as desirable and in avoiding altogether certain police-community relations factors that have been considered as peripheral areas of police activity. Is the completing of a crime report "after the fact" really a more important act than stopping crime before it occurs?

To be effective, we must place peace officers throughout the spectrum of community functions. We must make each officer personally and organizationally acceptable, through both implementing and continuing a wider variety of many so-called "nonpolice functions." The important note on which to end the discussion of the premise of increasing police activities is that we have avoided many areas of community contact to the detriment of the overall law enforcement function. As a recent survey so appropriately reports, "less than a third of the police departments studied have continuing, formalized community relations programs." [8]

Civil Strife and Unrest in the Community

As our vast metropolitan areas, if not the central cities, continue to experience a population explosion unparalleled in history, sociological factors to an increasing degree are creating grave problems for law enforcement. There is an immediate need for a greater understanding to be fostered between law enforcement and the various racial, religious, cultural, and ethnic groups; however, a primary part of the executive branch of government — that is, law enforcement — must maintain order in the midst of inflammatory situations that need containment and control.

Law enforcement officers must be trained from the outset to

---

[7] President's Commission, *Challenge of Crime*, p. 98.

[8] International Association of Chiefs of Police and the United Conference of Mayors: *Police-Community Relations Policies and Practices — A National Survey*. Washington, D.C., International Association of Chiefs of Police and United Conference of Mayors, p. ii.

understand this, as well as the supreme importance of and connection between civil rights and community relationships:

> One of the most fundamental elements in any police course in human relations is civil rights. This statement is applicable to police dealings with any and every citizen. It is imperative for all police officers to appreciate the civil rights acknowledged to the public by law.
>
> Research data strongly support the need for such course content in any police-human relations training program. For instance, it has been found that many police officers tend to be overly forceful when dealing with citizens who are ignorant of their civil rights. False arrests, illegal entries, and general denial of the civil liberties of the public are condemned as non-professional police practice.[9]

Growing awareness of the deep-seated feelings of inequality that exist in many groups is a fact of our time. To ignore it or to try to look the other way, hoping it will "go away," is to court disaster and attempt the impossible. One may witness manifestations of this in a burgeoning spectacle of community upheaval. It is only that the situation is accented in terms of race that race must be singled out as the most important individual factor demanding attention. A person only need look at the morning newspaper to read of protest activities; sporadically, riots still provide awesome laboratories for the study of mankind in crisis.

In civil disorders, the police are in the center of a dilemma. As Towler points out, "The success of a civil rights movement depends upon breaking down any resistance that seeks to retard it. By civil disobedience to a law, they seek to eliminate that law. Such action must necessarily be in conflict with law enforcement."[10]

The Mission of Law Enforcement

Amid the churning current of today's changing times, it is well for law enforcement to remember and reemphasize what is its basic mission, the first order of business, i.e. *to uphold individual liberty, freedom, and human dignity under the rule of law.*

We must not let ceaseless clamour and strife cloud reason and dim vision to that which is the anchor and objective of criminal justice — *ordered liberty under the rule of law.* All other crime sup-

---

[9] Arthur I. Siegel, Philip J. Federman, and Douglas G. Schultz: *Professional Police-Human Relations Training.* Springfield, Thomas, 1963, p. 14.

[10] Juby E. Towler: *The Police Role in Racial Conflicts.* Springfield, Thomas, 1964, p. 36.

pression endeavors are no more than necessary means to the accomplishment of this objective.

Tamm defines the need to maintain the correct perspective: "No public official is more immediately and personally concerned with the fundamental concept of liberty under law than the law enforcement officer. He is the human symbol of the law, from the Constitution down to the local ordinance. His daily life is devoted to the keeping of the public peace and safety, without which there is no orderly living and no untrammeled pursuit of happiness." [11]

Role of Law Enforcement in the Community

In the midst of this confusing tide of intense feeling and emotion regarding law enforcement and individual liberty, law enforcement faces a choice. It stands not at a crossroads, but rather it is perhaps best likened to a choice between a footpath and a superhighway. The former is simply a continuation of past efforts, without analyzing results or expenditures in terms of time and manpower. The latter — indeed, the purpose of this entire text — presents for each law enforcement administrator a picture of just what police-community relations means in terms of long-range police effectiveness. Each specific program dealt with later in this text is not a "must" for each area or each department; however, each program does involve one factor of vital significance — that it is being utilized and is thus regarded as effective by some police agency or agencies.

It is beyond the scope and thus is not the purpose of this book to analyze the proportionate effectiveness of a particular program. Rather, offered collectively, the programs serve as ready sources of information regarding the existence of such programs, together with certain key agencies utilizing them. The sampling is sufficiently complete to enable further exploration of those of interest to a particular unit; such exploration is a must for effective implementation.

Discussion Questions

1. In a recent news conference, the chief of police of America's largest police department wanted to increase the level of contact

---

[11] Quinn Tamm, former Assistant Director of the FBI: "Constitutional Law Enforcement." Address delivered to the International Association of Chiefs of Police.

between the police radio car officer and the citizen on the street. In your view, what are some ways to accomplish this?

2. What do you see as the future role and responsibilities of law enforcement?

3. What do you think could be done by a police administrator to convince the individual, front-line, uniformed patrol officer of the urgent need for good police-community relations?

Chapter 2

THE POLICE IMAGE

Objective: To understand the development of the police image (and role) and its influence on police-community relations.

- Public opinion and police image
- Widespread fear of crime
- Factors influencing police image
- Police policies in history
- Facelessness and automation
- Improving the image
- Community responsibility

the individual officer . . . the individual person-to-person day-to-day contact is responsible for the police image . . . (photograph by william e root)

←——————

IMAGE IS a term that simply defies the imagination! It is both specific and general, yet subject to what can only be termed as an often biased reason for public opinion. Historically, the phrase *police image* has not been given the credibility that now seems awesomely present. In recent years, it has become commonplace to hear the term *image*. The implication, whatever the field of endeavor, is that people are concerned with the overall view of a particular service or organization. The same is true for law enforcement; perhaps more than any other enterprise, policing must live with the good and evil parts of its heritage.

There are a few basic axioms that everyone interested in appraising the image of one's own policing agency should consider. The most important generality about an image is that it is, at once, highly individualistic, while at the same time it approaches near extremism in overgeneralization.

Inherent problems reflect on the public's perspective of the police. The public's views are not necessarily incorrect nor true, yet the consequences are manifold. Reality demands that police administrators understand a need for continuous and overt action. Bent addresses the situation:

> Public confidence in a police department is directly related to the image that citizens have of their police, and these images are formed from the impressions people gain about law enforcement. People—good, bad, and indifferent—are the concern of police forces; constant interaction with the public provides for the high visibility of the police. Policemen are observed during the performance of their regular duties: making arrests, patrolling, and providing assistance. The public also views them through the communications media and hears about them from each other. Thus, impressions are formed about the police from these direct and indirect contacts, and these impressions constitute the police public image.
>
> The building of public support and confidence is made difficult by the customary obscurity of police operations and administration. A positive openness about a police department's programs, problems, and goals can do much to improve relations with the public.[1]

Surveys of Public Opinion

In view of the growing national tendency to defy lawful authority, the results of a recent national survey conducted by the Na-

---

[1] Alan Edward Bent: *The Politics of Law Enforcement.* Lexington, Maryland, Lexington Books, Division of D.C. Heath & Co., 1974, p. 41.

tional Opinion Research Center (NORC) for the President's
Commission on Law Enforcement and Administration of Justice
were indeed surprising.

Contrary to the belief of many policemen, the overwhelming
majority of the public—with the notable exception of minority
groups—voiced a high opinion of the work of the police. The
NORC survey produced these answers to the following questions: [2]

Do you think that the police here do an excellent, good, fair, or a poor job
of enforcing the laws?

	Percent
Excellent	22
Good	45
Fair	24
Poor	8

How good a job do the police do in giving protection to people in the neighborhood?

	Percent
Very good	45
Pretty good	35
Not so good	9
No opinion	14

The results of other surveys are substantially consistent with this
one. A Louis Harris poll in 1966 found that 76 percent of the public
rated federal agents as good or excellent in law enforcement; comparable figures for state and local agencies were 70 and 65 percent
respectively.

The NORC survey disclosed that nonwhites, particularly blacks,
are significantly more negative than whites in evaluating police
effectiveness. In describing police protection, nonwhites rated "very
good" only half as often as whites and rated "not so good" twice as
often. According to the survey, these differences were not merely a
function of greater poverty among nonwhites: they exist at all
income levels and for both men and women. [3]

The omnipresence of crime does little to facilitate a feeling of
support for the *effectiveness* of law enforcement, and thus the police

---

[2] President's Commission on Law Enforcement and Administration of Justice: *Task Force
Report: The Police.* Washington, D.C., U.S. Government Printing Office, 1967, pp.
145-146.

[3] President's Commission, *The Police.* pp. 145-146.

image. Trends mentioned in Chapter 1 regarding crime require historical inquiry into the feeling about criminal activity, as well as a hard look at the actual amount of crime; then, too, this nation's populace tends to rank-order the problems of all types we face, and this too must remain a major concern for all governmental officials.

First, let us view crime of today and tomorrow in light of our recent experiences. The question is often raised regarding the viability of data compiled "last year." The prediction of future developments remains questionable, yet a brief view of more recent trends is appropriate and necessary.

In December 1972, Gallup Poll interviewers surveyed 1,504 adults, eighteen or older, in 300 localities across the nation, in an effort to measure the extent of crime. The poll revealed some significant findings, which are worthy of extensive review and reflection.

With crime now far and away the number one concern of residents of the nation's cities, this startling survey finding comes to light: One person in every three living in densely populated center-city areas of the nation has been mugged, robbed, or has suffered property loss during the last twelve months.

While the figures are lower for less urbanized areas, they are still frightening. For example, one person in five in the suburban areas of America has been the victim of one or more of the five types of crime covered by the survey, which measured the period of one year.

Findings are based on a nationwide survey in which interviews were conducted December 8–11 with 1,504 adults, eighteen and older, interviewed in more than 300 scientifically selected localities across the nation.

Sample surveys, by going directly to a sample of citizens, overcomes certain difficulties encountered in collecting data based on police records. Chief among these difficulties is the reluctance on the part of some victims to report incidents to the police, out of apathy, worry about having to appear in court, and, in some cases, fear of reprisal. In this survey, however, all persons who indicated that they had been a victim during the last twelve months were asked if they had reported the incident to the police. The findings show that in the case of certain of the crimes included in the survey, as many as a half of the victims did not report the incident.

Collection of data on crimes by the survey sampling method can provide information on certain types of crimes, such as acts of vandalism, not covered by other recording methods.

The survey sampling method also helps in determining the percentage of victims of multiple crimes. For example, evidence from the survey above shows that 21 percent of adults (18 and older) have been the victim of one or more of the crimes surveyed during the last 12 months, while 7 percent have been the victim of two or more of these crimes during this period of time.

The following questions were asked of the national sample of adults: "During the last 12 months, have any of these happened to you? [The card lists five types of crime.] Just read off your answer by letter or letters."

Each person indicating that he or she was a victim was then asked, "Did you happen to report this to the police, or not?"

Table I shows (1) the percent of adults mentioning each type of crime, (2) the projection of this percentage to the total adult population or to the total number of households, and (3) whether or not the crime was reported to the police.

Table I

Type of Crime	Percent in Survey	Projection* (Approx)	Said Reported To Police
A. Home broken into, or attempt made	7%	5,000,000 households	5%
B. Mugged/assaulted	2	3,000,000 adults	1
C. Money or property stolen from person or some other member or household	8	5,000,000 households	5
D. Home, car, or other personal property vandalized	8	5,000,000 households	4
E. Car, or car owned by member of household stolen	2	1,000,000 households	2

*The above projections are based on the total noninstitutionalized population, 18 and older, of approximately 136 million persons, or approximately 68 million households. It is important to bear in mind that the percentages reported are subject to some sampling error.

Analysis of these findings shows the incidence level for each of these crimes to be far higher in center-city areas than in suburban or rural areas and higher in the West than in the other three major regions of the nation.

Fear of crime grips Americans in many parts of the nation, affecting life-styles and distorting the day-to-day pattern of existence. Fear of physical violence has brought a flourishing alarm device industry into existence. Citizens are banding together to patrol potential crime districts in cities.

This survey shows that four persons in ten are afraid to walk alone at night in their neighborhoods. The proportion who hold this fear has jumped from 31 percent in 1968 to 42 percent today. As many as six women in every ten (61%) say they are afraid to go out alone in their neighborhoods at night.

In addition, one person in six nationally does not even feel safe and secure in his own home at night. Blacks are found to be more fearful than whites both in terms of walking in their neighborhoods at night and in terms of being in their own homes at night.

In assessing the situation in their communities, people believe crime to be increasing. Findings from the latest survey, based on interviewing in more than 300 localities across the nation, show half of all persons interviewed saying there is more crime in their areas than there was a year ago, while 10 percent say less. About three in 10 (27%) think the situation is about the same as a year ago, while another 12 percent do not express an opinion.

Figure 3 offers details of the survey.

Thus, Gallup provides historical and extremely valuable insight into the crime situation. Another factor of great concern and value is how our clientele rate crime, as compared to other problems this country faces. It no doubt comes as little surprise that this nation's concern with crime continues as the prime focal point. In July, 1975, Gallup then focused on the major issues of impact to the American people, and crime headed the list of major concerns among residents of the nation's largest cities.

Significant changes in public concern were reported by Gallup in 1977, when other factors became paramount in the view of the American public. [4]

---

[4] Gallup Poll: "Public's Concern on Energy Rises." *Los Angeles Times*, August 14, 1977.

CRIME[3]

Question: "Is there more crime in this area than there was a year ago, or less?"

	EARLY DECEMBER 1972				MARCH 1972			
	More %	Less %	Same %	No Opinion %	More %	Less %	Same %	No Opinion %
NATIONAL	51	10	27	12	35	11	42	12
SEX								
Male	47	11	30	12				
Female	54	9	24	13				
RACE								
White	51	9	28	12				
Non-white	48	22	18	12				
EDUCATION								
College	50	8	28	14				
High School	52	10	26	12				
Grade School	47	13	29	11				
OCCUPATION								
Prof. & Bus.	53	9	23	15				
White Collar	56	9	25	10				
Farmers	33	4	49	14				
Manual	50	11	28	11				
AGE								
18-24 years	52	13	20	15				
25-29 years	50	6	30	14				
30-49 years	54	9	24	13				
50 & over	48	10	33	9				
RELIGION								
Prostestant	49	11	29	11				
Catholic	55	8	26	11				
Jewish	X	X	X	X				
POLITICS								
Republican	52	9	28	11				
Democrat	48	12	28	12				
Independent	53	7	26	14				
REGION								
East	48	8	29	15				
Midwest	48	11	31	10				
South	54	12	22	12				
West	55	9	25	11				
INCOME								
$15,000 & over	58	6	22	14				
$10,000 - $14,999	52	12	25	11				
$ 7,000 - $ 9,999	50	9	30	11				
$ 5,000 - $ 6,999	49	10	30	11				
$ 3,000 - $ 4,999	48	5	29	18				
Under $3,000	44	18	30	8				
COMMUNITY SIZE								
1,000,000 & over	51	9	25	15				
500,000 - 999,999	54	9	26	11				
50,000 - 499,999	58	10	22	10				
2,500 - 49,999	56	7	27	10				
Under 2,500, Rural	38	13	35	14				

[3]George Gallup: *The Gallup Opinion Index*. Princeton, New Jersey, January, 1973, pp. 3-14.

CRIME

Question: "Is there any area right around here — that is, within a mile — where you would be afraid to walk alone at night?"

	EARLY DECEMBER 1972		1968	
	Yes	No	Yes	No
	%	%	%	%
NATIONAL	42	58	31	69
SEX				
Male	22	78		
Female	60	40		
RACE				
White	42	58		
Non-white	48	52		
EDUCATION				
College	42	58		
High School	42	58		
Grade School	46	54		
OCCUPATION				
Prof. & Bus.	39	61		
White Collar	46	54		
Farmers	12	88		
Manual	41	59		
AGE				
18-24 years	41	59		
25-29 years	37	63		
30-49 years	38	62		
50 & over	48	52		
RELIGION				
Prostestant	42	58		
Catholic	42	58		
Jewish	X	X		
POLITICS				
Republican	46	54		
Democrat	47	53		
Independent	33	67		
REGION				
East	42	58		
Midwest	34	66		
South	52	48		
West	41	59		
INCOME				
$15,000 & over	34	66		
$10,000 - $14,999	39	61		
$ 7,000 - $ 9,999	43	57		
$ 5,000 - $ 6,999	46	54		
$ 3,000 - $ 4,999	46	54		
Under $3,000	55	45		
COMMUNITY SIZE				
1,000,000 & over	46	54		
500,000 - 999,999	51	49		
50,000 - 499,999	51	49		
2,500 - 49,999	40	60		
Under 2,500, Rural	28	72		

CRIME

Question: "How about at home at night – do you feel safe and secure, or not?"

	EARLY DECEMBER 1972	
	Yes	No
	%	%
NATIONAL	83	17
SEX		
Male	88	12
Female	79	21
RACE		
White	84	16
Non-white	73	27
EDUCATION		
College	90	10
High School	82	18
Grade School	77	23
OCCUPATION		
Prof. & Bus.	88	12
White Collar	84	16
Farmers	94	6
Manual	80	20
AGE		
18-24 years	77	23
25-29 years	84	16
30-49 years	83	17
50 & over	86	14
RELIGION		
Prostestant	82	18
Catholic	85	15
Jewish	X	X
POLITICS		
Republican	86	14
Democrat	81	19
Independent	84	16
REGION		
East	85	15
Midwest	83	17
South	79	21
West	84	16
INCOME		
$15,000 & over	88	12
$10,000 - $14,999	89	11
$ 7,000 - $ 9,000	86	14
$ 5,000 - $ 6,999	74	26
$ 3,000 - $ 4,999	78	22
Under $3,000	75	25
COMMUNITY SIZE		
1,000,000 & over	82	18
500,000 - 999,999	83	17
50,000 - 499,999	83	17
2,500 - 49,999	85	15
Under 2,500, Rural	83	17

Economic problems are named most often as the chief difficulty facing one's family, followed by unemployment, illness, educating children, plans for retirement, concern over children's future, maintaining family harmony, and then energy shortages.

Problems relating to U.S. defense posture or to foreign policy are named next most often, by 10%. Then comes "crime and lawlessness," cited by 6%. All other problems are each named by 4% or less.

This question, asked at frequent intervals over the last 30 years, was put to a national sample of 1,516 adults:

"What do you think is the most important problem facing this country today?"

The results:

High cost of living	32%
Unemployment	17
Energy problems	15
International problems, foreign policy	10
Crime and lawlessness	6
Moral decline, lack of religious commitment	4
Dissatisfaction with government	3
Excessive government spending (for social programs)	3
Drug abuse	2
Race relations	2
Poverty	2
All others	27
Can't say	8
Total	121*

The Police Image: A Composite

Webster defines image as "a mental representation of anything not actually present to the senses." [5] The highly individualistic nature of imagery referred to earlier is reflected in this definition, and it is important to recognize that each person has a picture that is his or her own; it is affected by a great variety of outside influences, both personal and impersonal, but it is nonetheless beholden unto itself. Certain factors generally included as a backdrop for police image discussion are quite dependent upon the status of the individual: (1) economic status, (2) age group, (3) occupational background, (4) racial or ethnic group, and (5) educational background.

---

* Total adds to more than 100% because of multiple responses.

[5] *Webster's New Collegiate Dictionary.* Springfield, Massachusetts, G. & C. Merriam Company, 1961, p. 413.

Shading and influencing this personalized backdrop are any number of factors of a more general, yet highly important, nature. Those most germane include (1) conversation, (2) the news media — press, television, and radio, (3) personal contacts with the police, (4) movies and literature, (5) politics, and (6) prejudice.

For example, consider the public impact of a reported assault on police that the police honored:

> Jeffrey Nash tried to beat the heck out of two police officers, and they thought so much of his efforts that they nominated him for the Police Association's Citizen of the Year award. And he won.
>
> Nash thought the police officers, Tom Conner and Dan Gann, were trying to kidnap a 16-year-old girl. Conner and Gann were in plain clothes and were trying to arrest the girl for drunkenness.
>
> "The policemen were in plain clothes and the car was unmarked," said Police Association President Terry Osborne in presenting the award Wednesday. "Nash had no way of knowing the girl was arrested and not kidnapped."
>
> Gann and Conner nominated Nash for the award because they felt most people would have ignored the incident.[6]

Factors of Historical Significance

That mankind is shaped by the past is a fact evidenced by virtually all things that surround us today; each innovation represents but a present day adaptation of something, which, though new yesterday, may be passe today and antiquated tomorrow. The history of law enforcement is pockmarked with many ugly facades of justice. It has taken many centuries for us to rise to modern day, near-professionalism in this all-important branch of government.

The word *police* was coined from the Greek "politeia," meaning government-citizenship.[7] Policing as Americans know it today is a rather ancient profession, dating back to approximately AD 600. This marked the beginning of the Anglo-Saxon philosophy of local self-government. However, the framework of the Common Law, from which our own laws descend, was established centuries later by the Normans, during their period of English conquest (generally, AD 1066 to 1285).[8]

---

[6] "He's Honored for Assault on Police." *Los Angeles Times,* January 3, 1978.

[7] V. A. Leonard: *The Police of the 20th Century.* Brooklyn, New York, Foundation Press, 1964. p. 1.

[8] Raymond E. Clift: *A Guide to Modern Police Thinking.* Cincinnati, Ohio, W. H. Anderson Co., 1965, pp. 303-306.

The "third degree," i.e. torturing prisoners to extract confessions of guilt, was "perfected" during the period 1285 to 1500 AD in England. During this period, prisoners were brought into the Courts of the Star Chamber (King's Courts) and beaten before the bench until they confessed! Many believe that sophisticated versions of the third degree are still practiced in the United States today. The effect of this belief on the police image, in modern times, undoubtedly has impact. However, paradoxically, out of the Westminster Period came principles of freedom of speech and guarantees against self-incrimination.

True policing in the United States began in the early 1800s with the establishment of the New York City Police. The force consisted of 800 men, and it was not long before a spoils system was introduced. Among other evils of this practice were the accompanying disintegration of police discipline and public disfavor — certainly a profound influence on the image.

The Effect of Historical Practices Today

Today's police forces have inherited an inglorious past. Undeserved though much of it may be — having been as much the machinations of magistrates, politicians, and an apathetic public as that of the police — law enforcement must live with it.

A NORC (National Opinion Research Center) survey indicates that the tide of public opinion does not run as strongly against the police as many writers would have us believe. Still, most pertinent literature stresses the almost insurmountable·resistance of the public, relative to the policeman's task of enforcement and regulation. *Municipal Police Administration* discusses this rebellion against control, indicating that "The police are inclined to assume that unfriendly citizens are their natural enemies and that all citizens are unfriendly. Unfortunately, the police frequently act accordingly." [9]

Many writers, commenting generically on the police image, are inclined to consider what unfriendly pressure groups (which are always the most vociferous) are saying about the police, without balancing this with the many soft voices giving the police their support. To stress the traditional American resistance to regula-

---

[9] International City Managers' Association: *Municipal Police Administration*. Chicago, Illinois, International City Managers' Association, 1971, p. 456.

tion, as though we were still living in a frontier society, is to over-simplify and underrate the desire and respect for the rule of law, not of man, which democracy provides.

Still, police must face reality. In a historic address before scores of sheriffs and chiefs of police, a prominent member of the television industry, commenting on charges of brutality being used cynically as a propaganda technique, noted that, though sometimes warranted, the charges are most often exaggerated or distorted. Admitting that he himself realizes the incredibility of most of these charges, he still felt that "the public does look unfavorably at lawmen today." [10]

Image with Identity

"The police past," Parker points out, "is often one of alternating inefficiency, corruption and brutality." [11] Consider the part these factors have played in the history of policing and add to this the villainous role in which the modern police has been cast as a result of certain recent major court decisions, interpreted as crackdowns on unethical police methods. It sometimes seems miraculous that the police do not have a worse image.

Then, too, the facelessness of the modern police officer has undoubtedly affected the image. He or she seldom walks a beat or stands on a street corner where the public can be met face-to-face. The police officer now has an unfamiliar voice, and the "street-corner cop" has been replaced by the raucous sounds of revved-up engines and the siren's demanding wail. It thus becomes a mandate for law enforcement officers to seek out as many personal contacts as possible, to counteract this undesirable yet growing image of mechanical gadgetry. This "new era" of policing has already had its inroads in molding the image, and some aspects are excellent, while some are frighteningly questionable, from a police-community relations point of view.

We live in an automated world, surrounded by the efficiency of machines, the instantaneousness of computers, and the magic of electronic data processing. Modern man admires efficiency, and

---

[10] David M. Sacks: "Layman Looks at Lawman." Address presented to Police Chiefs Section of the 67th Annual Conference of the League of California Cities, San Francisco, California, October 11, 1965.

[11] William H. Parker: *Parker on Police.* Springfield, Thomas, 1957, p. 138.

this, with all of its machinations, is to be a part of the police image; but we must implement it in as positive a vein as is possible.

The Image: Vague and Distorted

A confidential survey of law enforcement in the metropolitan Los Angeles area revealed the general lack of knowledge regarding a major policing agency. The survey in one instance pointed out that *fewer than half of all respondents displayed even a reasonably correct understanding of the structure and function of the department.*

Other surveys have produced similar results. Too many citizens have little knowledge and less understanding of the function and responsibilities of law enforcement — a function that in some way touches everyone daily. This knowledge gulf, at a time when so much controversy exists about law enforcement, can be traced to a near total lack of formal education of the public about the police, the law, and the court system.

Then too, the so-called "average policeman" comes from a background that many claim affects traditional reaction patterns. Bloch and Geis, quoting from Gourley's *Public Relations and the Police*, point out how this may impact both police action and reaction:

> Many policemen come from the upper-lower and lower-middle classes, and they represent socially mobile individuals, although their mobility is slight rather than dramatic. Perhaps class congruence partially explains the fact that a survey of approximately 3,000 persons found that there is "a definite trend among the respondents with the least schooling to look most favorably upon the police, and for the college graduates to look upon them with the least approval." On the other hand, when respondents are divided by race, there is a clear tendency for nonwhites to be more critical of police than whites. A study in Hartford, Connecticut, for instance, found that slightly over two-thirds of the whites were satisfied with the manner in which the police were performing their jobs, compared to about half the Negro sample.[12]

The Extremely Personal Nature of Imagery

There are many ways to improve the image of law enforcement, but in the final analysis, the responsibility must be carried by each individual officer. Parker notes, "Every look, every word, every

---

[12] Herbert A. Bloch and Gilbert Geis: *Man, Crime & Society*, New York, Random House, 1970, p. 387.

motion made by every man in the organization, every comment of the day, communicates impressions to the public—and as such is public relations activity, good or bad." [13]

Few images are easily created. A television star, for instance, is but one person. An image of masculinity, or intelligence, or purity, etc., is generated through highly selective releases of information, personal appearances, and the like. Conversely, the peace officer is constantly before the public. In either instance, how many favorable impressions are required to obviate one poor one?

Improving the Image

What we must do for the officer in the field is create a favorable *image of law enforcement,* and this is no small task. Bruce Smith clarified the basic problem:

> Really favorable conditions will never be provided so long as misuse of police authority continues to bulk large in the public mind. Notwithstanding the rapid extension of a policy of moderation in the exercise of law enforcement powers, the tide of general opinion still runs strongly against police. The reasons for this condition are easily identified. Universal use of the automobile invites an increasing volume of restrictions upon the motoring public, and the old easy division of the community into lawbreakers and law observers is thereby destroyed. Today all are lawbreakers, and a large and important minority are deliberate offenders. [14]

Thus, the sheep and wolf are no longer clearly defined as black and white, but occupy a broad, gray area.

Community Responsibility

While the emphasis in the preceding pages has been on law enforcement's responsibility to upgrade itself (and in so doing, its image) there is a counterneed for the community to be willing to build an attitude of respect for the law and the men who serve as its administrative guardian. Blake makes an important point regarding the general public's attitude toward the crime problem: "In the national life it is the 'syndicate,' the Mafia, the juvenile gangs, or, in election years, the other party and its leaders. The general

---

[13] Parker, *Parker on Police,* p. 137.

[14] Bruce Smith: *Police Systems in the United States.* New York, Harper & Row Publishers, 1960, p. 9.

assumption is that there exists in the world outlaws and criminals who spoil the good world for all of us good people." [15]

Thus, we find the trite question of the citizen stopped for a traffic violation — "Why aren't you out arresting criminals?" — indicative of an attitude that the "bad people" are responsible for social decay. Blake further contends, "The major cause for the collapse of a society at any level may be traced to the sins of the 'good people,' rather than to the criminal activities of 'bad people.' This is not by any means to condone the evils of criminals. They exist. They must be thwarted. They must be punished. But, I repeat, they and their activities are not the major cause of the ethical disarray in American life." [16]

Only when the great majority of the American people willingly accept responsibility for socially acceptable behavior, together with concomitant acknowledgment that law enforcement officers must deal both with the hard-core criminal and situations that are going to affect the rights of the "good people," will the actions of policing agencies receive the willing, vigorous, and continuous support of the people served. This then is the other side of the coin. Law enforcement must do a great deal more, but so must the American people.

Discussion Questions

1. What are some of the things that the line officer can do to better the image of the police?
2. What programs might you suggest to bring about a better understanding between the youth and the police?
3. It has been suggested that the police must become involved in community functions to establish contacts and continuous relationships. Discuss some of the advantages and disadvantages of such involvement.
4. What are some of the reasons not discussed in this chapter for the negative image many people have of the police?

----

[15] Eugene Carson Blake: "Should the Code of Ethics in Public Life be Absolute or Relative?" *Annals of the American Academy of Political and Social Science, 363* (January): 9, 1966.

[16] Blake, *Annals American Academy of Political and Social Science,* p. 9.

crisis . . . an ultimate tragic development when the complex social structure breaks down . . .

Chapter 3

CRISIS AREAS

Objective: *To develop the awareness of officers and citizens of those areas of law enforcement which house a strong potential for violence, death, injury, and disorder.*

- Loss of faith in police
- Attention to community groups
- Verbal abuse
- Police-citizen contacts
- Professional attitude, training, and appearance
- Police brutality
- Police isolation
- Confusing laws

IN 1975, THE Federal Bureau of Investigation noted tragically that in the year 1974, 132 officers were killed in the line of duty. Assaults on officers increased; nationally, there were fifteen assaults for every 100 officers. During the 1974 crime reporting period, the FBI found a statistical crime rate increase of 18 percent, the highest rate of increase for years.[1] The decrease in certain reported crimes since then is promising.

What can be done with such varying developments? The first course of action is to understand what the problem entails. Realistically, one cannot ignore the findings of the President's Commission on Law Enforcement and the Administration of Justice and the National Advisory Commission on Civil Disorders regarding the cause of riots during the past decade, i.e. the action of a single or a few officers as a trigger.

It is obvious that police-community relationships are affected by a variety of factors. This chapter deals with the most common of what are termed crisis areas; the items discussed range from petty annoyance to irritation, dilemma, and finally crisis.

The United States in the late 1970s is and was comparatively quiet. The lessons of history can become lost in a lack of turmoil in virtually any social setting. A basic problem that American society must face is that a democracy requires public awareness, but it also demands public maintenance; Aristotle noted some 2,000 years ago, "the penalty good men pay for indifference to public affairs is to be ruled by evil men."

In Cohn and Viano's readings on police-community relations, they use a powerful excerpt:

> Loss of faith in the law enforcement establishment is increasingly manifested among the citizenry, especially minority group members, by increases in crime rates and riots; community indifference; charges of police prejudice, brutality, and disrespect for citizens; and complaints of lack of police protection.
>
> On the other side, police officers frequently appear to have lost faith in the country's leaders and the public. They charge that they are subjected to strong political pressures and undue restraints, are held accountable for most social ills, are accorded low status and respect by the community, have little opportunity for redress of grievances, and must perform a tremendously complex job under conditions which, at best, are frustrating.

---

[1] Federal Bureau of Investigation: *Crime in the United States.* Washington, D.C., U.S. Government Printing Office, 1975, pp. 45-48.

The escalation of antagonisms between police and citizens in certain sections of society has tended to induce the formation of two separate and distinct groups who communicate with and understand each other minimally, if at all.

These are harsh statements. To be sure, it must be recognized that the problem is complicated by inadequacies in housing, welfare, education, and employment. Yet, the magnification of these "opposing forces" is, in considerable part, a cause of the problems described. It threatens to undermine the basis of support from more temperate, sensitive, and rational people who constitute the essential communication links through which we can reclaim the middle ground necessary for the de-escalation of antagonisms and the resolution of differences.[2]

Quinney provides insight into the sociological dilemma that this crisis entails:

Maintaining order often involves giving support to some members of the community while denying it to others, controlling one member but lending support to another. Many disputes are handled by police intervention, which has been documented in a study of the calls received at a metropolitan police department. Nearly half were requests for assistance of some kind. The calls for support were about personal problems: requests for health services (such as ambulance escorts, investigation of accidents, suicide attempts), problems with children (complaints about trespassing or destructive behavior), and the problems of incapacitated persons. Other calls were requests for assistance in personal disputes and quarrels, violence or protection from potential violence, and requests for assistance about missing persons and behavior of youths. The policeman performs many actions that are not directly related to enforcement of the law but with other aspects of order in the community.[3]

OVERALL PROBLEM

Crisis areas are all too readily apparent when they erupt as a holocaust, in the form of a riot, and people ask, "What's happening?" It is of great importance to recognize that a specific situation may serve as a triggering device, which can result in a disturbance or a riot. While the situation or incident may have been only irritating or annoying in the beginning, the aftereffects become apparent when chaos strikes. Typifying this was the arrest on a drunk driving charge that took place at 116th and Avalon Streets in Los Angeles over a decade ago. The arrestee was a male black, close to

---

[2] Alvin W. Cohn and Emilio C. Viano: *Police Community Relations: Images, Roles, Realities.* Philadelphia, J. B. Lippincott Co., 1976, pp. 502-503.

[3] Richard Quinney: *Criminology,* Boston, Little, Brown & Co., 1975, p. 174.

home, who was soon joined by relatives; the arresting officers were Caucasian; a crowd gathered, the arrestee was taken to jail, together with persons who interfered. The incident shortly thereafter was believed ended, yet this "trigger" was not "the cause," but merely a device which released a multitude of pent-up emotions and wanton lawlessness. The Watts Riot began shortly thereafter.

Obviously, riots do not always result from irritating police-citizen contacts. The point to be emphasized here is that police-community relationships can be jeopardized, and it may or may not be the fault of the police or the citizenry. What this chapter seeks to do is discourage loose discussion of a fault-finding nature on police-citizen crisis areas. It is organized as a fact-finding presentation, designed to deal with crisis areas, not to establish blame. Certainly, if the police of this nation desire citizen awareness of critical areas, they must be willing to accept a joint responsibility and deal with matters that can result in crisis status.

Critical Role of Community Groups

Fortunately, most groups are made up of law-abiding citizens and exist for legal purposes. Unfortunately, at least from the standpoint of the police mission, any given person belongs to numerous groups, and the groups themselves are infinite in number, variety, and purpose. In some instances a person can belong to two or more groups whose purposes are sometimes at odds.

Groups that must be considered of prime importance include church, civic, school, labor, political, economic, and social organizations. ICMA notes, "Groups of citizens interested in special police activities (traffic, delinquency control, commercialized vice and crimes against retail merchants) appreciate efforts made by the police in the field of their special interest. By giving some attention to these groups, the police build good will and, in return, obtain the support of these groups, in solving the problems they have in common." [4]

Conflicting Group Interests

All groups have their own often highly individualistic goals. The

---

[4] International City Managers' Association: *Municipal Police Administration*. Chicago, Illinois, International City Managers' Association, 1971, p. 512.

police unfortunately are caught up in situations where maintaining law and order offends a major portion of those served. Today's college campus clashes between police and "crusading" students exemplify the perplexing position law enforcement occupies.

How to Influence Groups

Whatever the group, the law enforcement agency must make certain that whatever means are available to favorably influence group ideology are utilized to the fullest extent. Many times, law enforcement administrators living in this era of limited police budgets and personnel consider police-community relations an expensive luxury; the truth appears to be that police-community relations is expensive, but an absolute necessity. Past lack of attentiveness to *cost effectiveness* can be overcome. Only through continuous effective communication can a long-range understanding be established and maintained between the police and all groups.

The National Commission on Civil Disorders evaluated the need for police-community relations programs:

> We believe that community relations is an integral part of all law enforcement. But it cannot be made so by part-time effort, peripheral status of cliche methods.
>
> Improving community relations is a full-time assignment that must include the development of an attitude, a tone, throughout the force that conforms with the ultimate responsibility of every policeman: public service.[5]

Chapter 5 of this text deals at length with contacts necessary with community groups and their collective leaders. These contacts must be well organized, continuous, and all-encompassing. Failure to establish contact with a group—or more correctly, certain key groups—of itself becomes a form of negative police decision and action on the part of the policing agency that can have far-reaching repercussions.

Nationwide Action

On a national level, the National Institute on Police-Community Relations has held annual conferences since 1955. Many other organizations have also shown an interest; the United States govern-

---

[5] United States Riot Commission: *Report of the National Advisory Commission on Civil Disorders.* New York, Bantam Book Co., 1968, p. 320.

ment has recently expressed greater interest in the problems of law enforcement than at any other time in history. This is exemplified by former President Johnson's creation of the Commission on Law Enforcement and Administration of Justice, Commission on Civil Disorders, and the Office of Law Enforcement Assistance which allocates millions of dollars to further training and innovative programs in law enforcement (the latter is under heavy pressure to "restructure or retire").

The passage of the 1968 Anti-Crime (Safe Streets and Crime Control) bill initially provided 400 million federal dollars to help states and local governments cope with organized crime, riots, and other violent civil disorders. This allocation illustrates the concern and action, then and now, by this nation's highest officials. Today, nearly one billion dollars is allocated through this same source.

Police administrators must realistically face the dilemma of law enforcement in our time. Crime has continued to rise, as have arrests. Many people whom the police contact will be dealt a punitive blow to their freedom or their pocketbook. There is no magical or mystical way in which to avoid this type of police-citizen contact, but there is every reason to believe that the individual officer can improve his/her ability to deal with nonpunitive contacts, as well as those of a punitive nature. The idea of contacting groups, and of forming groups of key leaders, stems from recognizing that the police have a vital interest in fostering productive community attitudes. However, internal and highly individualistic orientation of each peace officer in this regard is also necessary.

THE CRISIS AREAS

Several areas are of critical importance in the maintenance of a peaceful society. An enlightened citizenry and law enforcement aware of the problem areas and the factors contributing to difficulty can do much to overcome the fostering of mountains from molehills.

Each and every peace officer must accept as a personal challenge the winning of public support and respect. Lip service to this goal is readily obtained; however, failures to follow through are legion. The areas listed in the following sections are considered basic if the police are to establish and maintain acceptance.

The attitude of the individual officer is perhaps the primary factor in community relations. ICMA points out:

> . . . Action is determined by frames of mind, and the police should scrutinize their own point of view to assure that it is a proper one. Their attitude will be determined by their concept of the police function—of their duty toward the public. They should recognize the line of demarcation between the police function and the court function. They should realize that the essence of a proper police attitude is a willingness to serve. They should distinguish between service and servility, courtesy and softness. They must be firm, but at the same time, courteous; they must avoid an appearance of rudeness. They should develop a friendly, impersonal, and unbiased manner, pleasant and personal in all nonrestrictive situations but firm and impersonal on occasions calling for regulation and control. They should understand that the primary police purpose is to prevent violations—not to arrest offenders.[6]

By its very nature, police work requires an officer to be suspicious, and this typifies a basic problem in attitude development: "By nature, training or experience, policemen are suspicious. Being suspicious helps to make you a good policeman. But this desirable quality can become a *rock in the roadway* to your getting along with people . . . Being suspicious may be no fault, but showing it is a great one."[7]

Conversation

The officer's manner and language when talking to persons deserves individual treatment, as these are perhaps more personalized than any other consideration. Terms used by police exert a tremendous influence on police-community relations, and "trigger" terms such as "nigger," "wop," "dago," or "boy" must be deleted from police parlance. These discriminatory terms produce both anger and strong counterprejudice among minority groups.

The Crime Commission Task Force stresses the crucial importance of professional noninflammatory conversation: "No matter is more important to Police-Community Relations than the manner in which police officers talk to people on the street . . . most persons, including civil rights leaders, believe that verbal abuse and

---

[6] International City Managers' Association, *Municipal Police Administration*, p. 481.

[7] Dan Hollingsworth: *Rocks in the Roadway.* Chicago, Illinois, Strombert Allen and Co., 1954, p. 27.

harassment is the major police-community relations problem today."[8]

Traffic

The most frequent personal contact a police agency has with the people is in the field of traffic. Remarks on the explosive and critical nature of this particular problem permeate this and countless other reports. It must be remembered that police influence the public in proportion to the number of contacts made: "Since the police make more public contacts in controlling traffic than in any other activity, it is especially important that continuous attention be paid to police attitudes in dealing with traffic offenders to increase respect and to improve public relations."[9]

Ladd feels there are two vital ingredients in a traffic program (or almost any police program): "They are *public information and organized support*. On the latter rests the entire structure of the program. It is the foundation which supports the official action. It gives organized backing to engineering, enforcement and education. Closely allied with this is Public Information, its most valuable instrument in developing the necessary informed public opinion."[10]

Courtesy

There can be no substitute for police efficiency in building a sound community relations program. Hand in hand with efficiency goes courtesy in carrying out each assignment. This is a key factor in face-to-face (police-to-citizen) contacts whenever practical and possible. One area too frequently overlooked in this regard is the fact that "relatively few police contacts involve punitive action."[11]

Thus, we have an excellent opportunity for friendly and effective fostering of sound relationships that is often ignored, or just overlooked. The National Commission on Civil Disorders cautions: "Unless carried out with courtesy and with some understanding of

---

[8] President's Commission on Law Enforcement and Administration of Justice: *Task Force Report: The Police.* Washington, D.C., U.S. Government Printing Office, 1967, p. 180.

[9] International City Managers' Association: *Municipal Police Administration,* pp. 418-482.

[10] Walter D. Ladd: *Organizing for Traffic Safety in Your Community.* Springfield, Thomas, 1959, p. 69.

[11] International City Managers' Association: *Municipal Police Administration,* p. 499.

the community, even the most enlightened patrol practices may degenerate into what residents will come to regard as harassment."[12]

The importance of courtesy in all public contacts was documented by the National League of Cities in its 1966 survey of 284 police departments. This survey found that discourtesy is the most frequent public complaint against peace officers.[13]

Appearance

The uniform and personal appearance of each officer tells those served of the care taken to present the police in the best possible light. Supervisors can materially improve the appearance of their men by holding pre-duty inspections daily and seeing to it that the men and their equipment are in good order. An unsewn button or unshaven face can have a detrimental influence on an entire department when viewed by the numerous citizens each officer deals with during a tour of duty.

Concern with appearance is not something that, once done, can be left alone. As is the case with most elements of police-community relations, it requires constant continuous attention.

The Telephone

Many police authorities contend that the most frequent contacts a law enforcement agency has with the public are through letters and telephone. Letters must be both courteous and informative. If a policing agency recognizes this, there is usually time to frame a reply that serves both purposes. However, the telephone offers one of the dilemmas for modern law enforcement: "The most common form of police discourtesy is encountered in telephone conversations. Indeed, public relations gets a jolt from which it is slow to recover when the telephone rings a number of times before one of our tired voices growls a 'Yeah?' at the other end of the line. This kind of reception is a 'slap in the face' to the caller who has telephoned concerning what is to him an important matter. We must

---

[12] United States Riot Commission, *Report on Civil Disorders*, p. 307.

[13] Raymond L. Bancroft, "Municipal Law Enforcement," *Nation's Cities*, February, 1966, 8pp. 15-26.

constantly fight the discourtesy that exists through the use of the telephone."[14]

When a distressed person calls a public agency, there is nothing more reassuring than a pleasant and sincere voice asking, "May I help you?" The recording of incoming calls at police facilities has aided both the police and the citizenry in lessening this basic problem area of police-community relations.

Training and Experience

There can be no substitute for a trained officer in the field. Usually, administrators concede that each officer must be conversant with the law, yet all too often we fail to indoctrinate our new officers with a philosophy of proper police-community relationships, and the "ten-pound badge" glares out at the public. It is imperative that we screen and train new peace officers in a professional manner, but it is equally important that we remember that this man or woman in the field must be an appropriate reflection of the proper police attitude, one year or ten years hence. Supervision is important, as is the attitude reflected by supervisors and high level police administrators, but so is the training and retraining program.

Physical Conduct

Self-control and calm judgment are the first requirements of any exercising of physical force. Misuse not only solidifies and escalates conflict between the police and minority groups, but it may also incite a riot. The National Commission on Civil Disorders points out that "Negroes firmly believe that police brutality and harassment occur repeatedly in Negro neighborhoods. This belief is unquestionably one of the major reasons for intense Negro sentiment against the police."[15]

Police departments must set forth clear and specific directives that the use of unnecessary or excessive force will not be tolerated. The Commission on Law Enforcement and Administration of Justice recommends the following: "To prevent physical abuse by police officers requires that all police departments take great care

---

[14] Raymond E. Clift: *A Guide to Modern Police Thinking.* Cincinnati, Ohio, W. H. Anderson Co., 1965, pp. 303-306.

[15] United States Riot Commission, *Report on Civil Disorders*, p. 302.

in selecting personnel, formulate strong policies on permissible conduct, dismiss officers who engage in physical misconduct, regularly review personnel practices, comprehensively investigate all complaints made against officers, and strongly discipline those who misbehave."[16]

Patrol Procedures

Misuse of patrol procedures such as field interrogations and "stop and frisk" searches are major sources of abrasive relations between police and minority groups. Law enforcement needs to exercise caution when using "aggressive preventive techniques" so as not to alienate respected members of the community.

> Aggressive, preventive patrol takes a number of forms but invariably involves a large number of police-citizen contacts initiated by police rather than in response to a call for help or service. One such practice utilizes a roving task force which moves into high crime districts without prior notice, and conducts intensive, often indiscriminate street stops and searches. A number of persons who might legitimately be described as suspicious are stopped. But so are persons whom the beat patrolman would know are respected members of the community.[17]

The President's Crime Commission commented upon this procedure which they felt is "particularly clouded in controversy": "If police were forbidden to stop persons at the scene of a crime, or in situations that strongly suggest criminality, investigative leads could be lost as persons disappeared into the massive impersonality of an urban environment. Yet police practice must distinguish carefully between legitimate field interrogations and indiscriminate detention and street searches of persons and vehicles."[18]

Citizen Complaints

The cry of police brutality typifies the headline-attracting type of citizen complaint that, all too often, a complete investigation determines is without foundation. However, damage of making the charge is done, and police live with a report of their alleged brutal actions, carried on page one of the local newspapers; the disproving

---

[16] President's Commission, *The Police*, p. 183.

[17] United States Riot Commission, *Report on Civil Disorders*, p. 304.

[18] President's Commission on Law Enforcement and Administration of Justice: *The Challenge of Crime in a Free Society*. Washington, D.C., U. S. Government Printing Office, 1967, p. 95.

of the complaint is usually covered or buried somewhere on the back pages of the same paper's last section.

Each police agency should have printed matter available, informing any interested party of the various procedures available through which a complaint of any sort may be lodged against improper police activity; if, for example, they may go to the district attorney, city council, board of supervisors, the attorney general, or other appropriate agencies, this should be pointed out. This type of data is contained in the widely distributed Police-Community Relations Policy Statement of the Los Angeles County Sheriff's Department.

Of perhaps greater importance is making the public aware of the fact that the policing agency is willing to accept complaints and take action, while informing them that these other recourses are available, if they are not satisfied. It is only in this way that the police can effectively dispel the cry of many groups seeking to establish citizen-police review boards. If police wish to prove that such groups serve no useful purpose, then channels of communication must be open, and recourse available to the unsatisfied; in most instances, this has been accomplished, but the public must be so informed.

Police Weapons

There has been a veritable avalanche of talk about what constitutes appropriate police equipment. The hand sap versus the palm sap, or no sap; the baton with a knobbed end or shock-producing apparatus; police dogs—all these typify discussion areas. Each locale must consider with great care whether or not the short-range effectiveness of a particular police weapon outweighs the long-range consequences of a resentful public. It is not so much that the weapon per se is available, but its use can make or break the public's attitude toward its law enforcement agency.

Response Time and Manpower Commitments

This text emphasizes the necessity to remove certain peace officers from line police duties so that they may engage in community relations activities of a wide variety. A basic problem facing most agencies is inadequate manpower, and thus police-community relations ironically serve to compound the problem. The response time, i.e. the amount of time between the placing of a call to request police service and the time of the arrival of that assistance, is a critical factor in terms of public reaction to their law enforcement officers.

Various agencies and individuals have dealt with the problem of police-to-population ratios, but nowhere has a concomitant problem, that of police-community relations manpower allotment, projected itself with such forcefulness, yet received such a lack of attention. There is a need to increase the number of police to serve a given population; only in this way can community relations programming be accomplished, together with the provision of prompt response to requests for emergent policing services.

Neither response time nor community contact lend themselves to categorical measurement of precise consequences, yet both offer long-range consequences for failure to correct inadequacies. Police administration goes beyond the structuring of the organization and the assignment of personnel to fill so-called vital and essential roles. In addition, there must be attention to other areas within the police field that are productive and positive and, perhaps most important of all, continuous. This, in the final analysis, means more personnel.

The Social Status of Officers

The peculiar nature of police work lends itself ideally to the formation of an intergroup fraternal type of structuring that extends far beyond the eight-hour working day of the police officer. He or she finds that social gatherings attended also by other known police personnel usually result in a variety of questions and comments from nonpolice guests. This varies in subject matter from conversations regarding a ticket received in the recent past to an officer drinking coffee consistently and for too long a period in a restaurant; it may simply be some remark that is derogatory about "some other police officer" or policing agency. The officer thus seeks the solace and companionship of fellow officers and their families. However, this voluntary isolation tends to create certain aspects akin to a leper colony, and even if people may also feel sorry for the plight of the officer, they still may decide they want nothing to do with him or her socially.

Law enforcement officers, both officially and unofficially, must branch out and deal more compatibly with the community they serve. This will require on-going programs to associate regularly with groups requiring the official contact of the department; it also means that the individual officer must accept a role of community contact which has been up to now largely ignored. This can only be accomplished if the department fosters the appropriate spirit in this regard, and if the officer accepts as a personal goal the establishment of a proper rapport with community groups with which he or she willingly and voluntarily associates.

Demonstrations

This country has witnessed a dramatic and alarming increase in the number of demonstrations — planned and otherwise — and riots that have taken place. An in-depth analysis of demonstrations and other nonviolent civil disobedience is presented in Chapter 10. This section briefly reviews police problems in handling demonstrations.

The pressing importance placed on civil rights issues seems to pinpoint the reasoning behind the demonstrations and riots, while at the same time it clouds many factors that are important from a policing point of view. This is exemplified by the ready participation of subversive elements and groups with individuals demonstrating for a just and proper cause. The Communist-front groups that can be readily identified will accept any platform that offers a forum from which to foster discord and disrespect for the American government. These groups and their parent organizations constantly strive to build up a mistrust between the police and the community. Any such breach is regarded as a major victory in achieving their goal to foster and perpetuate violence, hatred, and the eventual overthrow of our form of free government.

The police are thus placed in the unenviable position of attempting to police demonstrations sponsored by highly motivated and responsible American citizens; yet these persons are often joined by advocates of intolerable forms of government. The point to be emphasized here is not which "side" should take the first step, nor is it intended to dichotomize the police from the community. It is only that the failure on both sides of the fence has resulted in crises that must be admitted to and corrected.

The dilemma of the police in considering demonstrations is the same as that facing any enforcement arm of government. Police protect the rights of all persons. The fact that someone may consider it acceptable to violate a law that in good conscience he or she does not agree with, and is willing to accept the consequences, does not abrogate the fact that any police action against such a person is often regarded as martyrdom for the violator and an act of Gestapo-like terrorism on the part of law enforcement officers involved. This country was founded on a rule of law, the Constitution, not on the changing ideas of man. The same must hold true in regard to encouraging individuals to uphold the law of the land.

Riots

Riots cost so much in terms of police-community relations, to say nothing of lives and property damage, that we must continually assess and emphasize the vital role community and police leadership play in attempting to preclude riot-developing situations, as well as shortening their duration should they occur, and building police-community rapport in the aftermath if a riot does occur (*see* Chapter 11).

Laws

The inconsistency of certain laws may confuse the average American citizen. The confusion is compounded when a peace officer is called upon to deal with a matter that presents an inconsistency. Typical examples of this pertain to many vice offenses. In California, for example, it is a felonious act to engage in bookmaking, or the placing of a bet away from a racetrack. However, any adult can go to the track and gamble. The economics, sportsmanship, and other factors equally realistic or intangible notwithstanding, how does one explain to a child, or an adult, the "difference"?

The inconsistency is graphically portrayed by the President's Crime Commission in its remarks about gambling laws: "Social gambling affords a good example of the dilemma which police face. In most jurisdictions, all forms of gambling are illegal. Yet it is apparent that legislatures neither intend nor expect that such statutes be fully enforced. The consequence is that police are left with the responsibility for developing an enforcement policy for the particular community."[19]

---

[19] President's Commission, *The Police*, p. 21.

News Coverage

Radio, television, and newspapers afford the great majority of the American public the vast amount of information they receive on law-enforcement activities. Stories favorable to law enforcement offer no difficulties; but on occasion, slanted coverage of a certain incident can result in a proper and necessary police action being reported as such by one media, while it is given a damning twist in another. Chapter 6, on press relationships, deals at length with aspects of this, but because of the crisis-causing magnitude and importance of the matter, the reminder of the necessity of continuous positive contact on a routine basis with the press is herein indicated.

Peripheral Areas

The relationship between crime and employment, education and poverty has been the subject of a variety of sociological studies. From a long-range point of view, it would be impossible to consider police-community relations without recognizing the tremendous impact these areas have on any given individual or community.

Other agencies have dealt with the problem, and as Lohman pointed out many years ago, "The police are only one resource among several that must be utilized if we would master the problem of human relations and minimize the consequences of minority group tension."[20]

The problem of police-community relations remains to be solved. Suffice to say that the police administrator must work closely with other agencies that have as their primary responsibilities the alleviation of such crisis-building conditions as unemployment and poverty.

TOWARD TOMORROW

No area of police-community relations activities is as important as that which centers around the vital role played by the individual officer. The top administrators of policing agencies may well foster and espouse an attitude of image development and appropriate

---

[20] Joseph D. Lohman: *The Police and Minority Groups*. Chicago, Chicago Park District, 1947, p. 103.

responsiveness to community needs. Still, if this attitude is not reflected by the men and women in the field, the repercussions can be shocking. One "rotten apple" may not spoil the barrel, but it has an effect far greater than is desirable. Unquestionably, each officer must be thoroughly trained in his/her individual responsibility to reflect an attitude that will enhance the police role.

One continuing problem of police-community relations that overshadows virtually every area in need of consideration is *communication*. It is complex, illusory, and continuous. Harmonious relationships between the community and the police center on communications that in turn center on *conflict resolution*. Yet, it is important to note that *conflict* may be a part of our very nature. Jandt points out that "By definition, conflict involves two or more people, and only through communication can we engage in social conflict and the resolution of that conflict. Social conflict is not possible without verbal or nonverbal communication. Conflict is an important part of the totality of human communicative behavior."[21]

Positive communication can do much to eradicate complex problems involving police and community interaction. Lack of communication is a root cause of much of the social trauma plaguing this planet.

It must be remembered that we live at a time and in a nation where the individual liberties of the citizenry still are uppermost in the minds and actions of the people and their government. There is no easy solution to resolving the areas of crisis dealt with in this chapter, nor is there any reason for us to believe a utopia lies just around the corner. The long-range answers will center around the establishment of communication links between the public and law enforcement and continuous development of an attitude of respect for the law. This is no easy task, and it must be borne in mind by those who would change the attitude of the public towards the police, where it is not acceptable, that there is no overnight solution to a problem as old as time itself. This is not to decry efforts in this regard, but only to advise of the tremendous long-range responsibility the police and the public must share.

---

[21] Fred E. Jandt: *Conflict Resolution Through Communication*. New York, Harper & Row, 1973, p. viii.

Discussion Questions

1. Officer mannerisms or habits may sometimes incite hostility without the intention or knowledge of the officer. From your personal observation, what might be some examples of this? What can be done to alleviate this problem?

2. Misuse of patrol procedures, such as field interrogations and stop-and-frisk searches, are major sources of abrasive relations between police and minority groups. What can be done to overcome this problem without reducing the effectiveness of the police officer in the performance of his/her duty?

3. Communication is an all-pervasive problem that needs continuous attention?

4. What other areas not covered in this course might be considered crisis areas in police work?

PART II

ORGANIZATIONAL ASPECTS

organized police-community relations activities . . . traditional or team . . . a climate for the reduction of crime . . .

Chapter 4

ORGANIZATION FOR POLICE-COMMUNITY
RELATIONS ACTIVITIES: A MODEL

Objective: *To develop the officer's understanding of the functions and responsibilities of a police-community relations unit.*

- Adaptive and open organization
- Fundamental police responsibilities
- Community relations and crime reduction
- Police-community contacts
- Police-media contacts
- Productivity measurement

THE "TRADITIONAL" organizational chart preceding this section is suggested as a challenge. Some law enforcement administrators have attempted strict adherence to it, while others have evolved to the general notion of *team policing.* Neither seems to offer any absolutes relative to a solution for crime control. Both provide a valuable lesson to all police who care to view the prophecy of history that nothing lasts forever.

The need exists for an adaptive and open system of organization that does not allow power plays or over-zealous politicians or non-creative management styles to erode progress. A constant cry emerges for a "return to more cops on the street." This approach has failed nearly every element of American society. No local jurisdiction can afford the police-to-population approach of our nation's capitol on a continuing basis. Thus, we need to deal with crime in new fashions. *Community crime prevention,* an area dealt with later in this text, seeks to place officers in far greater numbers in an "uncrime" posture. Why deal with crime *after the fact?* Traditionalism has failed. Better methods can be developed and adapted to any given jurisdiction and prove to be cost effective.

What are the responsibilities of a police-community relations unit? What do the members of such a unit do? Just a few years ago this was a subject of little priority to the majority of police administrators. Events of the past decade have catapulted this traditionally downgraded and understaffed (if staffed at all) function to a position of foremost priority in the plans and policies of countless policing agencies. Openness to new ideas and methods is a primary requirement for police-community relations units. Central to their operations must be a conviction and commitment to experiment with and explore new and relevant approaches to near-revolutionary problems. This offers a number of consequences, and Eldefonso, Coffey, and Grace picture a series of factors worthy of note:

> Public criticism of law enforcement and its tactics is a favorite American pastime. This criticism, however, lacks validity and is comparable in some respects to reprimanding a doctor for his inability to save the life of a patient whose heart has been punctured by a lethal weapon. In this analogy, there are biological and physiological factors that play an important part in determining the patient's expiration, over which the physician has little control. The police are in a similar position. They are exposed in their ongoing battle against antisocial behavior, to cultural, social, and psycho-

logical forces over which they, as law enforcement officers, have little or no control. The social forces usually stem from the political structure of the community which includes: the efficiency and reliability of elected and appointed officials; the patterns of coercion, leadership, and responsibility of and between police officials and the political leaders; the capabilities, training, and experience of policemen; the attitudes and behavior of citizens toward the police; and the particular conditions or set of circumstances under which these forces interact.[1]

There is an imperative need for continued new approaches. With the escalation of urban crime, violence, and major disorders, public opinion has often emerged as a frightened and rigid stance of "stop crime at any cost." Combine this position with the near secessionist outlook of numerous militant minority (and majority) members in our society, and the need for progressive, creative police community relations remains at a crisis level.

This chapter defines what can be done by law enforcement agencies to positively contribute to alleviating a societal sickness — crime — and win the backing so necessary for their primary tasks.

A PHILOSOPHICAL NOTE

Certain fundamental responsibilities are common to law enforcement officers of all countries. They are responsible for insuring that the orderly activities of their particular society may proceed. In a democracy, people decree the extent of police activity through laws, social mores, and customs.

The broad purposes of police everywhere center around the necessity to control and/or apprehend those members of society who illegally do not conform and to assist other duly constituted agencies of government in the creation of an orderly environment. Dissident members exist in all societies and include, among others, thieves, burglars, robbers, murderers, and rapists. Such people commit *mala in se* crimes.

There also exist in every country peace disturbers, inebriates, traffic law violators (which probably includes most of us, at times), and nuisance-producing elements who do things which annoy and disrupt the orderly way of living, i.e. *mala prohibita* crime perpetrators.

Finally, there is a special conglomerate of *mala in se* and *mala prohibita:* subverters, saboteurs, and political opportunists who are

---

[1] Edward Eldefonso, Alan Coffey, and Richard C. Grace: *Principles of Law Enforcement.* New York, John Wiley and Sons, 1974, pp. 29-30.

a threat to the very existence of all free countries and may threaten the political, social, and economic structure of society.

If the non–law-abiding element of society can prevail, little need be said of the basic problems that pervade our system of freedom with justice. An often ignored approach is viewing crisis through negativism, but answers could be sought through such alternatives as a proposal of Cromwell and Keefer, entitled *Toward a Theory of Negative Contacts:*[2]

1. The police "power maintenance" function in society established dual organizational structures in police departments that are responsive to "legalistic" and "order" perspectives.
   a. Legalistic behavior is emphasized during periods of social stability in society.
   b. Order, or suppressive behavior, is emphasized in periods of social stress and acceptable during situational stress for the individual officer.
2. Police negative perceptions of minority groups are a function of
   a. concentrated visibility.
   b. extent of personal and social disorganization of the minority culture which is determined by the police on the basis of the
      (1) prevalence of perceived minority criminal deviance, and
      (2) prevalence of perceived threatening and challenging situations.
   c. pressure strategies utilized for effectuating changes in status.
3. Police negative perceptions of minority groups are perpetuated by
   a. selective recruitment from working classes of dominants.
   b. inadequate control mechanisms in the organization.
   c. reward (quantitative evaluations) structure of the organization.
   d. implicit and explicit socialization in the use of stereotyping as a skill requisite.
   e. danger-authority conflict of the police role.
   f. dominant group support and encouragement for the use of suppressive tactics.
   g. latent order structure which tolerates and reinforces situational order-oriented behavior by police officers.
4. Minority-group negative perceptions of police are a function of
   a. the "power maintenance" function of police.
   b. nonresponsiveness of police to minority needs and grievances.
   c. the perceived, and actual, verbal and physical abuse and harassment resulting from factors in hypotheses 2 and 3, and which create negative contact situations.
5. Minority-group negative perceptions of police are perpetuated by negative contact situations which reinforce c in proposition 4.

---

[2] Paul F. Cromwell, Jr., and George Keefer: *Police-Community Relations*. St. Paul, Minnesota, West Publishing Co., 1973, pp. 228-229.

6. Police negative perceptions of minority groups are also perpetuated by negative contacts which reinforce b in proposition 2, and factors c and d in proposition 3.
7. Repetitive and frequent negative contact situations lead to individual and collective polarization of police and minority groups, and individual and collective confrontation and violence.

POLICE FUNCTIONS IN THE UNITED STATES

In addition to basic tasks common to all police, law enforcement in modern American society has been given many additional responsibilities. These basically are service in nature, either to the government and relative to the performance of its general function or to the individual members of society. The police, for example, help find lost articles, give directions, and provide a host of other services to the individual. They inspect and issue licenses, perform many other regulatory services, sometimes fight fires, and even issue passports in some countries, as additional functions. Many of these duties devolve to the police because they are physically close to the people, available to perform the service, and because police are the government's sole executive agency organized and deployed on a usable basis at all times and in all areas.

Control of Conduct

The control role of the police is primarily concerned with the nonconforming members of society. The fact that full control cannot be accomplished by having a police officer on every corner is self-evident. Epstein summarizes the heart of this reality, as well as the challenge to each officer: "The policeman symbolizes the written law which he must enforce; he also is the symbol of the spirit of the law, which he must foster if his job is to be done effectively." [3]

Society needs an environment that will minimize disruption and disorder. Creation of such an environment should be accomplished within the framework of the social mores, customs, and laws of a country and with a purpose of serving the will of society as a whole. Police, in a free society, are agents of the people and must serve the people.

Community Relations and Crime Reduction: A New (?) Concept

As pointed out elsewhere in this text, there is a need for law

---

[3] Charlotte Epstein: *Intergroup Relations for Police Officers.* Baltimore, Maryland, Williams and Wilkins, 1962, pp. 173-174.

enforcement to establish and maintain rapport with a variety of community endeavors. Most of them do not relate to specific, short-range law enforcement objectives. The establishment and maintenance of liaison and communication are vital, however, if we are to deal with the basic police mission, accepting the premise that public cooperation and support are mandatory for effective operation.

The flexible structural model presented in this chapter is predicated on the assumption that complete programming in the field of police-community relations is necessary in order to achieve the following essential law enforcement missions: (1) establishment of respect for the law enforcement officer and the law and thereby reduce crime; (2) make public awareness and compliance with positive crime prevention a reality rather than a hope, and (3) create a law enforcement image that will facilitate the aforementioned in a rapid and permanent manner.

Although some departments unintentionally may omit certain functions listed here and disregard others because they believe the omitted functions are not advantageous, each activity listed here *is considered mandatory for a well-rounded police-community relations program.* The number of individuals assigned and the amount of time allotted for each of the functions should be based on the size of the department and the need for the particular function. Also, it must be remembered that no other policing function requires the high degree of skillful use of the finest of human relations talents, and infinite tact must be used in this field to promote professional and effective law enforcement.

Professionally organized and operational community relations programming can — in the long run — create a climate that in a very real manner will reduce criminal activities. The President's Crime Commission realized this when it recommended the following:

> Police departments should have community relations machinery consisting of a headquarters unit that plans and supervises the department's community-relations programs. It should also have precinct units, responsible to the precinct commander, that carry out the programs. Community relations must be both a staff and a line function. Such machinery is a matter of the greatest importance in any community that has a substantial minority population.[4]

---

[4] President's Commission on Law Enforcement and Administration of Justice: *The Challenge of Crime in a Free Society,* Washington, D.C., U.S. Government Printing Office, 1967, p. 101.

No law enforcement agency in the history of policing has, as yet, scientifically approached the problem of crime from the standpoint of complete public awareness and community support for police officers. Dictatorships have attempted the police state and they have failed; our democratic society attempts near extremism in respect for the right of the individual, and this has certain undesirable consequences.

Continuous and professionally organized community relations programming is a technique that has only recently received more than lip service from most peace officers. The time for implementing the techniques noted—in a well-organized, continuous, ongoing manner—is with us today. It remains for the law enforcement agencies with sufficient vision and imaginativeness to try this new approach to solving a crime problem, which is worse now than at any other time in the history of mankind.

The Ultimate Role of Police-Community Relations

This chapter defines what must be done by policing agencies everywhere if they are to provide a climate of public acceptance and support so necessary to accomplish tasks detailed and termed the basic police mission. The role of police-community relations is to provide an acceptable climate of community support and knowledge, coupled with an attitude on the part of law enforcement personnel that overtly shows its desire to uphold the rights of the people they serve.

There are, of course, a wide variety of functions that fall within the immediate purview of functioning police-community relations activities. These functions are listed in no particular order of importance; they deal with police-community relations in the broadest aspect of the concept.

SPECIFIC COMMUNITY RELATIONS FUNCTIONS

The headquarters community-relations function has certain general responsibilities. It should plan programs, conduct in-service training, represent the department with various citizen groups, and supervise departmental community relations efforts. Another important headquarters function is to keep all personnel aware of the community relations activities. By so doing, a better understanding is gained by all officers, rather than just the select few assigned to the headquarters unit.

Coordination at the Top

Regardless of the size of the department, all community relations activities must be coordinated through one central source. In small departments, this will be the director, commissioner, sheriff, or chief of police. In larger departments, this might be delegated to a ranking officer of the organization; regardless, *the person designated to command this function must have direct access to the top man in the organization.* Otherwise, he or she may well choke to death in red tape or drown trying to swim "through channels" if direct access is not provided. Other approaches can provide a dangerous source of screening and delay of information vital to the long-range best interests of the police.

The community relations coordination function must also be geared to integrate knowledge of major importance of all other internal operations of the department. Thus, the contacts of police-community relations personnel with civic leaders, government officials, other law enforcement agencies, etc., must be reinforced with current data in order to provide continuity of both programming and current working policy.

Civic Liaison

Various civic organizational activities—Lions, Kiwanis, Rotary, and a host of others—as well as governmental meetings, i.e. a board of supervisors, city council, an economic and/or youth opportunities agency, etc., will require and desire association with law enforcement. This function should be more than haphazardly accomplished and should use as a general criteria the following system: Responsible organizations making requests for liaison should be accommodated, provided that (a) each organization so obtaining participation has a logical relationship to the police function, and (b) the organization is of sufficient size and/or meets only as often as is necessary, thus justifying regular participation by law enforcement.

As a general rule, it is safe to say that the law enforcement administrator must weigh carefully the mission of the liaison to the police and the nature of the agency making the request, coupled with the number of other such requests with which he/she is confronted.

Perhaps most important, a method of recording these contacts and their results should be established. A running log on each organization, properly indexed and filed, and including intelligence information of pertinence, can be of immense value in determining the nature of the organization's activities, its leadership structure, and determining precisely who may be asked to help solve a problem confronting the police. The liaison thus ranges from presentation to the group of information relative to the police operation, to a direct request for the group to render assistance to the police in some particular major policing problem.

Key Community Liaison

Each major policing jurisdiction will also contain a wide variety of racial, religious, ethnic, social, sports, and other groups, each of which may or may not have a distinguishable power structure. The police-community relations function requires identity of, and many times with, these groups and their leaders. Contacts here must be continuous, and, again, a log is recommended.

The amount of attention each group receives is largely dependent upon the nature of the group's activities, both from a criminal and a community participation standpoint. The number of officers necessitated will thus be determined, in large measure, by how important and how many groups fall within this category.

The same rules apply to all groups of sufficient size and importance to warrant attention.

Communications Releases by Law Enforcement

Policy statements, press releases, and prepared speeches and handouts offer a ready source of information to the public. Their distribution will be discussed later in this chapter and in detail in Chapter 6. The major point of emphasis here is that they must be prepared professionally, and their dissemination should be to all concerned parties.

A college degree and/or prior experience in journalism can surely help the person or persons responsible for this communications activity; the extremely critical importance of presenting professionally written material is hard to overemphasize. Improper use of the English language, misspelled words, or simply an unaccept-able journalistic style—each of these items can hurt the police image. Suffice to say, complete perfection may be an impossiblility, but here is one area where the goal must be just that.

Written statements also require competent stenographic assist-ance and proper typing and reproduction equipment. These should also be the finest quality available—human and mechanical.

Many have downgraded these functions of a policing agency, using such attacks as declaring them to be "icing on the cake." There is much more to it, and Scott explains, "I firmly believe, however, that the public, which pays something over eighteen mil-lion pounds a year for the Metropolitan Police, is entitled to know what is being done by the Force and what value it is getting for its money." [5]

Information Released by News Media

Radio, television, magazines, and newspapers provide a constant source of information for the public. Too often the police ignore the fact that the communications media is also a source of intelligence data on both their image and activities and other factors of interest and concern to law enforcement. In some areas, because of sheer volume, it may be wise to employ a clipping service to monitor specific areas of interest for the policing agency. Regardless of whether this activity is actually accomplished by the department, or *for* them through other arrangements, the information should be systematically collected and its contents noted and disseminated to the appropriate members of the policing agency.

Photography

Crime photography is important to a police agency, but photog-raphy can also provide a more generic public service and be con-ducive to good community relations. A picture of a peace officer can be made available to the press when a story of interest involving the officer develops. When the officer is not engaged in undercover work, it is wise to have such photographs on hand and available to the press. There is also a need to have individualized photographs available to the press, on key occurrences.

---

[5] Sir Harold Scott: *Scotland Yard*. Tonbridge, Kent, England Tonbridge Printers, 1944, p. 84.

In addition to having individualized photographs available, each department should file a short biographical sketch of each officer. A personal note about the officer is interesting and may add to the human side of an otherwise stereotyped story.

The community relations photographic function may be continuous or part-time, but it must be professional. It may be accomplished by the regular crime photographer, or it may be someone with little or no previous photographic experience. In any event, the person assigned to the task must be skilled or must receive sufficient training. He or she should know the needs of various news services. For example, this officer may not be equipped to take motion pictures or video shots for television, but he/she must know that still pictures should be available on reproduction paper of a matte (dull finish) rather than glossy material. The photographer must know this in advance, and the shots must be both eye-catching and clear; of course, if a picture is to be worth a thousand words, it must tell a story.

Displays

The majority of police agencies participate in activities where a display board of demonstration projects can do much to improve the police image. Then again, participation in a haphazard fashion has the opposite effect. Display boards may range all the way from simulated narcotic paraphernalia, or the confiscated weapons of juvenile gangs, to photographs depicting one or many of the department's activities. They may be accompanied by a uniformed officer impeccably dressed and well versed in departmental activities, or the display may be self-explanatory. The general rule to follow in this regard is *How many people will view the display in a given period of time, and is the display of such a nature that further explanation is desirable?*

News Media Contact

News media contacts should be accomplished on a continuing basis with both top management and the beat reporters assigned to the police function. Only in this manner can rapport be developed that will allow frank discussion on both the propriety of articles and reports that may be questionable and continuously provide to them confidential information, which may be highly desirable from a publicity point of view but extremely detrimental to a police case if it were to be aired publicly. As in the case with other community contacts, a running log is suggested in order that regularity of contact will be a fact accomplished.

Continuous Availability

It is important to remember that a coordinated police-community relations effort does not end at 5:00 PM on Friday afternoon, commencing once again at 9:00 AM the following Monday morning. The program must be as continuous and never-ending as the patrol function. This requires that a responsible person be designated for coordination duty, to be available at all times throughout the course of a day and night, 365 days a year. Smaller departments may find that the desk man or watch commander can perform this function with eminent success. Larger agencies may require formation and/or maintenance of a special unit to which this responsibility will be delegated.

Training

One particular person must be charged with overall responsibility for training departmental members in the field of police-community relations. He or she should be an accredited instructor, fully conversant with the department's overall operation and intimately acquainted with every phase of the police-community relations program.

Speakers Bureau

Various groups request speakers; other groups should be contacted with a positive program to be placed before them by an appropriate law enforcement official. The speakers bureau concept (which may consist of several persons devoting their full time to this function, or the chief of police or sheriff speaking to organizations in less densely populated areas) requires that the persons making addresses be trained in public speaking. The basic rule is *send your best officers to represent the department.*

Tours

Occasional visitors to the police agency, as well as prescheduled visits by groups of students and other interested persons, provide a

constant source of image improvement for law enforcement departments. This can only be true, however, provided the police facility
is well kept and the tour guide is both knowledgeable and person-
able. It is better to have an old facility with a friendly peace officer
conducting a tour, than a new building with someone caught
"going off shift" trying to speedily traverse the halls or venting
his/her personal dislike for being caught by a visitor or school
group.

Each person assigned to conduct tours should have prior training
and instruction regarding points of interest, and a ranking official
should periodically conduct test runs to be certain that each tour
host's actions and attitudes reflect the best interest of the department.

The availability of tours through the police facility should be
publicized. Many organizations and interested persons are not
aware that their police facility may be inspected.

PRODUCTIVITY

An all-pervasive theme of the various police community relations
activities must be productivity, which necessarily requires measurement of proportionate effectiveness of differing approaches to the
problem of crime. Whisenand captures the essence of the factors
that must be considered:

Productivity denotes the return received for a given unit of input. To
increase productivity means that a greater return must be realized for a
given investment. The concept most often is used in reference to the production of goods, e.g., more agricultural products, automobiles, or tons of steel
per man-hour. Specialists argue over the precise definition of the term
"productivity," but it can reasonably be assumed to be a ratio of "output"
(or what results from an activity) to "input" (or the resources committed to
the activity). It is granted that police services are not as easily defined as the
process of producing a television set. In general, higher police productivity
means keeping the police department's budget constant and improving performance, or keeping performance constant and reducing the size of the
budget. Productivity gain can also mean increasing the budget but improving performance at an even higher rate. But the concept of productivity
cannot simply be transferred in a theoretical form from the economics of
production to the operations of a state or local police department. Thus, it
is proposed that increasing productivity in police services be considered in
the following four ways.

First, *increasing police productivity means improving current police practices to the best level known in order to get better performance without a proportionate increase in cost.* This means doing the things that are considered to be a necessary part of good police work, but doing them as well or as efficiently as the best current practices permit. For example, officers assigned to patrol spend a great deal of time on such activities as filling out unnecessarily long reports, or on activities that are important but that would require less time if they were better coordinated (e.g, the long hours spent waiting to testify at a trial).

Second, *increasing police productivity means allocating resources to activities which give the highest return for each additional dollar spent.* A police department carries out a range of activities, many of which are non-crime-related, most of which are necessary to its overall responsibility to the public. Beyond a given scale, however, expanding certain activities will give the force less value than initiating or expanding others. For example, experiments already in progress tend to support the contention of some criminal justice analysts that random patrol has a limited effect in deterring criminals. Thus, it may be possible to take, say, 10 percent or more of the patrol force off random patrol without any significant negative effect and shift them to activities that focus on preventing crime such as "hardening" likely crime targets (e.g., improved building security).

Third, *given the uncertainties of police work, increasing productivity means increasing the probability that a given objective will be met.* The professional police officer — from the chief to the patrol officer — must deal constantly with many unknown or ambiguous factors. He is constantly assessing the likelihood that this or that may happen, and consequently the more skillful he becomes at increasing the probability that each activity will result in useful accomplishment, the more productive the overall operation becomes. The clearest example of increasing the probability of achieving the intended impact is having personnel assigned when and where crime is highest or the calls for service are heaviest. Simple observation can indicate the "when and where" in general terms; careful analysis of available data can more accurately pinpoint likely times and places of crime occurrence, thereby significantly increasing the probability of putting officers where they are needed.

Fourth, *increasing productivity in police work means making the most of the talents of police personnel.* Sworn officers are better trained and more expensive than ever before. This means that they are capable of higher performance, that economy requires they be used more effectively, and that they expect to be treated with greater respect and intelligence.[6]

Thus, for effectiveness, crime becomes the obvious foremost consideration; the residual effect of crime control is improved police-community relations.

---

[6] Paul M. Whisenand: *Crime Prevention.* Boston, Holbrook Press, 1977, pp. 358-360.

Measurement of Productivity

A fundamental problem in dealing with crime is its measurement. Through the United States Bureau of the Census, major crime in the more populated areas of our country was measured and vastly exceeded officially reported incidents. This is no fault of the official reporting system of the Department of Justice and the Federal Bureau of Investigation; it simply means that more crime exists than is reported, as any new officer on patrol is well aware of, and causes a need for certain unofficial input for effective enforcement.

Nettler makes an important point regarding better knowledge of crime-reporting procedures:

> The imperfections of official statistics on crime have led sociologists to invent other ways of counting violations of the law. It cannot be said, however, that these measures *improve* upon the official tallies. Where the unofficial measures disagree with official statistics, no one knows which is the more valid. Where the official and unofficial tabulations agree, one is more confident of the facts with which explanations of criminality are built. Fortunately for theories of criminogenesis, official and unofficial counts of crime are in general agreement in mapping the social locations of the serious offenses.
>
> The unofficial procedures for measuring crime include (1) direct observations of criminal activity, (2) surveys of the victims of crime, and (3) studies of confessions of crime.[7]

The three suggested procedures should merit careful consideration from all jurisdictions.

Certain other basic problems of *productivity* and its measurement must be considered. Some of the essential elements noted by the Police Foundation involve the following:

1. The productivity of the individual police officer (or individual police employee, civilian or sworn).
2. The productivity of police units, such as shifts, police districts, neighborhood policing teams, or precincts.
3. The productivity of particular kinds of units, such as motorized police, foot patrols, investigative units, special tactical strike forces, canine corps, etc.
4. The productivity of the police department as a whole.
5. The productivity of the crime control system, including both police activities and private activities to reduce crime.

---

[7] Gwynn Nettler: *Explaining Crime.* New York, McGraw-Hill, 1974, p. 62.

6. The productivity of the total community criminal justice system, includ-
    ing the police, the courts, the prosecutor's office, corrections and social
    service agencies, and private sector crime prevention activities (such as
    use of locks, watch dogs, etc.).[8]

A FINAL THOUGHT

The philosophy and model program outlined in this chapter are
predicated on the assumption that certain functions are of such
significant importance as to demand attention from the top police
administrator. The philosophy of law enforcement demands action
of a sincere and positive nature.

The mere "keeper of the peace" role is not enough. As Gourley
explains, "The policeman . . . must always remember that law
enforcement is not an end in itself; but is, rather, a means to an
end — and that end is the maintenance of an orderly society."[9]

Finally, both the role and areas of concern must admittedly be
lumped into a form of collectivization: *To merely be a thief-catcher
or to present police-community relations programs is not enough.
The police must believe in what they are doing!*

Discussion Questions

1. In recent years, the community relations unit has catapulted to
    a position of foremost priority. What effect, good or bad, has
    the operation of this unit had on the line officer?
2. Discuss some of the qualifications or experience you feel any
    police-community relations officer must possess.
3. How extensive do you feel that the community relations unit's
    influence should be?
4. What other programs are noteworthy that were not discussed in
    this chapter?
5. Are there other specific ways to measure the productivity of
    police-community relations programs and personnel?

---

[8] John F. Heaphy and Joan L. Wolfle: *Readings on Productivity in Policing.* Police
Foundation, 1975, p. 90.

[9] G. Douglas Gourley: *Public Relations and the Police.* Springfield, Thomas, 1953, p. ix.

groups young and old . . . too often and too long ignored as available avenues through which to know and influence community sentiment . . .

Chapter 5

GROUPS AND LAW ENFORCEMENT

Objective: To develop the appreciation of both officer and citizen of the importance and urgency for police involvement and active participation with community groups, and to urge a stronger support for such activity.

- Man as a group member
- Influence of community groups
- Communication and prevention
- Working with juveniles
- Groups formed by the police
- Contact with group leaders
- NCCJ Institute on PCR

E ACH PERSON is a member of groups of various types, and his/her own individual and collective organizational goals—formal and informal—will sometimes be in conflict. A peace officer offers a splendid example of this: The officer deplores the type of "civil disobedience" that amounts to breaking laws a person does not agree with; he or she may also, however—and there are some current, noteworthy examples—belong to a group that advocates civil disobedience. The dilemma is thus pointedly clear, while the solution is not. Police strikes exemplify the problem, but if "binding arbitration" does not offer a solution, then just what does?

A group is sometimes likened to a conspiracy: It takes just two, but it can consist of millions. It has a reason or purpose, however noble or ignoble, for forming and continuing, and it will seek to accomplish its mission. Fortunately, most groups are composed of law-abiding citizens for legal purposes. Unfortunately, at least from the view point of police, any single individual belongs to numerous groups, and the groups themselves are infinite in number, variety, and purpose.

Leavitt approaches groups from the standpoint of organizational interdependence. He notes the basic problem of *change* and contributes to an understanding of the role of the individual within the groups:

> Anyone who lives in an organization is living in an atmosphere of dependency. He should therefore feel some love and some hate toward the organization. The intensity and direction of feelings should, in turn, vary with the ups and downs of organizational life.
>
> The morals of this tale are simple and important ones. Don't look for psychological equilibrium in organizations (or in marriage or in any other relationship, for that matter) . . . Look for variation and change. Don't look for statics; look for dynamics. Don't look for permanently "happy" organization; look for one that is self-corrective, that doesn't build up unexpressed grudges.
>
> Big brother (the organization) must always be frustrating as well as satisfying. He fools himself if he thinks he can be otherwise. But what he and the paralyzed brother can do is to limit the duration and build-up of frustration by providing mechanisms for expressing and acting upon it. Big brother had better also be satisfying as well as frustrating, because the dependency is mutual.[1]

---

[1] Harold J. Leavitt: *Managerial Psychology.* Chicago, University of Chicago Press, 1970, p. 131.

This section emphasizes the critical importance of law enforcement involvement and continuous effective liaison with identifiable groups of sufficient size and importance to noticeably affect community activities.

MAN AS A SOCIAL ANIMAL

Since the time man first appeared on earth, he has formed groups, especially family groups. Initially, self-protection was the primary motivating factor. More recently, social and psychological reasons have become increasingly important. It is of extreme significance to the peace officer that he/she recognizes that, with rare exception, every person is a member of many groups with a wide variety of purposes and ideologies. For example, a man occupationally may be a plumber, a member of a church, a participant in a Friday night dance group, and captain of a bowling team. In each instance, he is associated with other people, for a purpose. However, in each instance the group may discuss or treat matters quite divergent from the general aims of the formal organization. A "bowling team" may simply be a social gathering for competitive sport; however, this group can become a very potent force for many activities that have not one thing to do with bowling.

This chapter emphasizes the critical importance of law enforcement involvement and effective liaison with identifiable groups of sufficient size and importance to noticeably affect community activity. The role of police involvement with their groups' leaders was mentioned in Chapter 3 and will be considered in detail later in this chapter.

Two other aspects of groups will first be considered. The first consists of contact with those groups that, though formed for other purposes, are important enough to warrant regular contact by law enforcement. The second consists of groups that law enforcement itself forms in order to more effectively accomplish the police mission.

COMMUNITY GROUPS OF INTEREST TO LAW ENFORCEMENT

Adult Group Considerations

Almost every American policing jurisdiction contains a legislative body, a number of business and professional organizations, a chamber of commerce, church groups, social and sports organizations, and other such groups. These organizations constitute a vital segment of dedicated men and women whose efforts do much to structure the tone and tempo of the community.

The police administrator must develop appropriate data on these various groups. He/she must have information on the key members, size, formal and informal goals, functions, purposes, and activities. This information will determine how frequent and what rank-level of police should contact each group.

Many of these organizations have a variety of projects that support law enforcement, and a member of the police department must be available to work with them or their committee members on these programs.

These groups can also be very helpful when needed to sponsor programs and related activities in their support of law enforcement. The wise police administrator also remembers the advice of the *Ladies Home Journal: Never underestimate the power of a woman.* Women peace officers and women's professional and social groups can be utilized with excellent results.

PARTICIPATION: FORMAL AND INFORMAL. Many departments have found it highly advantageous to encourage departmental members to become active in at least one community activity. This does not in any way restrict them from being active in more than one; but too often, people—including officers—join organizations and do nothing more than carry a card or put in a periodic appearance. For example, the fact that a person is a member of a church does not insure attendance or participation in church activities.

There will be many groups with which the chief law enforcement officer of an area will wish to maintain regular, formalized contact. However, there will also be many others which the prudent police administrator will encourage department members to participate with on an unstructured and informal basis.

PRODUCTIVE GROUP CONTACTS. Law enforcement has too often and too long ignored available avenues through which to know and deal with community sentiment. Shortages of personnel notwithstanding, each group of sufficient size and importance to a community should be the subject of a regular contact by representatives of the police, for the establishment of rapport. In some instances it may be the presentation of an address on some interesting aspect of police work, on a subject timely to the community, or it may be periodic attendance, or it may be regular attendance at all meetings.

The need exists, but it is incumbent upon law enforcement to accept responsibility for initiating a formal program for this type of community group contact.

Working with Juveniles

Many police agencies have regularly scheduled school assemblies of all age levels in which a peace officer presents law enforcement's view to school children. This may take the form of a bicycle safety program or may simply be an explanation of the equipment in a police radio car.

Various other youth groups exist and deserve regular contact. Unfortunately, in today's mobile society, many persons arrive at the magic age of sixteen, obtain driver's licenses, and promptly have their first individualized contacts with the law.

CITIZEN AND THE LAW. With teenage crime rates outstripping those of adults, coupled with the fact that most first-time teen contacts by otherwise law-abiding youths come in the nature of traffic citations, a need exists at perhaps the eighth- or ninth-grade level in every school to develop and implement mandatory courses regarding law enforcement and its functions. The courses should be presented by a law enforcement officer who is also a credentialed instructor. Ideally it would be a regular duty assignment for him or her, and the curriculum might range from "The History of Law Enforcement" to "The Necessity for Issuance of Traffic Citations." Through such programs at these critical age levels, law enforcement can give positive impetus to more favorable acceptance of the role of police by the teenager of today, who of course becomes the adult of tomorrow.

Such a course entitled "Citizen and the Law" was activated in the late 1960s at the Temple City, California, Junior High School. The course, offered as an elective, was and is part of a unique experimental project created by the Los Angeles County Sheriff's Department, the City of Temple City, and the Temple City Unified School District. Its purpose is to provide the students with a realistic knowledge of the law and its administration. "Citizen and the Law" includes instruction on the need for laws, how they are enacted, the need for enforcement, how crimes are investigated, how criminals are captured, prosecuted, and sentenced, and how they are punished and rehabilitated. The dangers of narcotics and drugs are also emphasized.

"Citizen and the Law" has been offered now for over ten years. Evaluation of the first year's results disclosed positive increases in students' attitudes toward the law and its enforcement. In addition, in 1967, the National Awards Jury of the Freedoms Foundation at Valley Forge selected "Citizen and the Law" as the principal awardee in the local governmental unit activity category.

GROUPS FORMED BY THE POLICE

A police agency must execute its basic law enforcement duties with efficiency and professional competence. However, effective law enforcement is also achieved through overtly seeking and obtaining the confidence and cooperation of the community. It ranges far beyond the role of the early peace officer.

Formation of groups by the police, to accomplish this broadened police mission, is neither new nor revolutionary in concept. Various police organizations have formed a variety of groups. They range from reserve organizations to youth bands. The critical area centers around certain criteria:

1. Each group formed should be given continuous guidance.
2. The police administrator must regularly evaluate formation of a group in terms of time expended versus results obtained.
3. Continuous evaluation of the productivity of on-going groups, ethereal and otherwise, must be accomplished.

The following sections will present, from a police-community relations standpoint, the most important of police-formed types of groups.

Police Reserves

Many jurisdictions, because of shortages of police personnel, have found it practical to organize civilians from many walks of life to serve as part-time peace officers. Traditionally, there has been a widespread belief that the existence of police reserves is both temporary and undesirable. The shortcomings of police reserves can in large measure be overcome through (1) superior selection standards and (2) formal training programs.

Too often police administrators have ignored the most important aspect of police reserve organizations: Many members of the community wish to overtly assist in some type of community activity, and many public-spirited individuals would prefer to ride and serve in a police radio car eight hours per week rather than ring doorbells for a fund-raising drive.

A LINK WITH THE COMMUNITY. The furnishing of uniforms, payment (token or otherwise), and many other aspects of police reserve organizations are important considerations. Emphasis here, however, is placed on recognizing that police reserves can provide a vital, intrinsic link with the community, while at the same time they render measurable service in terms of hours of activity. Thus, from the vantage point of police-community relations, police reserves can be of finite, tangible value to the police organization. At the same time, they are providing another approach to the civic conscience.

Educational Groups

Typical of the new and innovative educational groups that are operating nationwide was a recent three-day Police-Community Relations Institute co-sponsored by the Department of Criminal Justice, California State University, Los Angeles, and the Southern California Police-Community Relations Officers' Association.

The Institute was directed to the patrol officer and first-line supervisor. Its primary mission was to illuminate and emphasize the personal significance and influence of these first-line "Ambassadors of Good Will" to successful police-community relations and the creation of the police image. Chapter 5 of this text summarizes its findings.

Advisory Groups

The police administrator is not a banker, newspaperman, public relations director, or an advertising executive. In most jurisdictions, key members of each of these fields (and many more) are highly desirous of maintaining good and effective law enforcement. This affords a golden opportunity for the police-community relations officer. Historically, police tritely acknowledge that the public must believe that their police are professionally organized and doing a highly competent job. Yet law enforcement has too often stopped here, instead of viewing the obvious: Responsible members of the community—persons of stature from all walks of life—can be formed into advisory groups.

In most instances community members willingly serve as consultants on issues vitally affecting the police image. Their view from the outside can provide law enforcement with insight that may alter a procedure or change an approach (or develop a new one) and thus assist in valuable and concrete form, in the improvement of police-community relations.

Law enforcement is viewed in its most exemplary light when it precludes trouble before the problem develops. Small and petty grievances can grow to irritation, then dilemma, and finally crisis. Why not act before the problem develops to stage two or three of such a continuum? Advisory-group contacts should be a first order of business for departments without them.

Citizen Advisory Committees

The President's Crime Commission, in recommending the formation of Citizen Advisory Committees, declared them to be "the most promising mechanism that has evolved" to reduce the isolation of the police from the community. "Effective communication between the police and the neighborhood is essential, and advisory committees offer an excellent means to achieve it."[2]

In noting that "existing committees have been seriously deficient,"[3] the Commission recommended the following practices:

1. Committees should attempt to attract as many participants as possible.
2. There should be at least one committee in each precinct, and more where precincts cover large areas or where community relations problems are serious.
3. Committees should involve not only ranking officers and community relations officers, but also the sergeants and patrol officers who bear the daily brunt of putting community relations into practice.
4. Membership should include not only the business and civic leaders who

---

[2] President's Commission on Law Enforcement and Administration of Justice: *Task Force Report: The Police.* Washington, D.C., U.S. Government Printing Office, 1967, pp. 156-157.

[3] President's Commission, *The Police*, pp. 156-157.

agree with the police or otherwise do not cause trouble, but also the people who harbor the greatest hostility toward the police, who most need an escape valve for their antagonisms, real or imagined. As explained by the Commission:

"Persons who are hostile may be argumentative, disruptive, or otherwise difficult to deal with. Allegations may be made which are, or which appear to be, radical or irresponsible. However this free discussion allows the committees to become vehicles for meeting conflict head-on in a controlled forum. The possibility of unpleasantness at a meeting is obviously preferable to leaving these confrontations to the streets."

5. Police must encourage frank and open discussion of controversial subjects. Complaints, whether or not they have basis, should be solicited and seriously considered. These meetings can dispel myths and uncover problems about police practices that, if left to rumor, would continue to create friction.

6. Police should use such community gatherings to discuss and elicit citizen views of police enforcement practices. For example, the use of dogs, saturation patrols, stop-and-frisk, and other practices all affect community relations. Consequently, citizens' opinions should be considered as one relevant factor in determining how these measures are used.[4]

Juvenile Groups

The rising crime rate in America offers many problems, not the least of which is the startling upward trend in crimes committed by juvenile offenders. There is a critical need for police agencies to accept a more active role in forming and participating with juvenile groups. This may take many forms, ranging from the youth band to an athletic league; it may entail assistance of, and participation with, already active juvenile groups, such as the Boy Scouts.

An excellent example of police participation with juvenile groups is the Los Angeles Police Department's "Law Enforcement Explorer Program." This program is intended to interest young Explorers (scouts) in a career in law enforcement and to develop an awareness of civic responsibility. The motto is "Learning to protect and to serve." Members are selected through a process similar to that employed in the selection of regular police officers. Training in basic law enforcement procedures prepares them to participate in various police-related activities.

---

[4] President's Commission, *The Police*, pp. 156–157.

Although chartered by the Boy Scouts of America, the program is law enforcement oriented and emphasizes good citizenship and character development. After training at the Los Angeles Police Academy, the Explorers participate in the following police activities: parade duty, bicycle licensing, department displays at public functions, tours of local police facilities, overnight trips, departmental service projects, and representing the Police Department at Boy Scout events.

FRINGE AREA YOUTH. In the effort to contact the youth, one must not overlook the "fringe area youth," the youngsters who are not qualified for the Boy Scout programs. These youngsters should not be abandoned to the underworld of crime and degradation. They can go either way, and we must initiate programs—and meet with them, for progress will be slow and many times frustrating—to direct these youths away from criminal environs and into the majority group of law enforcement supporters.

Skolnick and Gray pinpoint the basic problem that is at once legalistic and ecological:

> This ecological conflict thus has a legal dimension. The view of fighting held by gang boys, for example, is clearly a case in which the law and the customs conflict. The police are often called upon to break through layers of screaming girls in order to separate a pair of street-style gladiators, and one patrolman even suggested that the worst injuries he had sustained as an officer had been leg bites received from females on these occasions. Yet to gang boys, most of these fights are both honorable and necessary. They were either challenged, insulted, or hit first, and thus they are always bitter when penalized by the police . . .
>
> There are other situations, however, in which the formal legal status of a disorder is more ambiguous, and these situations can cause trouble when both the police and the gang boys lay claims to the benefit of the doubt. For example, when strangers or "unfamiliars" are being treated to gross violations of etiquette or to other such attacks on their faith in social order, the police quite naturally feel constrained to take action. Yet from a gang member's point of view, the legal issues involved in disorganizing a social situation are not always clear-cut.[5]

The author recommends that, in addition to having a mandatory course in law enforcement for all eighth or ninth graders, the police must participate more actively both with established juvenile

---

[5] Jerome N. Skolnick and Thomas C. Gray: *Police In America.* Boston, Educational Associates Division of Little, Brown & Company, 1975, p. 159.

groups and in the creation of police-sponsored programs such as summer camping, sport clubs, junior bands, and discussion groups. These youth programs enable the police and young people to engage in nonpunitive relationships while working and competing in sports and other positive educational character-building activities.

The police administrator may use the same techniques and devices to formalize contacts and formulate activities for the agency with both existing and needed juvenile groups that are used for adult group contacts.

The tremendous impact of our youth today appears certain to intensify this critical problem area, and it is imperative that action be taken now, as it is almost certain to require additional and expanded activity in the immediate future. A younger voting group requires many changes; action *now* can alleviate much of the trauma of "Future Shock."

THE GROUPS' LEADERS APPROACH

The final type of community group contact discussed here involves an approach that can prove to be highly productive. It centers around the necessity of bringing together leaders from the police field and leaders from the various power centers of the community. The meeting ground is all-important, and many so-called nonaction-oriented organizations, such as the National Conference of Christians and Jews, can provide an important and regularly programmed link through which contact may be initiated and maintained.

All too often, leaders in the police field have failed to contact important groups' leaders and thus have failed to gather vital intelligence on how these groups think and how they may act toward developing situations that are intimately linked with the functions of law enforcement.

Human Relations Commissions, B'nai Brith, the National Association for the Advancement of Colored People, the Japanese-American Citizen League, Council of Mexican-American Affairs — these are examples of racially, religiously, and ethnically oriented groups. There are many, many more, and it behooves the police administrator to engage actively in regular police-community relations conferences with the leaders of these organizations.

Groups: Collectivization versus Individual Contact

It is important to note the basic differences between having contact with individual groups and having contact with group leaders collectively, such as the conferences referred to, or some other gathering. The exchange between police and group leaders, properly conducted, may serve a fruitful purpose, particularly when the police are sincere in their desire to correct any real grievances. A further proviso is that community groups are willing to look realistically at problem areas and to assist in correcting misunderstandings that may exist in the minds of their members.

In summary, whether the group be a city council or a community coordinating council, whether it is racially, religiously, or ethnically oriented or simply a social club of stature or significance, the police should lend every effort to have regular and productive meetings with the responsible leaders of these organizations.

KEY LEADERSHIP CONFERENCES

Though a recurring theme of this text deals with police-community relations against a backdrop of a major social upheaval, it must nevertheless be emphasized that this very vital area is the continuous topic of less spectacular activities and attention. Numerous community groups, interested in promoting better rapport between the police and the public, have diligently labored to this end. That their efforts have not been entirely successful is evidenced by social turmoil; that their work has not been in vain may be presumed by the developing and generally excellent police-community climate in various areas of our nation.

Of these groups, few have been more energetic or successful in their endeavors than the National Conference of Christians and Jews (NCCJ). This section is based on excerpts from their Seventh Annual Institute on Police and Community Relations, attended by hundreds of key community and law enforcement leaders. The author was chairman of that conference, and in light of the nature of topical considerations, the most significant discourse of that meeting is offered, along with the general format. This type of meeting—community leaders and leaders from law enforcement— is offered as a model from which towns and metropolitan areas throughout the nation are encouraged to draw both format and actual data. The areas discussed by conference participants were those of most pertinence at that time. As police-community relations is a living, vibrant activity, highly localized in nature, each region must adapt to problems most acute to their region. The point is that, with key community and law enforcement leaders, such participation can help.

Organizing an Institute

The Institute to be discussed on police and community relations was co-sponsored by the University of Southern California, California State University at Long Beach, and California State University at Los Angeles, and was presented at the University of Southern California in cooperation with the Southern California Region of the NCCJ.

Several planning sessions were held during the year preceding the conference, with participation of community and police leaders in each session. Two months prior to presentation, literature and enrollment forms were provided each Los Angeles County police chief and the heads of key community organizations with an active and responsible interest in police-community relations.

The Discussion Groups

The theme of the Institute was "Law Enforcement—a Total Community Responsibility." As mentioned, hundreds of persons representing both law enforcement and the general citizenry attended.

Five topics were discussed by the registrants, divided into fifteen separate discussion groups:

1. *Demonstrations:* Who's in the Middle?
2. *Statistics:* Fact, Fallacy, or Fiction?
3. *Communication:* John Q. Public—John Q. Law.
4. *Police:* Conduct, Control, Complaints.
5. An *Orderly Society* with Individual Rights.

Two persons in each discussion group served as recorders. *One recorder represented the general citizenry, the other represented law enforcement.* At the "summit" session, the principal reporters' summaries were presented to the entire institute.

The following is the summary of the principal reporters. One should note the diversified background, as it provides depth, insight, and better understanding:

Topic Number 1: *DEMONSTRATIONS: WHO'S IN THE MIDDLE?*

Speaker from the community: Executive Director, Community Relations Committee, Jewish Federation Council.
Speaker from law enforcement: Inspector, Los Angeles County Sheriff's Department.

Defining the "middleman" in this case is not as easy as it might appear at first glance. In one sense, everybody is at times "in the middle," depending on the circumstances. Yet in a very real sense, law enforcement officers are the actual "middlemen" because the nature of their operation requires that they maintain law and order while at the same time protecting the rights of opposing sides of factions.

Problems Involved
1. Discerning whom to protect.
2. Legal problems involved in arrests.
3. Limits of civil disobedience.
4. Maintaining a good image under trying and difficult situations.

Possible Solutions
1. Coordination of plans with law enforcement.
2. Use of enlightened community resources (business, education, religious, etc.) to attempt to attack causes that prompt demonstrations.
3. Have law enforcement people formulate and share clear-cut policies.
4. Importance of responsible community support of law enforcement officials when they are carrying out the law.
5. Stimulate dialogue between law enforcement officials and responsible community leaders, including representatives of minority groups.
6. Importance of maintaining orderly demonstrations.

Topic Number 2: *STATISTICS: FACT, FALLACY, OR FICTION?*

Speaker from the community: Director, Youth Studies Center, University of Southern California.
Speaker from law enforcement: Lieutenant, Los Angeles Police Department.

It is generally recognized that statistics are an important aspect of almost every kind of organization or project. They are needed to determine need and location of services. They are needed for budgetary purposes. They are needed as a public relations device to help interpret the work and activities of a particular group or organization.

Problems Involved

The problem lies in the use and interpretation of statistics. Their value as tools of communication are limited because —

1. There is no standard or uniform language and interpretation.
2. The expense involved in separating out facts that would be of most help to a community or pointing out the problems of a specific group is considerable.
3. The collection of facts and the analysis of data are often one operation, thereby making objectivity difficult.
4. Differences in how arrests are written can be reflected in ultimate statistics on crime.
5. The fear of legal reprisal makes difficult at times the securing of needed statistics.

Possible Solutions

1. Attempt to achieve uniformity in language and interpretation.
2. Statistics should be related to some clear-cut purposes. They should be descriptive and objective, thus avoiding the tendency toward stereotyping certain groups.
3. Should consider "ecology of crime" — not where the suspect was arrested, but some data on the community in which he lives.
4. Give serious consideration as to how and where statistics are released and also the length of time an individual remains a "statistic."
5. Give further thought to sharing statistics with employers, the military service, or social welfare agencies.

Topic Number 3: COMMUNICATION: JOHN Q. PUBLIC— JOHN Q. LAW

Speaker from the community: Director, Community Workshop North Hollywood.

Speaker from law enforcement: Chief, Los Angeles County Sheriff's Department.

The lack of effective communication is an ever present problem in practically every organization and segment of our community. In spite of positive efforts by law enforcement and community organizations to improve communication, this area is one of continuing concern.

Problems Involved

1. Stereotypes both have of each other, thus making communication all the more difficult.
2. Occasional breakdown in communication within law enforcement groups themselves, i.e. squabbles with probation, FBI, etc.
3. Technological advances, which have about eliminated the man on the beat.
4. Irresponsible representations at times by the mass media and others in positions of authority.
5. The isolating of law enforcement people from a total community context rather than being an integral part of the community.
6. The problem of reaching the masses effectively.

Possible Solutions

1. Strengthen and extend courses in human relations, using more minority persons.
2. Strengthen interagency communications.
3. Broader participation of police *as citizens* in community affairs.
4. "Shake-Hands-with-a-Policeman Day."
5. Develop ways of communication with the most resistant persons and groups in a community.
6. Involve more of the clergy.

Topic Number 4: POLICE: CONDUCT, CONTROL, AND COMPLAINTS

Speaker from the community: Private Attorney, West Covina, California.
Speaker from law enforcement: Chief of Police, Arcadia Police Department, California.

Discussion on this topic is similar to touching a sensitive nerve and often sheds more heat than light on this usually explosive issue.

Problems Involved

1. Why does there appear to be a lack of coordination and communication among top local enforcement personnel?
2. Apparent lack of public understanding of the police function and intra-agency relations.
3. The almost universal opposition to police review boards and the feeling of many that the most direct and practical avenue of communication is closed.
4. Suspicion that internal policing and regulation is not always fair to the one aggrieved.
5. Feeling by a considerable number of people that different standards of law enforcement are used in different areas.
6. Police feel lack of support when courts don't convict.

Possible Solutions

1. Give public recognition when positive steps are taken to improve conditions.
2. Consider the development of a more systematic interagency approach in the Los Angeles area.

Topic Number 5: AN ORDERLY SOCIETY WITH INDIVIDUAL RIGHTS

Speaker from the community: Professor, California State University, Los Angeles, Department of Sociology.
Speaker from law enforcement: Chief, Newport Beach Police Department.

The following selected quotations from this group reflect some of their thinking on this subject:

1. The most orderly man in the world is the man in jail — but he must give up all of his rights.
2. In a democracy, individuals must abide by rules, but *basically* individuals resent agencies or individuals who enforce laws.
3. Our society is so concerned with *order* that the individual is loosing ground.
4. The image of the officer as a defender of civil rights is often blurred because he frequently uses judgments that seem arbitrary and represent questionable interpretation of the laws.
5. Tolerance and blindness by the appellate courts have taught all people that what is legally defensible is, in fact, not wrong.

Considerable concensus developed around these concepts:

1. There must be mutual respect for individual liberties and the police power. The unanswered question is, Where are these ideas brought into balance?
2. The protection of individual rights has become so strong an idea that some feel community rights must be emphasized and placed in a position of dominance (liberal interpretation of technical points by courts were cited).
3. Local communities must develop citizen groups who can assist in strengthening the concept of law enforcement, the police role, and the individual rights and responsibilities— even if imported leaders are used.[6]

Some Results

There was a general recommendation that the next police and community conference should involve some of the people talked about who were not present at the Institute. Perhaps some of these people could be helpful in trying to find answers to many of these problems.

From the written evaluations of the Institute, submitted by more than 50 percent of those who attended, a large majority of both law enforcement and non-law enforcement persons said they would like to attend another institute of this kind in the future. They also indicated they would encourage others to attend, and that concrete action in the community can be the long-range results.

The task facing both law enforcement officials and non-law enforcement persons in this revolutionary age is a momentous one, to say the least. It is not insurmountable, however. If all groups in our communities, law enforcement and non-law enforcement alike, view today's challenge as an opportunity rather than a detriment, we may see a new day in human relations in the not too distant future.

A COURSE OF ACTION

For truly effective community group contact, basic identifiable community problems will provide guidelines for the police administrator. He or she must attempt to reach, directly and indirectly,

---

[6] *Seventh Annual Institute on Police and Community Relations,* National Conference of Christians and Jews.

every person within the community in a manner that will enhance law enforcement's image. Human limitations on time and circumstances make the programming of personal, individualized contacts impractical, if not impossible. The police must reach persons in groups having the greatest impact on the community.

While this chapter emphasizes the three basic types of groups in which law enforcement must show interest, relative to police-community relations, there can be no question that overtly seeking and maintaining the support of the community, in the final analysis, is a responsibility the policing agencies of this nation can ill afford to abrogate. That the police and community share this responsibility is true, but for too long the police have waited for others to initiate appropriate activities to instill in each person this general respect for the law.

The groups that the police administrator organizes to do active police work, provide advice, or create rapport must be dealt with carefully, just as the people in a police agency who are to provide liaison with any group must be given appropriate attention.

The chief law enforcement officer of today must accept responsibility for initiating and continuing programs of contact with important existing community groups on a regular basis. In this manner, when a problem in the general area of police-community relationship arises, the administrator will know where to turn for guidance and support.

Discussion Questions

1. What role do you feel the police should play in community groups? Should it be on a formal or informal basis?
2. It has often been said that in order to maintain order, police need the backing and active support of the community. From the standpoint of the line officer, discuss some of the ways in which the effectiveness of his/her performance can be increased by this support.
3. What do you feel should be the role of the police in campus disorders?
4. What are some of the advantages and disadvantages of programs such as "block mother" and "coffee sessions?"

. . . the impression the public gains from reading, watching, and hearing has a direct correlation with the individual officer . . .

Chapter 6

THE PRESS

*Objective: To develop both the line officer's apprecia-
tion of the vital need for rapport and the departmental
policies and relationships that maintain good police-
press rapport.*

- Policies of notification of media
- Creating a favorable press
- Pressboards and press passes
- Press conferences
- Prisoner interviews?
- Written police-press policies

MARK TWAIN, with his usual tongue-in-cheek humor, wrote "There are two forces that can carry light to all corners of the globe—the sun in the heavens and the Associated Press down here." Oscar Wilde apparently felt otherwise: "In the old days men had the rack. Now they have the press." Edmunds Travis illuminated the role and objectives of a free and unbiased press as being "the protagonist and preserver of all rights, the foe and destroyer of all tyrannies. It insures every cause a hearing and every false doctrine a challenge." C.P. "Spud" Corliss, a veteran reporter who covered Los Angeles County for forty years, stated, "Despite a variance in viewpoints there is a common meeting ground between reporters and police because, after all, they should both be working in the public interest." [1]

History

The history of mass communication has been altered radically during the past 100 years; exponential progress is apparent everywhere, and not the least momentous transition has been the growth and improvement of public communication media. Only a few years ago, the newspaper stood alone as the only real means of "rapid" communication to the public. The telephone and telegraph did much to change this, although the major transition occurred with the advent of radio, then television.

Paradoxically, growth of the newspaper industry since World War II has been remarkable, and it serves as a basis for dealing with the concept of press relations. There are over 1,700 daily newspapers in this country. From 1947 through 1963, newspaper employment of personnel expanded from 248,000 to 329,000, a gain of 33 percent. In that time, total United States employment increased by 19 percent, and employment in manufacturing grew only 9 percent. Growth is also reflected in greater circulation, which in 1964 exceeded 60,400,000, compared to less than 51,000,000 in 1946. [2]

While no truly definitive studies have been done since this report,

---

[1] C.P. "Spud" Corliss: *Guideposts.* Hawthorne, California, Butler Data Systems, 1969, p.29.

[2] John G. Udell, Director, Bureau of Research and Service: *The Growth of the American Daily Newspaper: An Economic Analysis.* School of Commerce, University of Wisconsin, 1965.

a telephone poll reveals no appreciable change. Television, however, has taken on a new dignity — and overwhelming importance.

An important point is that people may be more numerous and better educated, but they are also more news conscious than in the past. We see it reflected through this cursory review of the newspaper trade; add to this the tremendous impact of radio and television, and a picture of police-press relationships begins to take form.

Equal Treatment: Notification Policy

Years ago, the newspaper stood alone as the great source of information for the general public, regarding both the routine and major activities of law enforcement. Radio and television have done much to change this as they have the ability to *present information on events as they are occurring.*

A police agency must recognize this, but it is also of extreme importance that all news media be notified of any incident of a news nature that results in a press notification.

It is wise for the police department head to have and utilize a clearly developed policy of notification, and this should be a matter of written, available record, for the information of all members of the department as well as the news services.

Types of Releases

News to be released to the press may be grouped into three types:

1. *Hot or instant news.* This would include a bank robbery, murder, a major traffic accident, or similar occurrences.
2. *Information news or written communications.* This type has no great importance from the standpoint of the absolute time of release. Typical examples are releases announcing openings for police employment, warning drivers to be cautious as summer vacation nears, and warnings to shoppers to watch their packages at Christmas time. These releases can be programmed through a tickler file, maintained on an annual basis.
3. *Feature story.* Usually a feature story results from either a reporter's interest in a particular departmental activity which has received little attention, or from the chief, public information officer, or any law officer with a nose for news. Examples of this would be human interest activities of members of the department.

    An officer may, on his own time, have organized a teenage softball team that competes with other similar groups in the community; or officer's career may have been marked with the solving of certain spectacular cases, and a news reporter may wish to do a story on this. Regardless of the incident, the key factor here is that the release is not instant news, nor the subject of a general release. The reporter prepares a feature story, and the normal practice is for it to be carried by one paper, radio station, or television channel.

Responsibility for Press Notification

The sheriff or chief of police bears ultimate responsibility for notification of the press on all items of major concern. In small departments, it may be possible and desirable to have the chief or an immediate subordinate release all news. Conversely, other departments, particularly the larger ones, have found it beneficial to follow a decentralization press notification system, which allows the individual officer at the scene of a major incident to make immediate notification. Whatever system is adopted, the singularly most critical area — and one of vital importance for any law enforcement agency — is to decide whether to allow the officer at the scene of an instant news-type incident to release information directly, or to call his/her supervisor or a press information officer for instruction, or to have the department head handle the subject.

Many departments have information officers to handle major news releases. Here, as is the case with the other alternatives available, the law enforcement administrator must weigh the value of instantaneous coverage against the possibility of a garbled release or, worse yet, the release of information that may help a criminal escape justice.

Whatever the decision, it is of prime importance to make hot incident notifications swiftly to all interested news media. A uniform policy must be established. Perhaps the radio dispatching desk will have a certain number of central locations or phone numbers that should be called when newsworthy items occur. A manned police pressroom may be located in the police facility. A centralized agency such as Los Angeles City News Service can be a tremendous advantage to a police agency, by notification through its wire services of countless news media locally, and when the occasion warrants it, this news service functions on a nationwide basis. Associated Press and United Press render outstanding assistance.

This problem of press release is by no means unique to police agencies: "Many companies spend a great deal on advertising, yet are not prepared to exploit what may be the finest advertising opportunity of them all: The *time* when something happens within the company to make it *news.*"[3]

One highly sensitive area requires elaboration: the scoop. Many times a reporter will come across a story of human interest and wants to deal with it as an "exclusive." As a rule, this is not a safe policy becaue, should this individualistic treatment occur on a hot incident, the head of the department can plan on all other media descending upon him or her with a vengeance. Perhaps the only practical dividing line is to make it a firm policy that all information given any news media regarding an incident of immediate or informational news value be given to all agencies.[4]

Creating a Favorable Press

A press favorable to a police agency can be quite difficult to obtain and always requires close attention. There can be no substitute for police work well done by an honest and efficient force of well-trained officers. There is no question that individual deeds of outstanding or heroic police work earn their own good publicity. Certainly no police agency can create proper news media relationships without first proving itself fully capable of handling its basic law enforcement functions.

THE CHIEF ADMINISTRATOR AND THE PRESS. The head of the law enforcement agency and the public information officers should make regular and reasonably frequent visits to the offices of the various news media. In this way, they will establish a personal relationship that can aid a great deal in facilitating good and proper coverage of events. The chief will also learn firsthand of areas where a breakdown in communications might, is, or may have been occurring.

Conversely, members of the press should be periodically invited to accompany the police in the field. This procedure would directly acquaint the press with the problems on the street that confront the police.

---

[3] Merchants and Manufacturer's Association: *Employers Press Relations Manual and Directory.* Los Angeles, Merchants and Manufacturer's Association, January, 1970, p.1.

[4] From a personal interview with Thomas C. McCray, Vice President and General Manager, National Broadcasting Company.

PERSONAL RELATIONSHIPS. All officers of the law enforcement agency will have personal contact with members of the press.
Therefore, it remains for police supervisors to set an example of
friendly, fair, and impartial treatment of all reporters. Mere lip
service is not enough. It follows that training conferences with
junior and senior police officers must go on continuously, and their
attitude must be observed constantly if proper demeanor is to be
obtained and retained.

A letter from the head of a police agency to a news media editor
or publisher in appreciation of a particularly favorable story and
commending the actions of a reporter can do much to create and
cement favorable relationships. In no case, however, should this be
considered a substitute for personal contacts, or should it consist of
idle, unwarranted flattery.[5]

Pressrooms and Pressboards

Policing agencies receiving frequent visits from members of the
news media will find it advantageous to have a pressroom for the
use of reporters. The room should be equipped with sufficient
tables and chairs, phone, perhaps typewriters, and certainly a
pressboard. The latter will contain a copy of major police reports
that may logically and legally interest the press, and thus the
public.

Any report upon which the department wishes to properly restrict
publicity, while still allowing the beat reporter to be cognizant of it,
may be marked by an appropriate stamp; or it may be retained in a
separate file and its review accompanied by a written or verbal
explanation that the matter is confidential. Proper rapport with
police beat reporters will result in such information remaining
unpublished.

Smaller departments may find no need for a pressroom as such,
but the concept and a pressboard are still a must.

Press Conferences

The press conference is a scheduled meeting with the press; it
may be programmed regularly—once a week, or once a month—or
it may be called when there is an announcement of major impor-

---

[5] Personal interview with Thomas C. McCray, Vice President and General Manager,
National Broadcasting Company.

tance that does not fall within the strict definition of a hot news item; it may be both of the above.

There are many advantages to including in a press conference an open-end question-and-answer period with members of the press. However, one must be prepared for every eventuality, as the questions can sometimes become quite eccentric. A policy used by several agencies holding press conferences is to request that questions be submitted in writing, shortly in advance of the conference.

Regardless, the press conference has great merit, and perhaps the best criterion on which to base the question of whether holding regular or "as needed" meetings is to consult with the news media serving a particular locale.

Role-playing and Press Information

Every competent peace officer learns to adapt his/her actions and attitudes as the situation demands. However, a strange "phenomenon" sometimes occurs when the officer in the field becomes the subject of a news interview. When this consists solely of a reporter with pencil and paper, then much is left up to the reporter in terms of both accuracy and presentability of the situation. Today, the telephone beeper for radio, the tape recorder, and the sound-on-film television camera have altered the situation radically.

The "phenomenon" previously mentioned refers to the curious deportment of many highly capable policemen when confronted with a microphone and/or camera. Lack of appropriate response can transmit an image of electrifying consequences, particularly when a nervous officer stammers through a taped interview.

The answer to "appropriate response" lies in adequate training for just such occurrences at the cadet and higher levels. It may be accomplished through an adaptation of role-playing techniques with tape recorders and, if fiscally possible, television equipment. Playback is enlightening, and practice is an all important factor.

In a day when police-community relations is receiving massive attention, it is vital for each officer to be as professional and competent in appearance as is humanly possible.

The Press Pass

Police press-pass issuance, usually done on a yearly basis by

ISSUING AGENCY

CALIFORNIA — 19__

PRESS

WHOSE SIGNATURE APPEARS ON
THE REVERSE SIDE HEREOF, IS AN
ACCREDITED REPRESENTATIVE OF

POLICE AUTHORITY   OVER

PHOTO

THIS CARD IS ISSUED ONLY FOR THE PURPOSE
OF IDENTIFYING THE HOLDER AS AN ACCREDITED
REPRESENTATIVE OF THE ORGANIZATION INDI-
CATED AND ENTITLES BEARER TO PASS POLICE
AND FIRE LINES. IT MAY NOT BE TRANSFERRED TO
ANOTHER PERSON AND IT IS TO BE RELIN-
QUISHED TO THE EMPLOYER UPON TERMINATION
OF EMPLOYMENT.

I ACCEPT THE ABOVE_____
                            SIGNATURE OF HOLDER

example of a press pass (front and back) used by the California Peace Officer's
Association

agencies utilizing such a system, offers a way of identifying reporters
working police beats. A rigorous screening process, developed in
close cooperation with top representatives of the news media,
insures appropriate issuance to authorized representatives of the
press. These passes serve to identify the holder but may also
authorize the bearer to pass through police and fire lines.

A Bit More on Press Policies

Each department must adapt its press policies to the needs of the
agency and news media. The factors mentioned in the preceding
pages should be reflected in any given agency in the adaptation that

best serves the long-range interest of their policing agency.

To do this effectively requires that the press policy be written, to serve as a continuous source of review with all personnel, and that members of the news media have full knowledge of just what is the current policy.

PRISONER INTERVIEWS. The subject of prisoner interviews illustrates this need for a well-defined, workable, and near universally acceptable press policy. Police agencies should not arbitrarily decide to restrict or provide prisoner interviews; rather, this should be worked out in conjunction with the press, the judiciary, legal counsels, and other concerned and responsible parties. In this manner, the law enforcement agency will not be placed in a position of arbitrarily determining a policy that at the moment might appear to serve the best interests of society, yet might create a highly undesirable long-range police-community relationship that abrogates substantially the beneficial effects of influential police work.

The Pursuit of Press Rapport

Many excellent documents have been written solely on the subject of police-press relationships. The factors mentioned in this brief analysis are those considered essential to the subject generically. The impression the public gains from reading, watching, and hearing of the actions of peace officers — today more than at any other time in the history of reporting — has a direct correlation with the "presentation skills" of the individual officer. The tape recorder and television camera make it essential for the officer to be a more versatile and capable "role-taker." He or she must not only present factual data but also must be able to do so with the clarity of Demosthenes and an appearance of supreme competence.

To retain relevance in the specific field of police-community relations and in order to keep the press fully apprised of PCR developments, a national publication of the National Conference of Christians and Jews, *The Hot Line,* is strongly recommended as a must on the mandatory reading list for both press and officers assigned to PCR. Subscriptions are inexpensive and extremely informative.[6]

---

[6] To obtain *The Hot Line,* write to the National Conference of Christians and Jews, 43 West 57th Street, New York, N.Y. 10019.

Written press policies — available to, adhered to, and known by all concerned — will do much to overcome difficulties that can arise as a result of news media contacts. These policies should be worked out in concert with the news media as well as other concerned branches of government. The essential characteristic of positive police-press relationships is a concern for the long-range program, designed to continuously foster and encourage the finest of police-community relationships.

Discussion Questions

1. What can be done to insure that good relationships between the press and the police continue, while at the same time insuring that both can do their jobs effectively?
2. What other activities not mentioned in this chapter cause police-press problems?
3. How would you initiate a *press policy* if you were the top official of a law enforcement agency?

role-playing . . . bridging the void between classroom and radio car . . .

Chapter 7

TRAINING AND EDUCATION
IN POLICE-COMMUNITY RELATIONS

Objective: To emphasize the necessity for continuous education of all peace officers at all levels—cadet, in-service, and command—to the long-range and immediate success of any police-community relations program.

- Major causes of police problems
- Better education for better justice
- Specific areas of PCR training (U.S. Constitution to public speaking)
- Peripheral areas (arrest techniques to role-playing)
- Continuous in-service training
- Management training

THE ONLY CONSTANT IS CHANGE

A continuous thread woven throughout this text is the admonition that times are changing and the police must change with them. They must modernize traditional methods and policies to meet new problems, demands, and responsibilities. Perhaps a more definitive delineation is in order at this point. Just what are these changes and problems and how do they affect law enforcement?

In the sense of community relations, today's community is vastly different from the community of yesteryear. This implies an urgent need for new concepts in police education and training, especially with regard to human relations, group dynamics, and the behavioral sciences. Law enforcement must examine its image and modify it from that of a repressive social influence to one willing to experiment with positive programs in a sociological context. Community crime prevention is a vital and dynamic part of this (*see* Chapter 13).

Deputy Superintendent John Nichols of the Detroit Police Department compares the position of law enforcement in today's complex and fast-moving community to that of the man who married a woman with seven delinquent children. Police did not create the problem, but they must live with it.[1] The seven "children" have caused profound and lasting changes and problems for the operations and administration of police organizations across the country and are as follows:

1. Supreme Court decisions that have made police investigations more costly in both manpower and equipment.
2. Burgeoning civil rights movement with its by-product of mass demonstrations, civil disobedience, and riots.
3. Increasing public demands for expanded service, yet often a public reluctance to assist the police in fighting crime.
4. Manpower depletions and difficulties of personnel replacement.
5. Rising crime rate and a nationwide breakdown in respect for law and order.
6. Major technological developments in communications and computer operations, which have increased efficiency and ease of operation but also increased isolation of the police from the public and further dehumanized police work.

---

[1] John F. Nichols: "Police Commanders Advised to Adapt to Changing Conditions." *Police,* May-June, 1967, p. 54.

7. Population mobility coupled with "crazy-quilt" pattern of over 40,000 separate police jurisdictions often creates fragmented, provincial police operations.[2]

Thus, *change* and the problem of remaining *relevant* join in a need to *know*. Now is not the hour, it is the whole array of time. Man plans to remain a factor in the destiny of the universe.

To progress and move forward demands a constant search for knowledge. This in turn demands training and education that exceeds minimal past approaches and looks realistically at the future. Law enforcement agencies must address the problem from both a financial and a moral standpoint. To overemphasize one to the ignoring of the other is both an exercise in "administrative amnesia" and an act of "administrative immorality."

Education is a broader parameter than training. Put into basics, it does not deny the need for an ability to accurately "fire a gun." Education implies that "when to fire" is more than a legal question but should involve courses of instruction involving humanistic demands on both victim and suspect that are mandatory for each officer.

From a broadened perspective, harsh criticism of simplified basic approaches to deep sociological problems is valid. Those who wish to put a totally security-minded, high school educated twenty-six year-old unemployed laborer (preferably with three children and a pregnant wife) into the forefront of those most desirable for maintaining law and order are illogical, but numerous. Education can and will create a finer and more rational level of justice; Bloch and Geis analyze the problem:

Presumably law enforcement officers with better educational backgrounds will feel less threatened by student demonstrators than those less well-educated and less secure personally. In addition, brutality directed against lower-class persons would presumably decrease as law enforcement officers developed more understanding attitudes toward sex offenders and drunks, among others, who appear to offend them more aesthetically than in actual fact. How to control retaliation against persons who present potential threats to the police appears much more complicated. For one thing, of course, persons might learn to deal with the police with more respect and less aggression; presumably, this would elicit better police behavior in return. For another thing, the police undoubtedly would have to learn to

[2] Nichols, *Police*, p. 54.

exercise more care and control of their own behavior if they expect others to treat them more respectfully.[3]

Training, education, and selection are the keys to future effective police activity. No areas deserve more consideration from those who view the troubled era in which we live. The impact and importance of education and training is the concern of the following sections as it relates specifically to police-community relations.

EDUCATION: A CONTINUUM

Today, there exist certain specific police-community relations educational needs in any policing agency. The areas of significance are dealt with in terms of command level, in-service, and recruit/cadet education. These three areas point out the importance of education presented on a continuous basis. All too often, in any field of endeavor, we find the shortsighted view, that once an employee receives basic indoctrination in subjects designed to make him or her proficient, then the task is done and "training" is completed. One need only view the rapid changes in laws of arrest, search, and seizure to recognize the fallacy of "completed" training in these areas, and then expecting a peace officer to "adapt," as the law changes, without guidance from the officer's own policing agency.

The same is true in the field of police-community relations. The size of the law enforcement agency will be a determining factor in the formalization of an internal training program to deal with police-community relations, just as is the case with other areas of instructional concern.

This and the generic topic of internally effective programs to enhance police-community relations require consistent, increasing attention. Kenney states, "In order to maintain high morale and good working conditions in the police department a good program of internal human relations is vital."[4]

The assistance of local colleges or universities, together with the aid of key community groups to deal with various aspects of police-community relations, can offer valuable insight to the police

---

[3] Herbert A. Bloch and Gilbert Geis: *Man, Crime, and Society*. New York, Random House, 1970, p. 399.

[4] John P. Kenney: *Police Management Planning*. Springfield, Thomas, 1975, p. 74.

administrator. Their assistance should be sought out; they can and have provided additional data and training, which, if otherwise confined to police talking to police, can become ingrained.

The remainder of this chapter will deal with specific educational areas — normally termed "training," and thus so named — which should be part of the police-community relations curriculum, in (1) recruit/cadet training; (2) in-service training, and (3) command staff training.

Cadet Training

Every police-citizen contact affords an opportunity for applied police-community relations. As noted previously, the majority of these contacts are of a nonpunitive nature, and the attitude of the public can be molded in a positive way if sufficient care is given to this aspect of our police-citizen contacts.

Training in police-community relations has two basic aspects. The first centers around courses of instruction that deal with this subject directly and exclusively; the second includes those courses of instruction designed to teach a specific aspect of law enforcement but that inextricably involve police-community relations in execution of field functions dealt with in the classroom.

Specific Areas of Police-Community Relations Training

The following synopsis deals briefly with each area deemed mandatory for cadet officers in the specific area of police-community relations. The model curriculum presented is given in no particular order of importance. It is to be emphasized that failure to train in any area can of itself allow the creation of a nonproductive community atmosphere, and thus the failure to take an action becomes an action in and of itself. For example, a small community may have little or no problems with labor strife. If, however, such strife were to develop and the officers serving the area were not conversant with how to deal impartially and practically with the problems that suddenly presented themselves, the results would be all too readily apparent. ——

The following are the mandatory course areas concerned specifically with police-community relations.

THE UNITED STATES CONSTITUTION.   The great framework of American law is found in the United States Constitution and its several amendments. Peace officers are not required to be "Constitutional lawyers," but a basic understanding of the provisions germane to law enforcement is vital.

COMMUNITY GROUP RELATIONS. Daily, officers contact members of "minority groups" while on duty in the field. This minority may be racial, ethnic, or religious, or it may be concerned with such interests as occupation and classroom situations. It is important to adapt training in this field to the specific needs of the area. It must be current and deal with realities. This is a preventative type of course designed to tell the new trainee of critical problem groups. The history of important groupings, together with their philosophies and attitudes, should be a part of the curriculum.

VOCABULARY. A peace officer must be proficient at rendering courtroom testimony. However, an officer's diction *in the field* is also a major part of verbal conduct, and proper use of the English language is a primary concern. Too often we overlook certain phrases or slang words that can antagonize a minority group unintentionally, i.e. "boy," "dago," "wop." Knowledge of the sentiments of some groups toward certain of these ethnic slurs can result in avoiding hazardous situations in the realm of police-community relations. Also, an officer should be sure to exercise self-control in the use of profanity; using foul or obscene language degrades the entire profession.

FIELD-PRESS RELATIONS. Field-press relations deal with specific departmental policies regarding the provision of news to the press by officers in the field. Departmental policies should be stressed, but not without emphasizing the critical importance of having a positive relationship with reporters. Each officer should be fully conversant with basic techniques, such as overtly seeking out press representatives at a crime scene, in order to give them proper information about a particular incident or in order to refer them to the appropriate departmental representative to provide this information.

HUMAN RELATIONS. "Community Problems and Social Progress," "How Human Relations Relate to Community Standing," "Family Life as a Desirable Social Structure" — these are basic areas of human-to-human contacts this area of instruction must emphasize. Each officer must recognize that every contact he or she makes with the public is a human-to-human situation. Thus, whether it be an arrest, the issuance of a citation, or simply the provision of information, each officer should present a police image that will project law enforcement in its finest light.

INDUSTRIAL RELATIONS. Large industrial regions know how explosive police-management-labor relations can become. Peace officers must be schooled in the history of the labor movement and the purpose of law enforcement at a strike, i.e. to be an impartial keeper of the peace (not a tool of management or a pawn of labor) and to maintain a strict neutrality and an impartial attitude.

OFFICER DEMEANOR. The personal appearance of the officer, whether in uniform or civilian attire, has a most important bearing on the reaction of the public to the officer's presence. Appropriate dress, coupled with the ability of proper expression, serves as the greatest set of working tools an officer can possess.

PUBLIC SPEAKER. Since the advent of policing, discussions have centered around whether we need peace officers with more brain than brawn, or vice versa. *Superior intelligence, i.e. well above the norm, must become a requirement for entry into law enforcement* if we are to speak of professionalization. This intelligence is manifested each time an officer persuades a noisy, intoxicated citizen into peaceful compliance without creating a brawl. The ability to speak well and understandably is thus essential to an officer's field work.

Public speaking, from the standpoint of the peace officer, involves the elements of good public speaking, both planned and extemporaneous. There can be no substitute for practice, but the elements of public speaking should be a part of every training program for peace officers.

ETHICS IN LAW ENFORCEMENT. Each new officer requires extensive training in the ethics of the profession of law enforcement. Departmental manuals dealing with this are becoming commonplace, and it is recommended that every department establish and maintain a current written manual and that each officer be thoroughly schooled in all of its aspects.

The *Police Code of Ethics,* together with departmental policies pertinent to police-community relations, should be explained and discussed in detail with each new officer, and he or she should be issued copies of key material.

Peripheral Areas in Police-Community Relations

Many training courses designed to give the new officer a background on the procedures and mechanics of law enforcement in a particular regard are inextricably tied to the field of police-community relations. Those of greatest significance are listed in the following sections.

ARREST TECHNIQUES. In addition to knowing the various laws of arrest, it is vital for officers to have an understanding of appropriate techniques for interviewing suspects, witnesses, and other parties. The basic factors center around the need for the working officer to be a *good practical psychologist.* Law enforcement academy training in this regard can be of major assistance, and both general and specific courses in psychology are available at many colleges and universities throughout the nation to augment specific training provided by policing agencies.

BATON USAGE. Historically, the baton or nightstick has been recognized as the policeman's weapon, a role not enjoyed by the hand or palm saps. It is vital to retain this baton image, and only through its proper and judicious use can this most effective police weapon retain its position or relative acceptance by the public.

MECHANICS AND PSYCHOLOGY OF TRAFFIC CITATIONS' ISSUANCE. More than any other police activity, the traffic citation symbolizes to the "average person" his/her vulnerability to punitive contact with law enforcement. It is imperative for peace officers to maintain as courteous and diplomatic an attitude as the situation will allow in this most critical area of police enforcement.

CIVIL LAW ENFORCEMENT PROBLEMS. Every law enforcement agency receives citizens' calls that fall within the realm of civil rather than criminal matters. The fact that a matter involves a tort, rather than a public offense, does not abrogate the duty of the police to courteously explain why a matter does not fall within their area or realm of jurisdiction.

CROWD CONTROL. Demonstrations are a fact of our time. Demonstrations become a way of life for many militant and quasi-militant organizations in the field of civil rights. Every policing agency must have a trained force to cope with such situations, whether they are large or small. The tacit and expressed attitude of the police involved in this activity can do much to calm or incite mob activity, and it is important that each officer recognize the psychological aspects of crowd control as well as tactics and procedural methodology.

DISORDERLY CONDUCT CASES. Persons who become drunk or disorderly in public view require police action. Many times a minor police incident that starts as a drunk arrest can end up as a "mob scene." Thus, the peace officer must be given extensive training in the use of the brain as well as brawn, in quickly removing drunken, disorderly citizens from a public place where many persons may observe the action and misconstrue the action, seeing only the "effect" and not the "cause."

DOMESTIC COMPLAINTS. Family disturbances require an inordinate expenditure of police time. Unquestionably, domestic complaints offer an area of police concern requiring infinite tact and appropriate training.

JUVENILE PROCEDURES. Community relations activities of a police agency are many times swallowed up by complete concentration in the field of juvenile offenders and potential wrongdoers. While this phase of community relations is of extreme significance — and indeed the law, judicial structure, and the crime prevention nature of juvenile work are closely allied with police-community relations — a point emphasized here is that this latter function also extends to adult contacts wherever and whenever possible.

VICE OPERATIONS. The control of public mores in the vice field (sexual behavior, narcotics, gambling, and liquor) is a field that has long created intense public interest. Two factions in the community ask law enforcement to accept roles at opposite ends of a spectrum. The one asks for strict enforcement of any and all of these vice regulations; the other wants absolute liberality. The great majority of public sentiment lies somewhere between these two extremes. Unfortunately, this apathetic attitude of the majority is a dilemma to the police, particularly in respect to the relations between the police and general public. Considerable attention should be given to the laws pertaining to "vice" in a particular area, but a great deal of attention must be rendered to the highly volatile community situation, which can erupt from an inappropriate handling of a vice matter.

ROLE-PLAYING. No treatment of police training techniques would be complete without mention of the need for practical application of all of the various areas of instruction. Role-playing for peace officers centers around the theme of practice before fellow police personnel, applying techniques explained through lectures in the classroom.

The great bridge such training seeks to span is that between the academic approach of the lecture hall and the applied police techniques necessitated by radio patrol-car duty. By placing cadet officers in various roles before their classmates and instructors, psychological pressure is exerted on them. This many times is similar to the pressure they will encounter in their earliest field assignment. Role-playing is considered a vital bridge and can be of great value in reducing the time necessary to develop a fully competent officer in the field.

In-Service Training

The human mind forgets. This is the reason we maintain documents of importance to remind us of the exact nature of events of the past. New developments continuously appear on the horizon, which, many times, are important to various organizations or individuals. For these two basic reasons — forgetfulness and new developments — it is imperative that no police training program ever be considered "complete." It must be continuous and must include the participation of every member of the department. This is usually referred to in police terms under the rather broad category of *in-service training*.

In-service training may take many forms: briefing prior to each tour of duty, prearranged courses requiring several days given periodically to every member of the department with a certain length of time in service, or some combination of the two may be utilized. Regardless of the procedure, certain areas of this type of training must include police-community relations reminders.

The fundamental rights of our citizenry and the protection of these rights are, in the final analysis, the overall objective of the police. To properly imbue each officer with this goal requires that initial training be reinforced with periodic courses to instill a sense of duty. Supervisory officers must also continuously see that subordinate officers reflect appropriate attitudes in their conduct.

Subject Matter

Rather than attempt to list a specific series of subjects together with individual course content, it is apparent that the basic areas of concern listed in the recruit training curriculum should contain the aspects of essential elements for *in-service training* at the line-officer level.

Notwithstanding this era of labor-management differences, no department stressing professionalization can afford to ignore the highly advantageous features of having officers report early for each tour of duty and receive semiformal instruction by their supervisory personnel, which will include information to assist them in the field. Many times, however, police administrators fail to utilize this same time to periodically retrain all personnel on matters of concern to overall departmental performance. This training may clarify departmental crisis areas, or it may present a refresher on crowd control and human relations. The content will be determined by a well-planned overview of major problems facing the particular policing agency, coupled with areas of public concern in the immediate future that may best be handled through utilization of highly trained and competent personnel.

Concentrated Programs

There are programs that may take veteran officers out of the field for a few days, utilizing semiconference techniques on specific subjects. Instruction may be rendered by both highly competent police training officers and personnel of stature from other fields of endeavors of concern to law enforcement.

One such far-reaching and creative program inaugurated by some agencies to improve police-community relations at the line level is the "Most Esteemed Officer" program. Based on the informal organizational influence of "peer group response," these programs strive to improve a line officer's community relations by gaining the support and commitment of the most esteemed officers. For example, a new officer reporting for field duty finds that he/she must conform to certain unwritten standards and behavior patterns. These patterns are largely set by the most esteemed officers working the station—that is, most esteemed by their fellow officers. These officers may or may not be observing good police-community relations.

Departments utilizing peer group response capitalize on the informal organizational influence by training these "most esteemed officers" in the need for and the advantages of good community relations. Time each month is devoted to orientation and training in the basic areas of police-community relations, including a review of citizen complaints and issues which cause unnecessary negative field situations. These selected officers will, hopefully, return to their units more supportive of police-community relations. The entire working staff will then see the most esteemed officers following a better response pattern. Thus, the entire unit will benefit.

Supervisory and Management Training

The supervisory and command personnel of each police agency will find a wide scope of training available to them. The importance of structuring this cannot be overemphasized. The top police administrator in any policing agency must take a leadership role both in developing training programs for supervisory and executive personnel of the department and also in insuring that every appropriate departmental member receives this training.

Police-community relations, particularly as imparted by supervisory and command personnel, will reflect *down* to the working peace officers and *out* to the community through both the officers and their supervisors. In many instances, training at this level can and should be coordinated with local colleges and universities and important civic and government groups. Such an approach can provide insight into the many aspects of community problems that, though far from the law enforcement field per se, have a vital bearing on effective long-range performance of the police mission to reduce crime.

THE EDUCATION SYNDROME

This chapter has dealt in some detail with the field of police-community relations education. In many instances, it is impossible to separate a curriculum designed for implementing aspects of field procedure without touching extensively on police-community relations. As indicated, there can be no substitute for a continuous educational/training program designed to refresh and implement new ideas. It must take place at all levels, and it must be a continuous process.

Improvement and maintenance of any mutual endeavor such as police-community relations requires that both sides sincerely seek to understand the problem issues and work together to resolve them. Education is an intrinsic element in any problem-resolution sequence.

Police agencies across the country have recognized the importance of and urgent need for continuous training of all officers in the concepts and practices of police-community relations, and they either have established or are developing the procedures to include this information in their schedules.

What education is the community receiving to help it improve police-community relations? The next chapter looks at one vital phase of community training, the schools; until recently, schools were somewhat ignored by both the police and the community in their continuing efforts to develop effective police-community relations.

Discussion Questions

1. In order to deal with new problems, the police must modernize traditional methods and policies. Discuss some of the specific areas in which you feel this modernization is necessary.
2. Discuss police operations and responsibilities at massive youth gatherings as seen at a rock music festival.
3. Many officers and police administrators think that police-community relations is "social work" and they are not social workers. Discuss the pros and cons of this viewpoint.
4. The quality of police service relates directly to the quality of the officer rendering the service. Discuss some ways in which the quality of the individual officer might be enhanced.

the author attempts to practice what he preaches . . . (photo by arthur parra)

Chapter 8

LAW ENFORCEMENT AND THE EDUCATOR

Objective: To develop an understanding of the relation-
ship between law enforcement, students, and teachers —
the way it is and the way it needs to be.

- Philosophy of early childhood education
- Reasons for police-sponsored school programs
- "Citizen and the Law"
- Teaching the teachers about law enforcement

THERE IS A growing concern for curriculum control on the part of law enforcement agencies, especially since communities develop their attitudes toward the maintenance of law and order through education in its broadest sense. These attitudes, whether favorable or unfavorable, developed early, become the foundation of loyalties and convictions.

The adult offender of today can often be traced to a child whose behavior spiraled from minor mischievous acts to serious violations of the law. However, in some children, simple mischief, if uncontrolled, is sometimes mistakenly seen as leading to disrespect for the law and its enforcers.

Though talked about for centuries, action today is necessitated because of the exponential growth of problems needing solutions. Education appears to offer the most viable approach and thus needs to be explored from the view of maintaining both an ordered society and justice. Isom suggests focusing on the youth of our nation:

> There is a need for a dynamic approach to educate youth to the problems of law enforcement. Various governmental and community agencies can no longer afford to operate independently of each other. Therefore, to encourage law-abiding behavior on the part of youth and citizens, a comprehensive plan of formal education through the schools dealing with law enforcement should be substituted for prevailing, random efforts of agencies and organizations. The school in its role as a liaison of culture is the best equipped resource to impress upon youth the necessity for a lawful society.
>
> Since the growing insulation of the police from the community is in part a direct product of attitudes, and since improvement of this situation requires an analysis and possibly an alteration of attitudes, it is of paramount importance that we focus at least part of our attention on the concept of attitude, assuming — for the sake of brevity — a basic knowledge of the term's meaning.
>
> The attitudes of children are less deeply entrenched than those of adults. So too, children have a non-negative situation. Therefore, a program of long-range objectives aimed at influencing attitudes should be directed toward the young. The ambition of such a program should not be deliberate attitude manipulation by propaganda; rather these programs should be designed to prevent formation of groundless but detrimental prejudices concerning law and its enforcement.[1]

This chapter further discusses the present situation between law enforcement and the educators, reviews current remedial pro-

---

[1] James E. Isom: "Law Enforcement Education in Public Schools." Police Chief Magazine, Gaithersburg, Maryland, March, 1974, p. 74.

grams, and suggests some action plans applicable to all law enforcement agencies and governmental institutions. The following section explains through a historical review our philosophy of instilling ideas and attitudes in the young.

Historical Perspectives

King Solomon of Israel, approximately 3,000 years ago, realized that the future of his expansive and wealthy nation depended in large part on the children of Israel. The borders of Israel at that time encompassed the entire Arabian peninsula, protected by the best-trained army in the world. Therefore, to continue Israel's prosperity and autonomy, Solomon set forth instructions on the care and raising of children; stated succinctly, he advised: "Train up a child in the way that he should go and when he is grown he will not depart from it" (Proverbs 22:6), or, according to a familiar maxim, "As the twig is bent, so grows the tree."

Solomon's instructions have been endorsed and repeated by various leaders, philosophers, and psychologists throughout the centuries. The Jesuit Society proclaims, "Give me a child until he is seven and I'll give you the man." Lenin said, "Give me the children and the seeds I sow will never be uprooted." And Arthur Schopenhauer warned that "wrong notions implanted early can seldom be rooted out." As our attitudes today are based on history, so are the attitudes of adults based on childhood training.

TODAY'S SCHOOLS—THE STORY OF AN AREA OF TRAGIC NEGLECT

One of our main training processes for children is the school. In its role as a liaison of culture, the school is the best equipped resource to dispel back-alley attitudes and short-sighted views about law enforcement. Inherent in its structure is the ability to instill in our youth an understanding of their responsibilities in upholding law and order. Yet, the effective channeling of this powerful reservoir toward the child's development of this understanding remains, to this date, a veritable virgin ground.

Equally untouched is the need for creative communication and rapport between law enforcement and teachers. We need to actively and continuously seek the support of the teaching profession, at all levels, in imbuing students with a positive understanding and respect for law enforcement.

Although the majority of law enforcement agencies conduct some type of school program to increase student-police rapport, too many of these programs are sporadic, token attempts. The President's Commission on Law Enforcement and Administration of Justice, reporting on a recent survey conducted by Michigan State University, writes that over 80 percent of the police agencies surveyed operate special school programs to tell pupils about police work or to explain special laws or problems which affect young citizens. The aim of such efforts is to portray the police officer as a community helper rather than as an antagonist.[2]

Typical examples of these excellent but inadequate programs at the grade school level include periodic visits to each grade to explain traffic safety, role and duties of the police officer, good citizenship, and safety rules to use with strangers. Films and other visual aids, including demonstrations of the radio car and walkie-talkies, and tours of police headquarters enliven the presentations.

New York City police have experimented with comic books about police work, training courses for elementary school teachers, and composition and drawing assignments for children on the role of police officers as their friends.[3]

Examples of programs at the high school level include teenage panels directing questions to officers at open meetings, integrated two-man teams visiting schools on an informal basis to discuss students' conceptions of the police, periodic lectures on the laws that affect juvenile conduct, police criteria for stopping or taking juveniles into custody, and the kind of processing a juvenile goes through, as well as its effects in later life.

These programs are commendable and should be continued and expanded on content and frequency of contact, but they are not doing the job. The current problems between police and teenagers, manifested by the teenagers' rising crime rate and increasing questioning of authority and hostility toward the police, indicate that the present programs are just not enough. More intensified training

---

[2] President's Commission on Law Enforcement and Administration of Justice: *Task Force Report: The Police.* Washington, D.C., U.S. Government Printing Office, 1967, pp. 160-161.

[3] President's Commission, *The Police*, pp. 160-161.

is necessary, including regular and thorough grounding in the principles and responsibilities of community law enforcement.

Police agencies chronically suffer from personnel shortages and inadequate funds, both of which seriously hamper creative and progressive school programs. One southern California police department has an excellent school program covering all grades, but because of the above shortages, their police-community relations officers visit each school twice a semester — hardly enough contact to implant lasting and loyal impressions.

The cost and complexity of keeping the peace in our communities dictates that governmental agencies must work together. They can no longer afford to operate independently, wasting resources and time in splintered and abortive efforts. To combat the onimous specter of lawlessness and win the race against crime, the schools, community governments, and law enforcement agencies must combine and coordinate their resources.

It is incongruous that many school districts require two semesters in driver's education and nothing in law enforcement education. People, particularly children, are not law abiding by accident or nature. To develop and maintain their commitment to law and order, the prevailing random and token attempts in our schools need to be replaced with full-time, comprehensive programs of formal law enforcement education.

Educators as Leaders

Educators, in both public and private schools, exert a tremendous influence on the American people. To realize that our youth spend more time in the classroom than in any other activity is to comprehend that compelling importance of the teacher's role in the nation's future.

In these times of crises and rapid social changes, teachers express their convictions either publicly or in the classroom. These convictions may range from their evaluation of our foreign policy to some instant situation concerning whether a single person or group or minority has the right to engage in activities contrary to institutional regulations or the social mores. We too often view with alarm — but not with remedy — educational leaders who help arouse students and faculty to vociferously protest a certain "establishment" policy. Resulting police "interference" to restore order may lead to angry allegations of police brutality, gestapo, filthy cops, or the current epithet — pigs!

There are other less dramatic examples of the educational influence that are negatively directed. One such example is the teacher who, when cited for a traffic violation, uses the classroom as a platform to criticize the officer's "goal displacement" — the officer should have been out chasing criminals rather than drivers. If repeated, these criticisms can and do adversely affect the students' concepts about law enforcement.

Educators exert a lasting impact upon our future citizens. Consequently it behooves us to assiduously search out new avenues to strengthen their understanding, respect, and support for law enforcement.

REVIEW OF REMEDIAL PROGRAMS

Every day society reaps the harvest of this tragic and traditional neglect of our schools as growing numbers of adults and young people openly resent and flout the laws of our country. This neglect, fortunately, need not continue.

A few vanguard police departments scattered across the country have recognized the enormous and lasting benefit to society by correcting this deficiency during our youths' formative years. These departments and their concerned cities have embarked on concerted and cooperative pilot programs to include law enforcement as a required course in the curricula of the junior high school.

An Innovation in Student-Law Enforcement Involvement

In September, 1967, three cooperating agencies — Los Angeles County Sheriff's Department, Temple City, California, and the Temple City School District — raised the benchmark of progress in police-community relations. These agencies activated a full-time, comprehensive program of formal law enforcement education, entitled "Citizen and the Law."

OBJECTIVES. After much investigation and many conferences, the participating agencies set forth these objectives for the "Citizens and the Law" pilot program:

1. To develop an understanding of society based on law and order.
2. To develop an awareness of the extent to which law violations affect the community.

3. To establish a genuine rapport between students and law enforcement.
4. To develop an appreciation for the courts as administrators of justice.
5. To develop a positive attitude toward upholding law and order.

The medium chosen to transmit these objectives to the students was the classroom, including field trips to law enforcement facilities, guest speakers, visual aids, and seminar-type discussions of the material covered.

The course was structured to teach certain key concepts with primary emphasis on one particular concept: The rights and freedoms guaranteed by the law must be accompanied by responsibility and respect for the law. Four other concepts unified the curriculum under this primary concept:

1. It is the right of the governed to do whatever they think best for their general welfare.
2. Laws mean little without some means of guaranteeing respect for them.
3. Courts interpret the laws and administer justice.
4. The law provides for punishment and rehabilitation of offenders.

Beginning a New Era

After nearly a year of planning and research, on September 11, 1967, for the first time in the history of education and law enforcement, a police officer entered a public school system as a full-time faculty instructor in law enforcement. Unlike past programs in which the officer just visited various schools, this officer-instructor imparted the critical areas of his knowledge and experience in a regularly scheduled class to junior high school students.

In addition to classroom instruction, "Citizen and the Law" included seven other responsibilities:

1. Preparing and presenting classroom meetings and assemblies in elementary and secondary schools.
2. Conducting weekly seminars with parents and other concerned persons.
3. Sponsoring additional activities such as student special interest group meetings.
4. Conducting in-service education of faculty members and administrators.
5. Coordinating special resources in law enforcement.
6. Representing the district on the school-community safety council.
7. Initiating communications with available resources at the county and university level in the development of evaluative plans for measuring progress.

EVALUATION OF THE PROGRAM. "Citizen and the Law" has been enthusiastically acclaimed by all participating agencies and other interested parties. During the first year the program fulfilled the objectives envisioned by its creators. The evaluation report prepared by the Temple City School Districts in cooperation with the county superintendent of schools documented improvement in student attitudes regarding the concepts of law enforcement. The report concluded, "In all areas measured, the instruction and experience in the law enforcement class had a noticeable effect upon students' attitudes."

The Idea Spreads

The use of the "Citizen and the Law" concepts and practices to head off student unrest and violence is spreading to other parts of the country. Harrisburg, Pennsylvania, and Cincinnati, Ohio, have developed curriculum on law enforcement for permanent use in their schools.

In 1968, Harrisburg, in cooperation with the county legal service association, inaugurated experimental classes in law and law enforcement at one of its high schools. The weekly classes are conducted by practicing attorneys—all giving their services free of charge. Attendance is voluntary and huge, with some students cutting classes to attend the law lectures.

The executive director of the county legal service association summarizes the reason why both the city and the attorneys decided on this new and innovative approach to develop better citizenship: "We haven't had any student violence yet and we don't want any. But there's so much unrest in our schools, so much irresponsible flouting of authority and law, we thought it might be important to give the kids a proper understanding of the law before it's too late. Most of them think of the law as a cop—their enemy. We're trying to show them that the law is not an enemy but is a vast and complex network of rules of conduct that's absolutely necessary if we are to avoid living in chaos." [4]

The classes have been so successful that the two other high schools in Harrisburg have requested similar lectures on law. The Pennsyl-

---

[4] John G. Rogers: "They Learn the Law—Before It's Too Late." *Parade,* Long Beach, California, Press-Telegram Newspaper, February 16, 1969.

vania Bar Association has asked for details of the program, and inquiries have been received from other states, including New York, New Jersey, Delaware, Massachusetts, and Florida.[5]

Education of Teachers in Law Enforcement

To leave the development of our children's attitudes toward law enforcement to chance is like playing roulette with their futures. They need to be guided into constructive channels while they stand at the crossroads of attitude development. As stated before and repeated here for emphasis, teachers are one of our greatest resources. They can impress positive concepts about the community and the student's role in it and also, at the same time, counteract the lawless, sinister forces that seek to convince the youth of our nation that the police are the enemy of the people.

This truth was demonstrated fifty years ago at Johns Hopkins University. A young sociology professor assigned his students to interview 200 underprivileged boys and predict their futures. The students, shocked by the slum conditions, predicted that about 90 percent of them would someday be imprisoned. Twenty-five years later the same professor assigned another class to check the predictions. Of the 180 subjects located, only 4 had been in jail. Why were the predictions so wrong? More than 100 of the men remembered a high school teacher who had an inspiring and lasting influence during their school years.[6]

Because teachers are one of the main cogs in the machinery that produces healthy citizens and healthy communities, their potential must be tapped to help produce healthy law enforcement. In 1952 Professor G. Douglas Gourley, California State College at Los Angeles, conducted an intensive survey of citizens' attitudes toward the police. A scientifically selected sample of 3,100 citizens answered a questionnaire containing three principal sections: biographical data, twenty-two multiple-choice questions, and voluntary statements concerning contacts with Los Angeles policemen. One of the most thought-provoking findings of this survey was the unfavorable ratings by housewives and female school teachers.

---

[5] Rogers, *Parade.*

[6] John Lagamann: "Self-Fulfilling Prophecy—A Key to Success." *Reader's Digest*, February, 1969, pp. 80–83.

Only 13 percent of the teachers, as compared to just 37 percent for housewives, believed that their police were habitually courteous to the public.[7] Gourley believed that these low ratings indicated the need for a public relations program directed toward women, since they greatly influence the attitudes of children—the citizens of tomorrow.

Every summer for the past six years, Gourley has taught a seminar entitled "The Teacher and Law Enforcement." Its purpose is to acquaint teachers with the functions, objectives, problems, and plans of their local police departments.

Much time is devoted to guest lecturers, field trips, visual aids, and discussing police work. The class is fully accredited and, though directed toward teachers, is open to all students. It is one of the few college courses in the county entirely structured to gain the teachers' understanding and respect for law enforcement.

PROPOSED COURSE OF ACTION

Law enforcement is a two-way street; it is everybody's business. Its effectiveness is entirely related to the support it receives from the community. Governments reflect the will of the people, and law enforcement is one of the vehicles used by the government to actualize the mandates of the people.

Let us begin to inculcate this support in the children, who harbor the nucleus of the future. Now is the time for educational and law enforcement institutions to look carefully at the remedial proposals reviewed in this chapter for possible inclusion in their own municipalities.

The following programs—two of which have already achieved efficacious results—would do much to correct the neglect between law enforcement and the educators:

1. Include courses such as "Citizen and the Law" as a required course in elementary schools, junior high, and senior high schools.
2. Develop programs such as "Law Enforcement and the Teacher" in colleges and universities across the nation to educate persons already in the teaching profession about law enforcement's operations and objectives.
3. Develop a college course, perhaps as an elective but hopefully mandatory, that will provide the essentials of the administration of criminal justice to prospective teachers.

---

[7] G. Douglas Gourley: *Public Relations and the Police.* Springfield, Thomas, 1953, p. 78.

Discussion Questions

1. Discuss some ways to strengthen police-teacher support and understanding.

2. A random sample of 3,100 citizens in Los Angeles revealed that women feel more hostility toward police than men. What might be some of the causes for this?

3. Why are juvenile arrests soaring? What can be done to impede the wave of juvenile crime?

4. How do you view programs such as the "Citizen and the Law"? What are some obstacles to the program's expansion?

PART III

Sociological Dilemma of Police-Community Relations

speed limit control by night . . . a major sociological problem all too prevalent in police work the world over is the isolation of the peace officer from the community . . . (photo courtesy of danish national police commissioner a baun)

Chapter 9

SOCIOLOGICAL ASPECTS OF
POLICE-COMMUNITY RELATIONS

Objective: To develop an awareness of the importance and influence of sociological conditions and principles in the functions of law enforcement.

- Police as scapegoats
- Sociological causes of crime
- Working with minorities
- Police caught in the crossfire
- Small group behavior
- Sociology and the law
- Social class as a control
- Police application of sociological principles

135

HISTORY DEMONSTRATES that humans are by nature and by need gregarious beings and, for the majority of their lives, interact — voluntarily or involuntarily — with other people in group settings. Their behavior, attitudes, and aspirations are initially formed and continuously modified by these groups.

The knowledge of sociological aspects or the understanding of humans, their social lives, and their communities are essential to meaningful police-community relations. Police officers who understand the influences of groups and society on human development and behavior are better equipped to understand human behavior, drives, and needs — their own as well as those of the people they serve.

The premise of this chapter is that knowledge of the sociological aspects omnipresent in police work can ignite a new awareness in every officer of the need for continuous, effective police-community relations. Application of this knowledge can help calm the unnerving whirlwind of unrest that is swirling across our country.

Some progressive police administrators, applying innovative courage and intelligent skepticism to traditional operating procedures, have harnessed aspects of sociology for the accomplishment of the police mission. As defined by one of these administrators: "Law enforcement procedures in today's tense world require a knowledge and a sensitivity that permit a feeling of the community pulse; that bestow the ability to note signs of majority group acts of aggression which are sure to invite reprisal; that provide an awareness of minority group motivations and tempers."[1]

Modern organization and management theorists are well aware of the importance of the social nature of man and structure their personal practices to satisfy social needs. The eminent sociologist Elton Mayo is quoted by Carzo and Yanouzas: "Man is basically motivated by social needs and obtains his basic sense of identity through relationships with others. The desire to stand well with one's fellows, the so-called human instinct of association, easily outweighs the merely individual interest."[2]

---

[1] Harold A. Lett: "Minority Groups and Police-Community Relations." *Police and Community Relations: A Sourcebook.* Beverly Hills, California, Glencoe Press, 1968, p. 128.

[2] Rocco Carzo and John N. Yanouzas: *Formal Organizations: A System Approach.* Homewood, Ill., Richard D. Irwin, 1967, p. 108.

Stuart Chase, a management consultant, refers to this urge to belong, to associate, and to participate as that "mysterious something" hidden deep in human nature.[3]

This chapter reviews the sociological aspects of a community that thwarts the police objective in general, and police-community relations in particular. It also describes the basis concepts and purposes of sociology that are applicable to law enforcement and closes with a brief look at some of the newer programs in operation across the country that seek to alleviate the police-sociological dilema.

SOCIOLOGICAL ASPECTS OF THE POLICE-COMMUNITY RELATIONS DILEMMA

Despite the fact that the main causes of crime are buried deep in the intricate mechanisms of our entire social, economic, and political system (poor housing, unemployment, inadequate education, family breakdown), many people blame society's inability to control crime on the police. The President's Commission on Law Enforcement and Administration of Justice comments on this enigma:

Public concern about crime is typically translated into demands for more law enforcement, and often into making the police scape-goats for a crime problem they did not create and do not have the resources to solve. The police did not create and cannot resolve the social conditions that stimulate crime. They did not start and cannot stop the convulsive social changes that are taking place in America . . . they do not enact the laws that they are required to enforce, nor do they dispose of the criminals they arrest . . . even under the most favorable circumstances, the ability of the police to act against crime is limited.[4]

The Commission further illustrates the limited role of the police in the interaction between the sociological aspects of community and the many-faceted complex of crime causation:

In communities where the instrumentalities of society whose success bears directly on controlling crime have failed — families, schools, job markets, and welfare agencies — the police must handle an enormously increased volume of offenses. It is when it attempts to solve problems that arise from the community's social and economic failures that policing is least effective and most frustrating. For, while charged with deterrence, the police can do little to prevent crime in the broader sense of removing its causes. On the

---

[3] Carzo and Yanouzas, *Formal Organizations*, p. 108.

[4] President's Commission on Law Enforcement and Administration of Justice: *Task Force Report: The Police*. Washington, D.C., U.S. Government Printing Office, 1967, pp. 1-2.

whole, they must accept society as it is — a society in which parents fail to raise their children as law-abiding citizens, in which schools fail to educate them to assume adult roles, and in which the economy is not geared to provide them with jobs.[5]

The fact that police represent only one factor in a complex sociological situation — albeit a critical factor — was consequently noted by former President Lyndon B. Johnson: "The only genuine long-range solution for what has happened lies in an attack mounted at every level, upon the conditions that breed despair and violence. All of us know what those conditions are: Ignorance, discrimination, slums, poverty, disease, not enough jobs. We should attack these conditions, not because we are frightened by conflict but because we are fired by conscience; we should attack them because there is simply no other way to achieve a decent and orderly society in America."[6]

In many instances, the fields of criminal justice and sociology find themselves with quite differing views. The sociologist points to groups and social problems as root problems that breed crime; the street policeman must deal with the here and now. Sociologist Harvey Brenner conducted an in-depth and complex analysis of factors related as causal to crime and other social trauma. His findings provide further evidence of a need for greater interaction and understanding between law enforcement and sociology. Drummond reports on some of Brenner's findings:

> Brenner's findings have been nothing less than startling. In testimony late last year before a congressional subcommittee, Brenner suggested that a 1% increase in the unemployment rate in 1970 had raised crime rates by the following magnitudes:
>
> - 40,056 narcotics violations of a total of 468,146 cases reported by the FBI that year.
> - 8,646 burglary cases of a reported total of 385,785.
> - 23,151 larceny cases of a total of 832,624.
> - 5,123 embezzlement cases of a total of 85,033.
> - 684 homicide victims of a total of 16,848.
> - 3,340 state and federal prison admissions of a total of 67,304.[7]

[5] President's Commission, *Task Force Report*, pp. 1-2.

[6] From a televised address to the nation by Lyndon B. Johnson, Thirty-sixth President of the United States, June 27, 1967.

[7] Bill Drummond: "Sociologist Links Unemployment, Crime." *Los Angeles Times*, March 5, 1978, p. 29.

Isolation—Sociological Dilemma in Police Work

A major sociological problem all too prevalent in police work is the isolation of the peace officer from the community he or she serves. The traditional view that the policeman is just a fellow citizen with the added responsibility to keep the peace has been either blurred or completely forgotten by many people. The majority of this country's over 500,000 police officers are social isolates who associate only with other police officers. Under the innovative direction of the former Chief of Police of Riverside, California, R. Fred Ferguson, in a city where Mexican-Americans constitute much of the population, officers spent time living and being with minority segments of the community. To cite from specific experience, Officer Steve Taylor offered some potent comment:

One particular family we visited has a son who is in the 11th grade. This young man is very outspoken and very anti-police. He blamed the police for most of the problems on the East side and confused the police with the authority of the government on such problems as housing owned by the government from which people were evicted or forced to leave for non-payment. This is enforced by the police, so, therefore, the police caused the problem.

All in all, this was a very worthwhile program and I would not hesitate to do the same again at a later date. It is my personal opinion that other officers of this department would profit with meaningful experiences by involving themselves in the same program.[3]

Ferguson further explains this innovative program:

From its inception, officers became a part of the program. Additionally, officers have also participated in a "Total Immersion Spanish Language Program" offered by the University of California at Davis—in Ensenada, Mexico. Two Community Relations officers work full time to provide new communication links and interpersonal experiences for policemen and barrio youth alike.

It is too early to expect measurable results. We have made some positive observations, are receiving some positive feedback and sense some positive behavioral change. Rocks and bottles are still thrown and policemen continue to have difficulty in dealing with some barrio elements.

We are learning, however, that a few unmanageables do not represent a community and that we do have many friends, people who need us, in the barrio. And, that we are more alike than different.

Lastly, specific needs of the barrio residents have become more apparent from our early assessments of the program. One of these needs, we believe, can be filled by expanding our own staff to include an expert in fraud who is

---

[3] Officer Steve Taylor, Riverside Police Department Training Report (1975).

also bi-lingual. Such an expert would be trained to work in the field and assist not only the Mexican Americans, but also the non-citizens of the barrio, who are subject to exploitation by the larger community and/or their own people. The development of such a staff position is presently under study.[9]

. . . "I looked down the distant road and I saw a rock. As I drew closer, I saw that it was a man. As I drew even closer, I saw that he was my brother."[10]

Police administrators realize that self-imposed isolation by police officers is a root cause of many problems in achieving effective police-community relations. The late Doctor John Pfiffner identified three results that must be corrected to ease the confrontations at the police-community "frontline." These results include resistance to change, withdrawal from society, and formation of a closely knit, closed police fraternity.[11]

CONFIGURATION OF CAUSES. While there are many complex and nebulous reasons for this isolation, perhaps one of the most frequent and underlying causes is the "cross-fire" between the government and the public that too often finds the law enforcement officer right in the middle.

As the most visible agent of government, the police officer symbolizes security to some and threat to others; to some he or she is brutal and unfeeling and to others soft; some want strict enforcement, and others, none at all. The police officer is bound to bring offenders to justice, yet equally bound to observe the full legacy of their constitutional rights in doing so—no matter how volatile the circumstances. When times are tranquil, the officer is ignored; when turbulent, he/she is maligned. The police officer must enforce the popular and unpopular laws and operate within a framework of statute and doctrinal dogma. He or she is pressured by the political structure on one side and various vocal and incendiary groups on the other. As a result of these many "cross-fires," police gradually and somewhat unconsciously socialize with just other policemen, thus further alienating themselves from the people.

---

[9] R. Fred Ferguson: Policemen: Agents of Change—A Crime Prevention Report. California, Crime Prevention Review (California Attorney General's Office), 1975, p. 13.

[10] Anonymous.

[11] John M. Pfiffner: The Function of the Police in a Democratic Society. Occasional Paper 8No. 1, Los Angeles, California, University of Southern California Press, 1967.

Resolution of this roadblock constitutes one of the foremost aims of police-community relations. Ways must be found for law enforcement and the public to get to know each other, to talk together, to air and analyze hidden concerns and existing mutual problems, to build respect and understanding — for these interactions comprise the warp and woof of good police-community relations.

SOCIOLOGY—WHAT IS IT?

Sociology is the study of societies, past and present, in their entirety or in smaller units of analysis. The sociologist studies groups and institutions as they relate to each other and to society as a whole. Primarily interested in developing behavior patterns of the entire group, the sociologist observes how and why people interact with each other within the group.

Sociologists examine social processes and progress, social order and disorder, social control and social interaction. They attempt to identify characteristics common to all social systems that explain the continuity of the system; for example, how does the family maintain and perpetuate itself through the ages? They are also interested in police groups — how they interact among themselves, as well as how their actions affect the general population.

Through scientific observation and study, sociologists attempt to remove opinion about human behavior and replace it with knowledge, to distinguish between value judgments and facts. They accomplish these purposes by observing and analyzing the group or society under study by one or all of four basic methods: geographical environment, culture of the group, biological endowment, and the results of social interaction. Major emphasis today is on culture of the group and social interaction.

Sociology of Small Groups

The small group — society's building blocks — furnishes the essential ingredients of socialization and the basic source of social order. It further provides the major source of values and attitudes that individuals possess, both criminal and noncriminal.

This brief analysis of small groups applies to both law-abiding and law-violating groups. The basic processes of structure, interaction, and commitment are much the same for both, as are the satisfactions and objectives — only their means may differ. For example, the group formed because of common interests and for mutual benefit that steals for money has many fundamental principles and processes in common with the group that conducts a rummage sale for money. It is important that this similarity be remembered when studying small groups.

SMALL GROUP INTERACTION. The small group—the most important of which, for our purposes, is the family—usually consists of from two to twenty members. Conversely, collections of fewer than twenty individuals may actually contain several small groups.

Small groups serve a mediating function between people and the larger society. Examples include the family, car pool, work group, street gang, committee, lunch group, prison cell, a golfing foursome, and a bowling team. Groups are held together by a sense of common identity and a similarity of interests.

Members of a small group tend to formulate and follow group norms. The norm specifies a type of behavior expected of a group member. Most members tend to converge toward agreed-upon behavior as they interact and become aware of one another's judgments. If an individual's actions agree with those of the group, his/her behavior will be approved. If a person's behavior conflicts with the group norms, he/she will have to conform, change the norms, remain a deviate, or leave the group. Such an individual may be ostracized and/or banished from the group without his/her consent.

Conversely, some groups encourage diversity as long as there is a base of similarity, i.e. research group or discussion group. If membership in the group is important, the individual may subvert his/her own standards and goals to promote those of the group. The small group can exert potent pressure on the individual, but it can also sustain each person's uniqueness.

Sociologists are interested in obtaining and identifying all available knowledge about the small group and its social interaction in order to predict the group's behavior. Their research has resulted in much of the modern-day thinking on human relations, group dynamics, and related subjects.

Social Control and Law Enforcement

Social control is the aspect of sociology that concerns law enforcement. It is those organizations, institutions, groups, and persons that regulate the actions of people.

Human behavior is largely controlled by the customs and conventions of the society in which one lives. These social controls may be conscious or unconscious, formal or informal, internal or external, lawful or unlawful. Specific forms include folkways, mores, and laws (both civil and criminal).

Folkways include ways of acting, dressing, eating, etc. They are not usually morally or legally wrong if violated. Society does not attach too much importance to their conformity. *Mores* are behavior norms to which society attaches moral judgments. *Laws* are established by the political government to enforce folkways and mores. Laws rule certain behavior as legally wrong.

MOBILITY OF PERSONS AND COMMODITIES. The increased mobility of today's society has weakened the institutions that formerly exercised adequate social control. The large family and the homogeneous neighborhood — principal agencies of social control — have been replaced by the small family, detached from other relatives, in a heterogeneous neighborhood, where the behavior of one person is a subject of indifference of other persons.

Mobility also intensified the problem of control by extending the boundaries of frequent and effective interaction from the local community to the nation in the form of commerce, travel, and many means of direct communication.[12]

Sutherland and Cressey evaluate the few studies on the relationship between mobility and the crime rate as inconclusive. "They have been directed toward analysis of the direct effects of mobility in a contemporary situation. They fail to measure the full significance of mobility, for the effects of this process on criminality are principally indirect and are diffused over a period of time and over a wide area."[13]

Sociology of Law

The sociology of law in the classic manner, which tries to discover fundamental relationships between law and society in their varying

---

[12] Edwin H. Sutherland and Donald R. Cressey: *Principles of Criminology.* Philadelphia, J. B. Lippincott Company, 1955, p. 88.

[13] Sutherland and Cressey, *Principles of Criminology,* p. 88.

historical settings, has not flourished in the United States. The major American contribution to a sociology of law has been a pragmatic one: to argue a law in terms of its effects, or to support arguments in court with more than reasoned appeal to general experience.

The American way inquires into the actual working of the legal system, into the effects of the rules upon those immediately involved and upon society in general. The American sociologist believes that since the law serves social interests, there is a general interdependence of law and society, and legal rules must be tested for their practical effects.

Sociologists and legal scholars of the last two generations have dealt with legal concepts and doctrine from a sociological viewpoint. They directed their efforts toward communicating specific sociological knowledge about nonlegal phenomena and applying sociological analysis to particular problems of legal doctrine and legal institutions.

RESULTS. The outcome of this interaction spans the twentieth century. In 1908 Judge Louis Brandeis (who later was appointed to the U.S. Supreme Court), fortified with the social science data of the day, authored an appellate brief that limited the working hours of women.

In 1954 the United States Supreme Court in a landmark case overthrew the principles of "separate but equal facilities" *(Brown v. Board of Education, Topeka, Kansas)*. The Court cited several social psychologists and sociologists in expressly rejecting the old rule.

Perhaps the most far-reaching decision affected by sociological thinking is the Bail Reform Act of 1966, Public Law 89-465, which became effective September 20, 1966. Specifically, this Act established release of subjects on personal recognizance or unsecured appearance bond as the preferred forms of release in federal cases pending trial. This new conceptional approach replaced the previous one where a prisoner had to guarantee appearance by cash or property bond.

The Humphrey-Hawkins Bill of 1977-1978 would *require* a significantly lower rate of unemployment. Sociologist Harvey Brenner is a central figure utilized by the Bill's proponents (*see* Footnote 7 of this chapter).

The advent of the sociologist upon the legal scene, and the formulation of "legal realism" or "social jurisprudence" as concepts acceptable to some legal faculties, has inculcated much distrust among the more traditional members of the legal profession. They charge that, armed with the knowledge of behavioral science, judges invent the law and ignore precedent in their decisions.

LAW IN TRANSITION. This belief in law as a self-sufficient discipline is waning; it is no longer viewed as a static condition or social order. With each decade the influence of the sociologist upon it seems to be growing stronger.

SOCIOLOGICAL ASPECTS OF CRIME
Free Will Versus Determinism

Sociologists identify two major approaches to crime and delinquency: free will and determinism; although these approaches link and overlap, they also conflict.

FREE WILL. This approach assumes that people are responsible for their behavior. Law and order are maintained by force, punishment, and, more important, punitive prevention. The courts and law enforcement emphasize personal responsibility as a fundamental pillar in the edifice of protection for society.

DETERMINISM. Adherents to this approach conceive behavior as caused by social forces, environment, and heredity. They believe that if an act is bad, one should remove the causes that lead to the need or desire to commit the act. Prevention is emphasized, through the removal of sociopathic causes that lead to crime.

Behavioral Science Causal Approach

Behavioral scientists categorize the causal approach to crime behavior into three models: nonconformist, conformist, and anomie.

The *nonconformist* model recognizes that all people have needs. When these needs are blocked, frustration results, and the search for satisfaction enlarges. The chosen way out of the frustration is usually delinquent or criminal behavior. Remedies include removing the obstacle or substituting a nondelinquent way out.

The *conformist* person does not conflict with his/her world but conforms to it, as his/her world conflicts with society because it is a criminalistic subculture. This model postulates that criminal behavior, as with all behavior, is learned in interaction with other persons, principally within intimate personal groups. This model is the most prevalent, and while it lost momentum in the 1940s, by 1955 it was resurrected for the poverty program.

Anomie is a feeling of alienation from other human beings—a normlessness, loneliness, and inability to form an maintain satisfactory relationships, frequently connected with poverty and racial discrimination. The French sociologist Emile Durkheim pointed out that the central theme in our society is lack of control over the social order, i.e. no caste system. Our existence is built on science, with society motivating people to excel by promising future rewards. For many, these rewards do not materialize, and the person must grapple with the conflict of culturally instilled aspirations and social realities. Sociologists propose that this lack of coordination, with society promising benefits it cannot always fulfill, leads first to anomie—a personal disorientation or loneliness—and then to alienation.

Examples of the psychological and permanent damage caused by the anomie-alienation syndrome are the high school dropout and the delinquent street gang; one protests by committing economic suicide and the other institutionalizes alienation.

Social Stratification

Society compares and ranks individuals as groups. When groups are ranked with some degree of permanence, social stratification exists. It develops when humans compete for food and other tangible goods, and also for the intangibles: power, privilege, prestige, and reputation.

Social stratification or social class depends on the values of the culture and may vary from place to place and from time to time. Variables of class consistency today are occupation, income, education, social acceptance, heritage, ethnic origin, competence, and residence. In other societies and at other times, different attributes were important, such as age, degree of nobility, and physical strength.

Some sociologists stratify people into four classes: upper, middle, working, and lower. Others recognize six classes:

Upper-upper. Usually requires many generations and hierarchy of birth and wealth.

Lower-upper. "The elite" — wealth, but without lineage.

Upper-middle. Substantial businessmen; civic leaders with good homes.

Lower-middle. Small businessmen, clerical employees, and skilled workmen, called the "affluent middle-class."

Upper-lower. Poor but honest; semi-skilled factory workers, respectable.

Lower-lower. Persons with bad reputations and those opposed to middle-class values.

Sociologists disagree on the concept of social class. Is it substantive or classificatory, real or artificial? For example, in rural stratification, property determines social position much more than in urban stratification where occupational position predominates.

People in a given social class generally share the same values, enjoy the same activities, and live in the same type of environment. Studies to determine the barriers that separate the various classes suggest that social interaction is the most significant. Do members from different classes intermarry, socialize, eat together, and live together in the same neighborhoods?

Social Class and Social Control

Sociologists state that one's social class at birth strongly influences the development of delinquent or nondelinquent behavior and attitude patterns. The middle class emphasizes orderly habits, propriety, thinking and planning ahead, self-sacrifice for later rewards, and responsibility. These traits differ from the lower class where behavior is learned in environments and personal contacts where delinquent patterns frequently exceed nondelinquent patterns in acceptance, frequency, and priority.

ASCENDING THE SOCIAL LADDER. Some studies of stratification identify two primary prerequisites — money and family — as keys to the doors of society. Others suggest that social mobility and modern technology are obscuring the earmarks of class. Both schools agree, however, that as one ascends the social ladder, one's life-style changes in noticeable, almost predictable ways. The changes most frequently observed encompass the following:

- Infant mortality decreases.
- Health and life expectancy increases.
- Visits to the doctor increase.
- Occupational status increases.
- Level of education increases.

- Selection of dating and marriage partners remains constant.
- Age at time of first marriage increases.
- Warm and permissive treatment rather than punishment of children.
- Knowledge of political issues increases.
- "Justice" in courts increases.
- Likelihood of social and religious prejudice decreases.
- Status anxiety increases.

IN SUMMARY. The United States enjoys an open society with social mobility. Education is considered the key for the "pyramid climber," and individuals are encouraged to climb as far as their talent and ambition will allow.

POLICE APPLICATION OF SOCIOLOGICAL PRINCIPLES

Police agencies are becoming increasingly aware of the influence of sociological principles on police-community relations. This section describes some of the police programs in various cities that were created to facilitate better communication and understanding between the police and minority groups.

New York City

The New York City Police Department has become closely involved in a variety of activities. Included among these are the Boy Scout group, youth clubs, and baseball and basketball leagues, all under the auspices of the Police Athletic League.

In troubled areas, community relations patrol officers have organized regular neighborhood community "workshops" where interested parties meet the precinct captain and staff to discuss problems and grievances.[14]

Los Angeles

Considerable effort has been expended to establish liaison with militant minority group organizations—often little more than loosely organized gangs—to channel their interests and activities into useful community projects. This liaison provides for prompt

---

[14] Leonard Powell: *A Study of American Police Experience of the Problems Involved in Dealings with Minority Groups and Young People.* A Research Report by New Scotland Yard, London, England, 1968, pp. 9-10.

action on valid complaints of current police procedure. The advantage of prompt action to prevent a minor problem escalating into a major one is self-evident.[15]

Chicago

Some of the more striking measures adopted in Chicago include organization of neighborhood "Better Business Bureaus" to supervise ghetto business, consumer education courses in the schools to educate young people in comparative shopping, efforts to develop black ownership of retail outlets, and greater enforcement by government agencies of fraudulent merchandising practices.[16]

Washington, D.C.

To evaluate the isolation of police from the people, which too often accompanies mechanized patrol, Washington, D.C., has planned and implemented a new and thought-provoking project: the model precinct. In a selected precinct, the police make a determined effort to get closer to the people. Foot patrol and twenty-four-hour referral service is available at the police station to advise the people on issues of interest to them.[17]

Neighborhood service centers have been established in tense, high-crime areas, in easily accessible locations such as storefronts or public housing projects. Staffed by police officers, their task is to provide information and service. "This gives the local resident a clear, simple contact for official advice . . . [and] gives the police the opportunity to serve, . . . not merely enforce the law."[18]

Inspector Leonard Powell of New Scotland Yard visited one of these centers and enthusiastically praised the idea and the dedication of the officers who manned it:

> The police-community workshop I visited was situated in a high-density, low-income housing area and was housed in a flat which had been donated for the purpose by a property company.
>
> Two Negro patrolmen staffed the center and provided everything from a youth club and coffee evenings, to a forum for adult meetings. They also

---

[15] Powell, *Study of American Police Experience*, pp. 17-18.

[16] Powell, *Study of American Police Experience*, pp. 21-22.

[17] Powell, *Study of American Police Experience*, p. 26.

[18] Powell, *Study of American Police Experience*, p. 26.

ran a "surgery" where the local populaton, normally reluctant to visit a police station, could attend to seek police advice and assistance.

I was impressed by the dedication of these officers—who had clearly devoted a great deal of their own time and ingenuity to the project.[19]

Atlantic City

A Crime Prevention Bureau has established a good relationship with the community, particularly the young people. According to the National Advisory Commission on Civil Disorders, "It has concentrated on social services, persuading almost 600 drop-outs to return to school, assisting some 250 hardship cases with food and work, arranging for dances and hydrant showers during the summer, working quickly and closely with families of missing persons. The result is close rapport with the community—and recruits for the department."[20]

In Retrospect

Regardless of what aspect of law enforcement a person is involved in, it is essential to have a working knowledge of the factors of social significance that range beyond the immediate purview of law enforcement. Sociology is not new or startling, and its principles can be utilized to great advantage.

Police offices today must take a new look at some old problems to understand certain causal conditions that profoundly affect their role as guardians of the social order.

Discussion Questions

1. The role of the officer in the community has often been referred to as that of a street corner sociologist. Discuss this view.
2. Many people blame society's inability to control crime on the police. Is there justification for this belief?
3. What can be done to correct police isolation from the public?
4. Has the impact of sociology on police work been overemphasized?

---

[19] Powell, *Study of American Police Experience,* p. 26.

[20] United States Riot Commission: *Report of the National Advisory Commission on Civil Disorders.* New York, Bantam Book Co., 1968, p. 320.

civil disobedience . . . demonstrating for causes . . .

Chapter 10

CIVIL DISOBEDIENCE:
CONCEPT AND PRACTICE

Obective: To develop better understanding of civil disobedience by analyzing its history, philosophy, current use, causes, and relationship to law enforcement.

- Philosophy of civil disobedience
- Civil disobedience as a step to anarchy?
- Lao-Tzu to Martin Luther King
- Causes of civil disobedience
- The weapon of prejudice
- Civil disobedience as a front
- Role of law enforcement

THE AMERICAN PUBLIC AND CRIME

THEORY AND practice often clash in the harsh reality of life. In no aspect of world tradition is this more true than when we try to deal with the somewhat elusive concept of civil disobedience.

The purpose of this chapter is to acquaint the reader — police and nonpolice alike — with the concept, philosophy, and practice of civil disobedience. It is intended to present both sides of the picture, which has become multiphased and multicolored through centuries of practice. Both its uses and misuses create trauma for law enforcement as the police stand as the visible and viable agent of government and are caught between demonstrator and nondemonstrator, regardless of the cause.

The problems within our democracy need to be identified. *Sensing* of the population throughout our nation offers a semblance of rationality in truly feeling out what the major concerns of the American people are all about. A recent Gallup Poll reveals the pulse of the nation:

Crime heads the list of major concerns among residents of the nation's largest cities . . .

In the latest survey, 21% of residents of cities of 500,000 or more cited crime as their community's major problem. Nationally, the figure was 15%.

Buttressing this concern, the FBI announced . . . that crime had risen 18% during the first three months of 1975 over the same period a year ago. That compares with a 15% increase during the first quarter of 1974 over the same period in 1973.

Dramatizing the change in urban worries, a 1949 Gallup survey of residents of cities of 500,000 or more found that poor housing, traffic congestion, unsanitary conditions, high taxes and corrupt politics all rated ahead of crime. Only 4% named crime as the worse problem.

Even in medium and small cities, crime is seen as the No. 1 problem. In small towns and rural areas, however, crime is superseded by other troubles.

Although nonwhites have been particularly hard hit by the economy, they are nearly twice as likely as whites to say crime is the greatest difficulty facing their community. Similarly, persons in lower income groups are more inclined to name crime than are persons in upper-income groups.

This is the question asked by Gallup interviewers: *"What do you regard as your community's worst problem?"*

Here are the results based on the views of residents of cities 500,000 and over:

Crime 21%
Unemployment . . . . — 11
Transportation-traffic 7

Education 6
Poor housing-slums.. 5
High cost of living 5
Drugs 4
High taxes 4
Unsanitary conditions...................................... 3
Ineffective police.. 3
Juvenile delinquency....................................... 3
Lack of civic pride... 3
Other problems... 28
Don't know — No Answer 5

The total adds to more than 100% because some persons named more than one problem.

When the survey results are examined in terms of the nation as a whole, crime again emerges as the top problem. The following table compares the views of the nation as a whole with residents of the nation's largest cities:

	National	Largest Cities
Crime..	15%	21%
Unemployment	11	11
Transportation	9	7
High cost of living	5	5
Education	5	6
High taxes	4	4
Drugs	4	4
Poor housing-slums..................................	4	5
Unsanitary conditions...............................	4	3
Ineffective police...................................	3	3
Other problems.....................................	36	34
No opinion...	6	5

The results reported today are based on interviews with 1,558 adults in more than 300 localities during the period June 27-30.[1]

Note the number of factors mentioned in the Gallup Poll that have been known to cause protests and civil disobedience. Civil disobedience, as well as many of these instigating problems, is ancient. Historically, in almost every part of the world — from ancient Greece and Rome to New York and Los Angeles — there has been

---

[1] George Gallup: *A Poll of Urban Issues, Special to the Los Angeles Times.* Los Angeles, California, 1975.

civil disobedience, some violent, some nonviolent. This chapter looks at the so-called nonviolent type, such as demonstrations, sit-ins, picketing, and marches.

AN ANALYSIS OF CIVIL DISOBEDIENCE

From the beginning, we must state the obvious regarding civil disobedience: Our present age offers no answers or solutions. What we do have are too many police agencies tailoring their actions to handle each new incident in crisis fashion with little creative research of the problem from a causative point of view.

This analysis of civil disobedience—its philosophy, historical development, and possible causes—is designed to promote better understanding and perspective and to present some methods to cope with this baffling phenomenon that has beleaguered established governments since antiquity.

Review of the Philosophy—and Rebuttal

The philosophy of nonviolent civil disobedience is based on the theory that certain laws and/or practices and/or institutions are evil, and that the individual has the right and duty to evaluate and determine their moral propriety. It theorizes that evil laws must be resisted after the government's system is found too slow or ineffective. It must be done publicly and nonviolently, with the individual willing to suffer the legal and social consequences—including self-sacrifice.

Modern day American followers of this philosophy claim that it is based on the First Amendment of the Constitution, which guarantees freedom of speech, assembly, and the right of redress of grievances:

> Congress shall make no law respecting an establishment of religion, or prohibiting the free exercise thereof, or abridging the freedom of speech, or the press, or the right of the people peaceably to assemble, and to petition the government for a redress of grievances.[2]

The primary prerequisites or tools of this type of disorder include total commitment to the cause and nonretaliation (turn the other cheek). The disorder must be performed outside the governmental framework and in public to elicit sympathy for the cause.

In summary, then, *civil disobedience is a course of illegal con-*

---

[2] *Constitution of the United States*, First Amendment.

duct undertaken by a like-minded or homogeneous group for the purpose of obtaining redress of alleged grievances.

REBUTTAL. This view and philosophy has a host of opponents. Among these is United States Supreme Court Justice Hugo Black, who condemns civil disobedience as the first step to anarchy. He declares that no individual has the right of privilege to take the law into his/her own hands, as there are sufficient legal remedies for redress.

Justice Black and other opponents further state that civil disobedience weakens the foundation of democracy. Certain sanctions must be imposed on citizens by other citizens, for personal security and the preservation of life, property, liberty, and civil rights; without effective laws, law enforcement and individual civil rights are useless; civil disobedience increases crime, applauds the law breakers, and promotes disrespect for law and order.

HISTORICAL DEVELOPMENT

Civil disobedience probably started when the first organization began to oversee and decide the affairs of man. We do know that nonviolent protests were practiced 3,000 years ago in China when Lao-Tzu, founder of Taoism, emphasized love, moderation, and nonviolence. He exalted the ethics of nonretaliation and taught that the most loving, humble, and harmless person is, in the long run, the most powerful.

Another noted but later practitioner was Jesus Christ. He confounded the religious and civil leaders of his day with his teachings of brotherly love and "love thine enemy." Some centuries later, Christians of the day saw Martin Luther split their church with tactics of civil disobedience.

Civil disobedience, as we know it today, originated with Henry David Thoreau, who believed that it was evil to obey an unjust law. To his own mind, the only possible moral action to a law that conflicts with one's conscience is to instantly disobey.[3]

Perhaps the most successful and most imitated practitioner of nonviolent civil disobedience was Mahatma Gandhi. India is free from colonial rule today, in large measure because of Gandhi's persistent and effective adherence to its principles. Basing his

---

[3] Henry David Thoreau: *Essay on Disobedience,* 1850.

behavior and philosophy on the teachings of Christ and Thoreau, Gandhi led literally millions of Indians in sit-down strikes and other forms of passive resistance against the English Colonial government. After nearly twenty years of refusing to fight but effectively stalling the entire economy, Gandhi in 1947 won independence for India.

In the United States the late Martin Luther King, Jr., was the most persuasive and effective advocate of civil disobedience. Following the methods of Gandhi, he achieved many legal and social benefits for blacks. King believed that passive resistance was complementary to government action, and that disobeying a bad law and obeying a good one showed greater respect for the law than to simply act in robot fashion and obey because it is the law.

Passive Resistance in America

Passive resistance of Oriental and Middle Eastern origin has, for the most part, failed in America. "Turn the other cheek" behavior is alien to the average American participating in or viewing such behavior, and with the potential for violence always present, many "nonviolent" movements have erupted into violent confrontations.

In India, leadership of the noncooperation movement was vested in one party, represented by coordinating leaders. In America there is no single, overall ruling group or individual. The leadership is fragmented among several groups who jealously compete for power and recognition.

INVESTIGATION OF THE CAUSES

The goal of civil disobedience is to alter the established social or political system and thus gain some desired objective. For Lao-Tzu it was power; for Christ it was brotherly love; for Gandhi it was independence of India; for King it was equal rights for his race.

Disobedience is usually precipitated by a minority group, which believes that it has been discriminated against by the majority. On the college campuses some dissident groups believe they should have more representation in the administration of the school; minority groups believe that they should have equal opportunity in jobs, housing, education, and advancement.

Prejudice

Perhaps the basic, most prevalent cause of civil disobedience is prejudice—that is, prejudice of the majority, or the group in power, toward some minority struggling for a certain objective: religious liberty, racial equality, national recognition, independence, or just a more equitable distribution of our world's limited wealth.

Just as civil disobedience has occupied a prominent and continuous position in the affairs of men and women, so too has prejudice. Whether it be because of religion, race, class, or nationality, this text and many behavioral scientists suggest that the most frequent underlying cause of civil disorder—if traced to its root beginnings—is the nebulous yet powerful force of prejudice.

Definition

Prejudice is briefly defined as a preconceived judgment or opinion based upon a faulty and inflexible generalization. It may be felt or expressed; it may be directed toward a group as a whole or toward one individual because he or she is a member of that group. A prejudiced idea is one so firmly imbedded in the mind of the believer that it cannot or will not be changed—even in the face of scientific fact.[4] A good example of the volatile nature of prejudice is the hatred generated against the Japanese-Americans during the Second World War.

Noted author Gordon Allport traces the evolution of the word prejudice in this manner:

> The word "prejudice," derived from the Latin noun "praejudicium," has, like most words, undergone a change of meaning since classical times. There are three stages in the transformation: (1) To the ancients, "praejudicium" meant a precent—a judgment based on previous decision and experiences. (2) Later, the term, in English, acquired the meaning of a judgment formed before due examination and consideration of the facts—a premature or hasty judgment. (3) Finally, the term acquired also its present emotional flavor of favorableness or unfavorableness that accompanies such a prior and unsupported judgment.[5]

Development

Prejudice generally develops in social systems through conflicts between groups within the system. For most purposes, these groups

---

[4] Gordon W. Allport: The Nature of Prejudice. Reading, Massachusetts, Addison-Wesley, 1954. p. 6.

[5] Allport, Nature of Prejudice, p. 3.

can roughly be divided into two basic segments: majority and minority.

Societies are divided into strata based on the majority, minority classification. The division is not a simple dichotomy of two groups, but extends to group after group until the entire social system is carefully ranked. A nation or government that includes all these strata must unite to control them because each individual or group is constantly struggling for the limited quantities of power, prestige, and income attendant to the whole. Governments tend to hold individuals and groups in place by the use of folkways and mores, which are buttressed by tradition and often maintained by force.

To understand modern prejudice, one must understand conflict between groups in society. For example, Ruth Benedict writes, "Social change is inevitable, and it is always fought by those whose ties are to the old order . . . those who have these ties will consciously ferret out reasons for believing that their group is supremely valuable and that new claimants threaten the achievements of civilization. They will raise a cry of right of inheritance, or divine right of kings or religious orthodoxy or racial purity or manifest destiny. These cries reflect the temporary conditions of the moment . . . none of them are based on eternal verities."[6]

Uses of Prejudice

Some forms of prejudice, whether economic, psychological, religious, or racial, have been practiced throughout history as instruments of group control. Prejudice is a formidable and effective weapon of control, and majority groups have frequently resorted to it to resolve and stabilize problems of social organization and order.

The nature of prejudice is such that it affects the psychological make-up, cultural background, and the economic ability of the minority group.

Current Practice of Prejudice

Race has become — or, some would argue, remains — the most prevalent criterion to use in inflicting prejudice on minority groups. Today's problem of minority group prejudice has gravitated to the urban areas, where the institution of prejudice holds the black

---

[6] Ruth Benedict: *Race: Science and Politics.* New York, Modern Age Books, 1940, pp. 220-223.

minority within areas that are boiling cauldrons of rebellion. Harold Lett describes the situation that exists in many ghettos: "To be denied the right of earning a livelihood for one's family, or to be deprived arbitrarily and capriciously of needs, because of an accident of birth, produces a kind of emotional shock that in turn, creates a deep, smouldering rage which arises out of blind, helpless frustration."[7]

When this rage boils up and overflows, the subsequent civil disorder may be nonviolent or violent; either way, law enforcement is in the middle.

Prejudice and Civil Disobedience: Some Misuses

Many well-meaning Americans are today caught up in a mire of hate, which is being formented or led and financed by persons not necessarily desirous of continuing the American way of life. This was cogently brought to mind by the late and much maligned J. Edgar Hoover, then Director of the Federal Bureau of Investigation, when he warned, "The growth of black extremist organizations constitutes a potential threat to the internal security of the nation, partly because there has been an expansion of foreign influences in these groups . . . the thrust of the New Left Movement is to completely destroy our form of government."[8]

This is not to say that all civil disobedience has a subversive undercurrent; it is, however, to remind the American people and police officers alike that there are certain factors under the surface that appear today to have a unity of purpose in creating civil unrest that does not appear to be wholly a spontaneous or unrehearsed type of activity or plan. Many well-meaning students and teachers and other Americans are brought into these activities while honestly believing they are fighting for a just cause or situation (or, other times, a legitimate human rights group is spoiled by one radical member). This does not alienate the fact that many so-called causes are directly intent on undermining the government of the United States.

Thus we have a curious paradox: Millions of well-meaning Americans are joining causes today that while appearing pure on

[7] Harold A. Lett: "Minority Groups and Police—Community Relations." *Police and Community Relations: A Sourcebook.* Beverly Hills, California, Glencoe Press, 1968, p. 124.

[8] "Hoover warns on Terrorism by New Left." *Los Angeles Times,* January 1, 1969.

the surface are something like an iceberg of intrigue and are often unseen subversive causes. While it is true that police over-reaction has been a factor in certain riotous situations across the country, the fact remains that there appears to be a hard-core cadre operating within this nation intent on turning any so-called nonviolent demonstrations, marches, and the like into clashes between the agents of government (the police) and the agents of the movement (the demonstrators). When conditions of this nature prevail, then it goes almost without saying that the peace officers of this country will face prolonged and continuing involvement of a critical nature within these movements.

Ronald Reagan, former Governor of California, commented on the similar strategy used by hard-core cadres of campus agitators who did seek to disrupt—and openly boasted of destroying—the higher educational system of California:

> The tactics change and will continue to change. But from SKS, PLS, BSU, YSL and other radical organizations, we find a common design:
> 1. Find a few "core" people on a campus.
> 2. Train them in the tactics of insurrection.
> 3. Have them find the issue of potential strain on their particular campus, whether it's the food in the cafeteria, campus rules regarding the use of facilities, or visitation rights in the dormitories.
> 4. Seek out support in strategic places in the community.
> 5. Push constantly for just a little more than is allowed.
> 6. Harass the local administrators verbally, as well.
> 7. Wait for the mistake you produce.
> 8. Paint the administrators as rigid and authoritarian.
> 9. Be prepared to win either way—you either win the building or you point to police brutality if you are removed from it.
> 10. Be willing to nibble, because each success makes easier the next one.
> This is the strategy of take-over.[9]

The tactics do not always remain constant. However, few times have they been so well articulated on the general theme of civil disobedience.

THE ROLE OF LAW ENFORCEMENT

Since understanding usually leads to better performance, it is imperative that law enforcement know something about the goals of

---

[9] Ronald Reagan: "Freedom vs. Anarchy on Campus—Warning from Governor Reagan." *U.S. NEWS and World Report*, December 30, 1968, pp. 47-49.

the protesting groups, the grievances that precipitate a protest, and the methods the group uses. Each member of a law enforcement agency should be trained in the philosophies and ideology of the various organizations currently operating in their respective areas, their general feelings toward law enforcement, and what law enforcement can expect of them, as well as how to recognize signs of community tension, and how to handle protests when they occur.

A causal approach to what really caused these riots to occur and all of the civil disorder presents a theme involving four basic factors:

1. Inadequate housing
2. Insufficient education to obtain needed jobs where they would be employable
3. Inadequate employment
4. Poor community-police relationships

Many feel that the frustrations to people, particularly minorities that are in plagued areas where the first three are all existent, are probably responsible for much of the bad feeling toward the viable and visible sign of government—the police. Peace officers can frequently prevent civil disobedience through thoughtful and meaningful explanation of a disliked law or procedure. If prevention is not possible, they can supply their department with information essential to effective operating procedures.

Paramount in the framework of any action plan to cope with civil disobedience and the prime directive for all law enforcement personnel is fair and impartial enforcement of the law in a Constitutional manner. In the long run, this is the only really workable way for law enforcement to build community support and remain a neutral, stabilizing force during these times of crisis.

Discussion Questions

1. There appears to be a fine line between civil disobedience and criminality. Who should determine when this line has been transgressed?
2. What are some peaceful alternatives dissidents might use to attain their goals? Are these alternatives effective?
3. Numerous responsible and informed individuals have warned that lawful demonstrations have become the vehicle for extremist groups to disrupt the country. What evidence can be offered to support or deny that warning?

riot . . . the specter that stalks man's footsteps as he searches for solutions to society's ills . . .

Chapter 11

RIOTS: A TWENTIETH CENTURY PLAGUE

Objective: To develop an understanding of the police practices used to control riots; to emphasize the vital importance of each peace officer in preventing riots.

- Commission studies
- Use of military assistance
- .Soliciting community support
- Recruitment of minorities
- Position qualifications
- Policies for reporting information
- Controlling rumors and receiving complaints

165

HISTORICAL PERSPECTIVE

DEFINING A TERM such as "riot" requires a great deal of tact. What exactly constitutes civil disobedience is elusive, but *riot* may be even more difficult to dissect. A riot in the legal sense may involve as few as two people or an many as thousands. The police role is never more perplexing than attempting to handle a "riot" at the local bar, as opposed to the "riot" of vineyard workers—by the hundreds—who seek out violence to make their point. Yet, the use of counterviolence on the part of law enforcement, to keep or restore order from chaos, should be viewed as a last resort. While certain actions might well be legal in the strict construction of that term when confronted with a near-riotous situation, several factors merit review. As Turk points out:

> Confronted with a defined normative problem, the greatest temptation and the easiest recourse for authorities is to attempt solution of the problem by legalization—which is tantamount to attempting to solve all interpersonal problems by announcing ultimatums and threatening violence unless one gets one's way. The point is that the most explicit and forceful strategy is not always, or even usually, the most effective. Violence, in particular, can be effective when used infrequently and selectively; but violence is a dangerous approach, whose effectiveness diminishes and whose counterproductivity rises when it is used too often and too indiscriminately. Before they assume the costs and risks of legalization, sensible authorities will require evidence that the problem is objective as well as perceptual, that it is necessary for them to deal with the problem, that legalization is the only or best control strategy, and that a particular degree of legalization is called for, knowing that legal sanctioning used blindly may well be the greatest of all threats to legal authority.[1]

Civil disobedience can explode, and often has exploded, into riot. Thus the law enforcement officer must be intensely aware of the infinitely varied aspects of both.

There is no evidence historically of just when the first riot took place. In our country, a number of riots occurred during our first hundred years as a nation; the late nineteenth century gives us a point of departure.

On October 24, 1871, Los Angeles, California experienced the "Chinatown Massacre." One evening cost eighteen lives, and it was recorded as "the worst such upheaval" in American history.

---

[1] Austin T. Turk: *Legal Sanctioning and Social Control.* Rockville, Maryland, National Institute of Mental Health, 1972, p. 75.

That was over a century ago; more recent riots have left various cities of the United States in ruin. The "Age of the Riot" had its beginning on August 11, 1965, in Watts, followed nationally by Atlanta, Bridgeton, Cambridge, Chicago, Cincinnati, Detroit, Elizabeth, Englewood, Grand Rapids, Houston, Jackson, Jersey City, Milwaukee, Nashville, Newark, New Brunswick, New Haven, Oakland, Paterson, Plainfield, Phoenix, Rockford, San Francisco, Tampa, Tucson, Washington, D.C., again in Los Angeles, and so on and on.

These disorders, usually taking from two to seven days to run their senseless destructive courses, clearly illustrate to those who have studied them — and to those in law enforcement who have lived them — that policing efforts alone, though dedicated and well intentioned, are simply not enough. The events of these human and economic catastrophies have taken their toll in human life and limb, property, and a suspicion, fear, and hatred that cannot accurately be assessed or completely erased. To avert these mushrooming and sinister tragedies in the future, more emphasis must be focused on their prevention and on solutions that treat causal factors more accurately and thoroughly. To accomplish this difficult task, we must first recognize the need for exercising extreme care and skill in police dealings with fellow human beings. Law enforcement officers must be sensitive to their sworn obligation to protect all citizens without regard for class, culture, or complexion. This becomes a great deal more than mere verbiage to be expounded upon; should the public or police fail in what must be a joint endeavor, we might be witness to a resurgence of rioting and the misery that attends its aftermath.

COMMISSION APPROACH

Immediately following the now historic Watts Riot, a Governor's Commission was appointed and charged with the responsibility of investigating its causes and effects. The observations in this penetrating study have materially increased the available knowledge upon which modern law enforcement must focus. Following the even more bitter racial disorders of the summer of 1967, the late President Lyndon B. Johnson established the National Advisory Commission on Civil Disorders and charged that Commission with the responsibility of investigating the causes and consequences of such disorders in a national context.

The McCone Commission immediately following the riots in Los Angeles spent several months interviewing various persons who had been there, both from a civilian and an enforcement standpoint, as well as fire, electric companies, etc. They concluded, after this study, that when four major causes come together in an explosive fashion, chaos can result. The four factors overly simplified are (1) inadequate education, (2) inadequate housing, (3) inadequate employment, and (4) poor community-police relationships.

Since that time two other federal commissions have been formed to investigate this plague of the twentieth century: the National Institute of Law Enforcement and Criminal Justice and the National Commission on the Causes and Prevention of Violence.

The National Institute of Law Enforcement and Criminal Justice interviewed students, college spokesmen, and city police officials as the initial part of a long-range program aimed at reducing violence. The National Commission on the Causes and Prevention of Violence has sponsored several studies on violence.

A CLOSER LOOK AT THE PROBLEM—AND SOME SOLUTIONS

The areas considered in the remainder of this chapter are based on the observations of the President's Commission on Law Enforcement and Administration of Justice, the National Advisory Commission on Civil Disorders, and the United States Attorney General's Commission on Standards and Goals for the Criminal Justice System. These areas are designed to present police administrators and others with an opportunity to consider both the crisis areas and some suggestions for overt action.

Utilization of the Military

PREMISE. Law enforcement agencies and the military should develop contingency plans so that in future situations of an emergency nature, there will be a better method of assuring the timely commitment and rapid deployment of troops.

ANALYSIS. When major civil disorders develop within the purview of law enforcement, the availability of instantaneous control forces—sometimes beyond the personnel and equipment of the affected jurisdiction—is of extreme importance. Due principally and traditionally to the statutory restrictions on the use of federal forces and limitations imposed on the state police, the complement and material resources to assist the local agency in riot control measures must be thoroughly defined in advance. Utilization of the National Guard or other military units is realistically determined by conditions of the moment. The head of the law enforcement agency confronted with the emergency must, therefore, have immediate access to some designated person who is authorized to commit troops. Having such a person available at all times, with full authority to initiate action, provides one possible solution to the problem.

The rapid deployment of troops generally presents no problem. Obviously, the precise manner in which to accomplish deployment will depend on the situation of the moment, and thus continuous liaison is necessary between the various agencies participating in any emergency situation.

Civil disorders of extraordinary proportions may require commitment of federal troops to assist state and local agencies. State and local officials should appraise themselves of the exact procedures to be followed in requesting federal troops, the number that would be available, estimated times, and the command responsibilities and relationships that would exist between the interacting control forces.

Police-Community Relations Programs

PREMISE. Programs structured to improve the relationship between law enforcement agencies and the various minority communities need greater emphasis. Each policing agency should continually seek a high degree of rapport with every segment of its jurisdictional community. Each officer entering the department should receive extensive instruction regarding individual responsibility to establish and maintain this rapport.

Current public interest, civil rights disturbances, and demonstrations point to the urgent need for improved liaison with minority groups, as well as community leaders, at the "grass roots" level. This liaison is mandatory to maintain effective police control.

ANALYSIS. The police officer—both inside and outside the "ghetto"—symbolizes not only the law, but also the equities and inequities of the entire system of criminal justice. Indeed, as a symbol of government (particularly in the ghetto), the police officer often represents the good and the evil of the entire governmental process. Cast in this role — perhaps unfairly — the policeman often becomes the target of inflamed pressure groups, who with some justification feel victimized by the social process. In this difficult role, the law enforcement officer can either distinguish or destroy the qualities of patience, courage, and character.

If the police are charged with the primary responsibility of securing the life and property of the public they serve, and if it is axiomatic that effective achievement of that goal necessitates community support, then it is absolutely essential that the police actively solicit the support of community groups vitally concerned with the course of police conduct. In this regard the following steps should be considered:

1. Develop and maintain liaison with civil rights and other sizable groups concerned with police-community relations in its broadest context. Dialogue with groups expressing differing philosophies may be traumatic, but it is an absolute essential.
2. Interpret the philosophy of these groups.
3. Identify leaders, members, and objectives of extremists groups.
4. Specialize in community relations problems.
5. Develop and maintain liaison with government and community agencies that are connected with community relations close to law enforcement.
6. Check crime reports for racial or similar incidents and make follow-up investigations, as necessary.
7. Assist station patrol officers and detectives or other police or government agencies with cases having racial, religious, ethnic, or other identifiable overtones; this to be on a request basis.
8. Identify and classify potential problem areas.
9. Assist in the education of officers in community relations problems through inservice training.
10. Develop and maintain liaison with the public and parochial schools regarding incidents of tension.
11. Establish and maintain a record system regarding pertinent problems and tensions, community groups, and individuals involved in community and racial problems.
12. Keep the department informed of the above information for policy making in the handling of civil rights demonstrations.
13. Lecture to all recruits on appropriate topics relative to police-community relations.
14. Lecture on police-community relations to outside police agencies on request.
15. Check news media for information regarding racial and similar inci-

dents. Review, clip, and file all pertinent articles on these problems.
16. Keep all concerned personnel advised on problems in specific police-community relations areas.
17. Create an award system designed to credit officers who minimize potential for disorder by improving the police relationship with alienated members of the community.

Recruitment of Minority Group Members

PREMISE. Law enforcement agencies should stringently seek to increase their existing officer complement of Black, Mexican-American, and other minority group members.

ANALYSIS. Unfortunately, in the overwhelming majority of law enforcement agencies, the percentage of minority group members employed in police departments does not approximate the percentage of minority group members in the general population that they serve. This situation is disturbingly acute at the entrance level and is even more marked as we examine the vertical command structure. This proposed premise, though desirable, is complicated by the reality of recruitment problems. To recognize the difficulty of qualified recruitment and promotion is not, however, a license to ignore the obligation. Every available media of communicating law enforcement's personnel needs to be constructively and continuously utilized. It is further recommended that on-going review of departmental promotional policies be embarked upon in a visibly integrated, equal opportunity police force.

Position Qualifications

PREMISE. Employers should reassess job qualifications and determine the feasibility of increasing employment opportunities for persons with arrest records; blanket rejection of such persons should be discouraged.

ANALYSIS. Recruitment standards for any given agency are governed by statutory dictates. As an example, view the requirement of our nation's largest county: In the County of Los Angeles, police personnel are recruited in conformity with rules and regulations set forth by the United States, the State of California, and the County of Los Angeles. Section 13510 of the California Penal Code authorizes the California Commission on Peace Officer Standards and Training (POST) to establish the following minimum recruitment standards:

1. Citizen of the United States.
2. Minimum age of twenty-one years.
3. Fingerprinting of applicants with a search of local, state and national fingerprint files to disclose any criminal record.
4. Shall not have been convicted by any state or by the Federal Government of a crime, the punishment for which could have been imprisonment in a Federal penitentiary or a State prison.
5. Good moral character as determined by a thorough background investigation according to specifications entitled "The Personal History Investigation" published by the Commission.
6. Graduation from high school or a passing of the General Education Development test indicating high school graduation level, or a score on a written test of mental ability approved by the Commission, and equivalent to that attained by the average high school student.
7. Examination by a licensed physician and surgeon. Only those applicants who are found to be free from any physical, emotional or mental condition which might adversely affect performance of his duty as a peace officer shall be eligible for appointment. The applicant's findings shall include but are not limited to all of the items set forth in the specification entitled "Physical Examination" published by the Commission.[2]

Los Angeles County Civil Service further clarifies and restricts employment of personnel:

The Secretary and Chief Examiner, subject to the right of any person aggrieved to appeal to the Commission as provided in Rule 5, may refuse to accept an application or to examine an applicant, or may withhold the name of a person from the eligible list or an eligible from certification, or the Commission, after notice, may remove the name of an eligible from the eligible list:

1. Who does not meet the requirements set forth in these Rules or in the bulletin announcing the examination.
2. Who is physically or mentally unfit to perform the duties of the position which he seeks.
3. Who is addicted to the use of intoxicating liquors, of narcotics or habit-forming drugs.
4. Who is addicted to gambling or immoral practices or habits.
5. Who is guilty of conduct not compatible with county employment, whether or not it amounts to a crime.
6. Who has been convicted of a crime.
7. Who has been dismissed or has resigned in lieu of discharge from any position, public or private, for any cause which would be a cause for dismissal from County service; or whose record of employment has not been satisfactory in the County service, or with any other agency or firm.

---

[2] Administrative Code of California. Title II, Chapter 2, Section 10002.

8. Who has abandoned any position in County service or been absent from duty without leave of absence duly granted.

9. Who has made any material false statement or who has attempted any deception or fraud in connection with this or any other civil service examination.

10. Who refuses to execute the oath as prescribed by law.

11. Who fails to present himself for fingerprinting as required by the Commission.

12. Who has assisted in preparing, conducting, or scoring the examination for which he applies or who has in any other manner secured confidential information concerning such examination which might give him an unfair advantage over other applicants in the examination.

13. Who fails to present himself for or fails to pass the medical examination prescribed by the Commission.

14. Who advocates, or who is knowingly a member of the Communist Party, or of any organization which to his knowledge is a successor of such party, regardless of its name, or who is knowingly a member of any organization which to his knowledge now advocates the overthrow of the Government of the United States or of his State by force or violence of other unlawful means, or who now advocates the support of a foreign government against the United States in the event of hostilities.

15. Who has been discharged from the Armed forces under conditions other than honorable.[3]

Thus, many factors beyond a police agency's immediate control influence hiring procedures, as Los Angeles County is typical in this type of regulatory machinery. It is to be emphasized, however, that many cases falling within this purview have other, positive aspects. The *exception principle* should apply in all applicable instances, particularly today when many of society's standards are being openly questioned.

Standardization of Information

PREMISE. A region-wide "data bank" should be created to centralize and standardize the information and statistics that numerous federal, state, and local agencies collect concerning various areas of the country.

ANALYSIS. Many notably successful policing agencies operate according to a formula that makes reporting districts synonymous with census tracts. This system has proved to be extremely efficient and is of great value in that it allows effective correlation with all

---

[3] Los Angeles County Civil Service Rules and Regulations, Section 7.04, 1978.

federal data released in connection with the national census program.

Through such a program, information is available concerning
income levels, types of employment in specific areas, family sizes,
and other information of significance when correlated with the
incidence of various types of crime.

This system of reporting — *the census tract basis* — should be
adopted by all law enforcement agencies and be made available to
whatever responsible central agencies are interested in correlating
and analyzing the resultant data.

Disaster and Inflammatory Incident Reporting

PREMISE. Members of the police, press, public officials, and
community leaders should meet and establish guidelines, both
procedural and policy, for reporting disasters and inflammatory
incidents.

ANALYSIS. The nature of police work creates continuous
interest from the news media. With the exception of incidents so
rare they do not warrant discussion, police requests for cooperation
and appropriate reporting have been honored in an outstanding
manner.

In view of the recurrent call for reporting accuracy — particularly
where disaster of inflammatory incidents are involved — and the
peculiar position the police enjoy to supply the press with accurate,
reportable data, the police and the press must be fully conversant
with the hazards, under riot conditions, of gathering and indis-
criminately releasing such information and, under riot conditions,
the constitutionally protected rights of the press and the public to
be fully informed.

Improved communication between the police and the press may
be accomplished by community leaders, police, press, and public
officials orientation sessions designed to acquaint or reacquaint
participants with the problems that may be encountered by each.
To maximize the effectiveness of such meetings, participants should
be representative of an adequate cross-sample of affected personnel.

Following these preliminary discussions, an opportunity should
be afforded the police to introduce the availability of an emergency
information center and the designation of public information

officers. Such centers and officers maximize press access to accurate information about emergency operations pertinent to the concerned department's activities. National news media representatives should also be fully informed about such centers in the event of conflagrations.

Rumor Control Clinic

PREMISE. The majority of information to and from the black community comes from reporters who are directly connected to police and news media of the establishment. An information center should not intensify this dependence. Properly conceived, a clinic can supplement on-the-spot reporting in supplying news about official action.

ANALYSIS. Rumors aggravated tension and disorder in more than 65 percent of the riots studied by the President's Commission on Law Enforcement and Administration of Justice. The Commission cites the power of a rumor by the one that swept the Watts area in the 1965 Los Angeles riot: "Two white policemen were beating a colored lady like a dog."[4]

According to the Commission, "This incident, which was thought by many people to be the cause of the Los Angeles riot, never occurred."[5]Indeed, rumor has proven such an incendiary element that several cities — notably Chicago, Detroit, and Los Angeles — have set up Rumor Control Clinics.

The Los Angeles Rumor Control Clinic came into premature existence a decade ago to handle a shooting incident between the police and alleged Black Panthers. The Clinic played a major role in disseminating the truth and thus helped forestall an explosive situation.

The Los Angeles Clinic informs the community of any problems and also of information that might help to develop realistic and practical approaches to community problems. It assists the black community further by supplying information on services available to it.

The Clinic is a private organization and independently financed.

---

[4] President's Commission on Law Enforcement and Administration of Justice: *Task Force Report: The Police.* Washington, D.C., U.S. Government Printing Office, 1967, p. 147.

[5] President's Commission, *The Police,* pp. 147-148.

Many consider it the only source of information the black community will trust.

Citizen Complaint Procedures

PREMISE. One of the prime requisites to any adequate community relations program is an effective system by which aggrieved citizens can lodge their complaints.

ANALYSIS. A citizen intent on lodging a complaint against any member of any law enforcement agency should be permitted to do so through a variety of channels and without excessive formality. Perhaps as important to the citizen as the ease of access to the grievance process is the belief that his or her complaint will be thoroughly and impartially investigated and the real sanctions will be imposed against officers found derelict.

The multiple-channel approach many departments utilize exemplifies such a grievance mechanism.

A complainant can approach *any member* of the department and have the complaint officially investigated. Complaints may be lodged with the unit commander of the employee being complained about or with ranking members of the department. They may also be brought directly to the head of the department or the department's personnel bureau.

Registration of the complaint is promptly followed by a thorough and impartial investigation, and the *complainant is advised of the results.*

Should the complainant feel that the grievance is not receiving appropriate attention or does not elect to complain directly to the police agency, he or she may lodge the complaint with the Commission on Human Relations (hundreds now exist throughout the country), the district attorney, grand jury, Civil Service Commission, attorney general, city attorney, or the Federal Bureau of Investigation; many other channels exist in specific geographical localities.

Aggrieved citizens are understandably reluctant to formally complain about police misconduct. This feeling results in part from the belief that the police tend to "stick together." Legitimate police declarations that officer misconduct will not be tolerated — that the police do not enjoy any special immunity — may in time discourage this reluctance to complain and justifiably restore public confidence in the internal grievance mechanism.

A CONCLUDING NOTE

This chapter analyzes a major problem of today. Not all aspects are dealt with, yet these are crisis areas that must be continuously considered. Development of policies and practices beforehand can preclude many traumatic situations before they burst into prominence elsewhere. In a very real sense this is preventive police-community relations of the finest order and highest quality.

The problem is of course not new to this world, nor to Western civilization. Quinney notes:

> Some modern nations have been police states; all, however, are policed societies. Practical men have never underestimated, though they have often distorted, the importance of the police. Sociological theory in the "social control" tradition, however, has usually slighted the police in favor of normative or voluntary processes. The significance of the police, for our purposes, can best be understood as they appeared to a generation for whom modern police were an unprecedented innovation — Englishmen in the middle third of the nineteenth century.
>
> The London police, created in 1829, were from the beginning a bureaucratic organization of professionals. One of their tasks was to prevent crime by regularly patrolling beats, operating under strict rules which permitted individual discretion. The police also had a mission against the "dangerous classes" and political agitation in the form of mob or riots. On all fronts they were so successful that initial and strong objections to them rapidly diminished; from being a considerable novelty, they quickly became a part of "British tradition."[6]

Since the Watts Riot occurred, this country has witnessed racial bitterness and strife unparalleled in its history. Rhetorical protestations of a "new" police-community relationship by the police or promises of a "new" social order by dissidents do little to bridge the gap that concededly exists between the police and the public — and the public and the police.

Responsible police leadership — and this is a foremost concern — must span this police-public gap with programs designed and implemented to instruct, by example and practice, present and future police officers in acceptable modes of police conduct. This problematical approach will inexorably shape police attitudes into a likeness appropriate to their changing social service role.

---

[6] Richard Quinney: *Criminal Justice in America.* Boston, Little, Brown & Company, 1974, 8pp. 156-158.

In major cities and regions throughout the nation, countless thousands of hours are now being devoted to police-community relations. Perhaps this continued effort is the real key to new hope, nationwide, for a permanent improvement of these relations.

Discussion Questions

1. To what do you attribute the relative lack of violent social unrest of the past several years?
2. Discuss some programs for preventing riots or civil unrest not mentioned in this chapter.
3. Using some of the major riots of the last fifteen years discuss some ways in which you might have handled the situation differently.

PART IV

POLICE-COMMUNITY RELATIONS TODAY AND TOMORROW

the slammer has proven to be dysfunctional as a contemporary means for crime control . . . we need to explore alternate methods more thoroughly . . .

Chapter 12

DIVERSION

OBJECTIVE: Noting a "philosophy of need" to channel efforts toward crime reduction in an old but unofficially accepted direction.

- Definition
- Origination of diversion
- Juvenile diversion
- Treatment instead of incarceration
- Problems with diversion programs
- Pros of diversion
- Labelling and overcriminalization

INTRODUCTION

THE CRIMINAL justice system in this country is currently considered to be in a state of crisis. The system as a whole—the police, courts, and corrections subsystems—has been a recipient of voluminous criticism. The criticism originates from numerous sources, including the public, news media, law breakers, and representatives of the system itself.

Law enforcement, both as a totality and on an individual basis, has been criticized for virtually every aspect of police operation. The attitude of police toward the communities they serve has been widely attacked.

Minority groups, in particular, have complained about police methods. Charges of selective enforcement, harassment, and brutality aimed at particular groups have been widely circulated.

The courts too have their critics, perhaps the most vocal being the police and attorneys. Congested calendars and backlogged cases have led to charges of inefficiency. Judges have been described as soft or overly lenient because of their sentencing procedures. Many decisions of the courts, especially those relating to human rights, have been extremely unpopular with police and prosecuting agencies.

Public criticism of corrections agencies has been awesome. The failure of these agencies to rehabilitate inmates has been decried by both the public and the inmates themselves. Attention has been directed at conditions in the various corrections facilities by numerous inmate protests and riots.

Many of the problems faced by the criminal justice system have grown out of the inability of the various agencies to work within the limited budgets and personnel available to them. Lacking the means to obtain additional funds, the agencies have been forced to seek alternative methods to cope with current problems. *One of these methods is that of keeping offenders out of the system or removing them from the system at some point prior to completion of the total criminal justice cycle, encompassing arrest, adjudication, and incarceration—in a word, diversion.*

TRADITIONAL APPROACHES

The traditional methods of "removing" an offender from the

system are probation and parole. Recent years have seen the growth of plea bargaining (much to the dismay of many criminal justice personnel) in the courts as an additional approach. By allowing a defendant to plead guilty to a lesser charge (than that alleged), it has been possible to move him or her through the adjudication portion of the criminal justice cycle more rapidly than if the case were to go to trial.

Realistically, plea bargaining has enhanced a defendant's chances for probation or reduced sentence; thus the defendant may be removed from the system more quickly. Discretion of the prosecutor and the court play a large part in the plea bargaining process. Their ability to properly evaluate individual situations is often severely hampered by lack of both sufficient information about a specific defendant and clear standards for plea bargaining. Decisions must be made as to whether the criminal act charged is sufficiently serious as to merit prosecution and a criminal record, or whether the offense can be ignored. If the latter extreme is chosen, the risk of appearing to condone the behavior in question must be faced.

THE GENESIS OF DIVERSION

Diversion programs have been developed as a response to the need to remove offenders from the system, without seeming to condone their actions. In recent years we have seen a tremendous outgrowth of such programs. In 1967, the President's Commission on Law Enforcement and Administration of Justice discussed diversion and recommended the institution of such programs. Since that recommendation was made, so-called diversion programs have been embraced by numerous agencies in the criminal justice system. Diversion programs have grown from that recommendation in much the same way that programs designated as police-community relations grew out of racial conflicts throughout the nation in the sixties — that is, at an epidemic rate.

One of the biggest problems encountered in a discussion of diversion programs is defining the term "diversion." Numerous agencies within the criminal justice system have instituted programs of various sorts, many of the programs having little in common with one another but for the word "diversion" in their title.

Defining Diversion

Raymond T. Nimmer defines diversion in two different ways: "The channeling of criminal defendants into programs that may not involve incarceration,"[1] and "the disposition of a criminal complaint without a conviction, the noncriminal disposition being conditioned on either the performance of specified obligations by the defendant, or his participation in counseling or treatment."[2] Although both of those definitions are applicable to many diversion programs in operation today, each presupposes the arrest or charging of the defendant. For that reason, diversion programs operated by the police are, in effect, excluded by those definitions.

The National Advisory Commission on Criminal Justice Standards and Goals, in its report on Community Crime Prevention, defines diversion in a very different fashion: "the process whereby problems otherwise dealt with in a context of . . . official action will be defined and handled by other nonjustice system means."[3] For a general discussion of diversion, this definition is appropriate. It is broad enough to encompass diversion at any point in the criminal justice cycle.

OPERATIONAL PROGRAMS

Diversion programs in use today are generally directed at four types of offenders: (1) juveniles, (2) those involved in personal disputes, (3) those having little or no past record, and (4) those who are mentally disturbed. Included in the latter group are drug users and alcoholics.

The programs generally seek to help the offender by referring him or her to agencies outside of the criminal justice system. The agencies are charged with the responsibility of supervising the behavior of the offender and contributing to the settlement of personal problems.

---

[1] Raymond T. Nimmer: *Diversion, the Search for Alternative Forms of Prosection.* American Bar Foundation, 1974, p. 3.

[2] Nimmer, *Diversion,* p. 5.

[3] National Advisory Commission on Criminal Justice Standards and Goals: *Report on Community Crime Prevention.* Washington, D.C., Government Printing Office, 1973, p. 59.

A Working Theme of Diversion in General

One major United States police agency, in a section of its policy manual entitled "Alternatives to Physical Arrest, Booking, or Continued Detention," states the following:

> Once a violator has been identified, it is the function of the Department to initiate the criminal process; however, there are circumstances when a crime may occur and the Department will not make a physical arrest. There may be a report written and an application for a complaint made; or in some cases, when the offense is of a minor nature, a verbal warning or other direction may be given. The decision not to make an arrest will be guided by Department policy and the factual situation involved, not by the personal feelings of the officer. An arrest does not dictate a booking, and a booking does not dictate continued detention. When circumstances so indicate, an arrestee should be released, without being booked and, if booked, should be released from further detention.[4]

Juvenile Diversion Programs

Youth services bureaus, defined by the National Advisory Commission on Criminal Justice Standards and Goals in its report on Community Crime Prevention, are "neighborhood agencies providing community services for young people"[5]They are being developed and used to divert juvenile offenders from the criminal justice system. The bureaus provide various services, including medical care, counseling, employment, and educational aids and referrals. Juvenile diversion seems to have replaced the *parens patriae* or substitute parent doctrine of the juvenile court; this latter doctrine has been all but lost as the court has taken on more and more of the qualities of the adult court: "When the first juvenile court was established nearly 75 years ago, it was an outgrowth of the movement at that time to advance the welfare of children — in education, protective services, and child labor laws. Its goals were similar to those proposed for youth services bureaus today. One goal was to provide individual treatment and social services for children coming under the Court's jurisdiction, instead of primarily dispensing punishment. Court proceedings were to be informal, nonadversary, and confidential."[6]

---

[4] National Advisory Commission on Criminal Justice Standards and Goals: *Report on Police.* Washington, D.C., Government Printing Office, 1973, p. 606.

[5] National Advisory Commission, *Community Crime Prevention,* p. 51.

[6] National Advisory Commission, *Community Crime Prevention,* p. 58.

Personal Disputes

For many years, the police have, without so calling it, diverted from the criminal justice system persons involved in personal disputes with other family members or neighbors. Instead of arresting such persons, officers will "counsel" them. "The establishment of Family Crisis Intervention Units within police agencies simply formalizes, makes visible, and provides some control over long-standing practices."[7]

The development of neighborhood agencies to which such persons might be referred by the officers is just another step in the diversion process.

Past Criminal Records

The diversion of those offenders with no past criminal record or minimal records is an attempt to separate them from the more sophisticated criminals and to provide them with some individualized attention and help. By so doing, it is hoped that the high recidivism rate of offenders previously incarcerated can be avoided.

Narcotics and Mental Trauma

The diversion from the criminal justice system of narcotic addicts, alcoholics, and mentally ill persons is simply a matter of humanity. It is imperative that these people receive the help they need. Although such programs as they exist today are far from being totally successful in the "curing" of such persons, the effort must be made. There are numerous projects operating throughout the country to divert such persons to treatment centers both before and after trial and to avoid penal incarceration:

A number of states have developed procedures and accompanying facilities for civil commitment of narcotic offenders similar to the procedures used for the civil commitment of mentally ill persons. Here, as an alternative to conviction and sentence in the formal criminal justice system, the addict-pusher 'voluntarily' submits to incarceration in a nonpenal facility and to participation in accompanying treatment programs. In return, he escapes the onus of a conviction record and avoids going to a traditional prison or other correctional facility. However, his term of commitment is related to his 'condition' rather than his offense, and sometimes incarceration is

---

[7] Donald J. Newman: *Introduction to Criminal Justice.* Philadelphia, J. B. Lippincott Company, 1975, p. 390.

shorter but more often longer than the period of confinement provided in the penal law.[8]

The Dilemma

There are many limitations and problems associated with the development of successful diversion programs. These have become apparent as the *diversion trend* has spread and errors in past programs have been discovered and acknowledged.

The acceptance of diversion programs is not universal in the legal community. One important criticism from that profession is that diversion programs may fail to afford the defendant the due process protections accepted as indispensable in the criminal justice system: "The formal criminal process operates only with statutory authority; it rests on matters of evidence and proof, has built-in procedural safeguards, and, in general, has an elaborate set of checks and balances designed to minimize errors, to accurately separate the guilty from the innocent, and to exercise controls over the treatment of even the most guilty and dangerous. Diversion techniques often bypass these procedures and controls—indeed some diversion practices are deliberately utilized to avoid challenge and to bypass proof . . ."[9]

SOLUTION

In order to eliminate legal challenges to diversionary plans, which could eventually destroy the entire diversion concept, whenever possible due process problems must be isolated and programs devised in such a manner as to neutralize these problems. In California, this has been accomplished in the narcotics offenders diversion process established by Sections 1000 (et seq) of the California Penal Code. Before a defendant is allowed to participate, he or she must consent to the diversion and waive the right to be brought to trial within sixty days. *This waiver enables the authorities to bring the defendant to trial at a later date should he or she fail to successfully complete the diversion obligations.*

Resources—and Problems

Diversion programs have been severely hampered by a lack of

[8] Newman, *Criminal Justice*, p. 390.

[9] Newman, *Criminal Justice*, p. 390.

resources, including facilities and treatment personnel. For this reason, many programs have remained modest, accepting only offenders selected by extremely stringent standards. As a result, two things have occurred. First, the numbers of offenders processed through the programs has been so small as to make little or no noticeable impact on the overcrowded criminal justice system the program is attempting to relieve. Second, by placing stringent restrictions on those eligible for the programs, success or failure rates obtained cannot be applied to less restricted groups as justification for expanding or eliminating the programs. Those rates are representative only of that particular group, whose members will tend to share a variety of common characteristics, including age, past record, present offense charged, or race.

To eliminate these limitations, a program must have sufficient resources to handle a broadly based group of offenders. The group itself must be large enough to both justify the expense of the program and to impact the system the program is attempting to relieve. This will require progressive administrators who share not only the generally accepted belief that the system has been a failure, but a willingness to risk new ways of doing things.

Because of the "helter skelter" manner in which many diversion programs have grown, other problems have arisen. Diversion programs have become something of a "fad," and every agency seems to have started one. However, there has been a general failure on the part of those agencies *to plan and, more importantly, to set goals for their programs.* As a result of that failure, it is impossible to adequately evaluate the programs or to identify strong and weak points within them. In addition, there is no way to judge the extent of success or failure of any given program.

The inability to judge the success or failure of many diversion programs has led to still another problem: It has left the proponents of diversion little ammunition to rebut the charges of opponents that diversion does not reduce crime. For diversion programs to succeed, adequate financing will be necessary. If proponents fail to show the *taxpayers* and government officials that diversion does, in fact, reduce crime, it is not likely that such money will be forthcoming.

A final criticism of diversion programs is voiced by Donald Newman: "Diversion tends to diffuse control and accountability.

Individuals 'disappear' from the criminal process so that there is no easy way to keep track of them, to monitor their treatment, or to assess the effectiveness of diversionary alternatives."[10]

A Need and An Answer

Programs can be devised in such a way that treatment and behavior can be monitored so that the individual does not "disappear" from the system. The planners of the program must provide for some manner of control and feedback. One possibility is the requirement that treatment facilities report periodically to the diverting agency.

TOWARD A BETTER SOCIETY

Proponents of diversion cite advantages to both the offender and the system from its use. The most common benefit cited is monetary. It is expensive to process an offender through the criminal justice system. It is more expensive to maintain an offender in incarceration. In addition to supporting the offender, the taxpayers may be required to support his/her family. If an offender can, indeed, be diverted more cheaply, the cost benefit is obvious. Before citing the cost effectiveness, however, one should determine that there is an actual savings, not just a transferring of costs from one agency to another.

Crime Reduction

There is little doubt that diversion will be widely accepted, as well as handsomely funded, if it can be proven that it does reduce crime. If the diversion program is in any way successful with the offender, it should, at the very least, reduce recidivism. Community-based treatment programs are being widely heralded by sociologists as a successful alternative to incarceration. Diversion programs falling into that category are certainly apt to receive a large body of support from the sociologists.

Another advantage of diversion to an offender is a partial elimination of the labelling process by which he or she is officially designated a criminal. An offender, especially a juvenile, who is called by such a label for very long frequently comes to accept the label. In a discussion of felons, John Irwin notes:

---

[10] Newman, *Criminal Justice*, p.275.

Only a minority of felons are strongly and exclusively committed to a deviant behavior system when arrested, convicted and imprisoned. The majority, even a majority of "criminals," have participated to some degree in both criminal and conventional systems and are to some extent ambivalent in commitment. The process of being diagnosed and classified by official agents, however, tends to polarize those who stand in the middle, ambivalent between a deviant commitment and a conventional commitment. Probably most of the relatively uncommitted shift toward a deviant identity. Some, however, do shift toward a conventional one, or remain ambivalent.[11]

Frank Tannenbaum, in his article "Point of View," further discusses the labelling process:

The first dramatization of the "evil" which separates the child out of his group for specialized treatment plays a greater role in making the criminal than perhaps any other experience. It cannot be too often emphasized that for the child the whole situation has become different. He now lives in a different world. He has been tagged . . . . The process of making the criminal, therefore, is a process of tagging, defining, identifying, segregating, describing, emphasizing, making conscious and self conscious; it becomes a way of stimulating, suggesting, emphasizing and evoking the very traits that are complained of.[12]

Labelling poses a special danger to an offender who is being processed through the criminal justice system for a minor or marginal crime; the person can become a victim of *overcriminalization*. A person with no previous record, arrested for possession of a small amount of marijuana, can still be charged with a felony in many jurisdictions. Putting this individual in contact with and treating him or her in the same manner as hardened convicts is a classic example of both labelling and overcriminalization. How many Vietnam veterans returned untouched by narcotics? The use of diversion programs to eliminate inappropriate response patterns by the criminal justice system is advantageous.

A FINAL NOTE

The success of a diversion program depends on multiple factors. Some were previously mentioned as responses to problems and criticisms of diversion programs.

Realistically, for a program to operate effectively, there must be

[11] John Irwin: *The Felon*. Englewood Cliffs, New Jersy, Prentice-Hall, 1970., p. 36.

[12] Frank Tannenbaum: "Point of View." In Rose Giallombardo (Ed.): *Juvenile Delinquency, A Book of Readings*, 2nd ed. New York, John Wiley & Sons, 1972. p. 85.

authority for its operation. This sanction can be statutory or from an official empowered to approve the action. Once authority for the program is established, agencies must be formed or found that are willing to act in accordance with the design of the program. These agencies must be provided with facilities and resources necessary to carry out the goals of the program. So provided, the agencies must offer effective counseling and treatment for those referred to them for such action.

Another important factor determining the success of a diversion program is the establishment of its credibility. Responsible members of all participating agencies must be made to believe, through results, that the program is serving a useful purpose. Without that cooperation, any program will surely fail.

Discussion Questions

1. Is the Criminal Justice System *really* a failure?
2. Other than diversion, how would you suggest improving *law enforcement's* ability to deal with crime?
3. What diversion-type programs do you believe the police should be involved in (other than the "cop on the beat")?
4. Can diversion, as defined and dealt with in this chapter, really work?

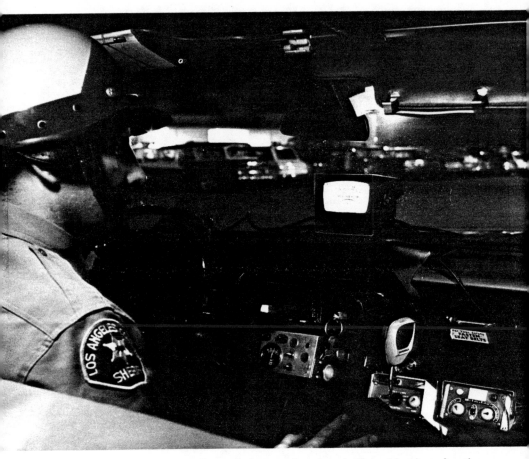

. . . pre-crime . . . un-crime techniques rather than dealing with crime after the fact and without total community involvement . . .

Chapter 13

COMMUNITY CRIME PREVENTION

Objective: To develop a citizen involvement concept for permanent pre-crime (un-crime) action.

- What is Community Crime Prevention?
- Specific crimes to impact
- Social improvement-law enforcement
- Commitment to the cause
- Public awareness
- Individual responsibility (self-help programs)

INTRODUCTORY DATA

COMMUNITY CRIME PREVENTION is a theme that is old in years, but pointedly youthful in terms of its development. It is a concept, a thought, and a dream, and law enforcement agencies throughout the nation must adopt it. It is an attack on crime in very unorthodox ways, and what it means is that for the first time in the history of our country there will be an attempt at near total citizen involvement in the factors that do bring about a reduction in the ability of the criminal to prey on the average citizen.

Seeking the impossible, i.e. a crime-free socity, is unrealistic and too often put forth as a goal for the criminal justice system. This in turn points to the further need for community involvement, in order that an understanding of the *problem* and *logically based answers* stand out:

> Written in police manuals, guides, and rules of procedures in thousands of cities across the United States and Europe are the goals of the police. Although written differently in all of these cities, it is: "To prevent and deter crime." When this is not achieved and instead crime rises, the police are blamed and the arm of the law becomes the ass for everyone to kick. When a fire occurs nobody blames the fire department, when crime occurs the police are blamed for failing to deter and prevent crime. In the face of this, the police department accepts the goal of preventing and deterring crime and hopes to go out there and "make a difference." Preventing and deterring crime by the police alone are unreachable goals forever out of their grasp. Reaching for it will continue to result in low job satisfaction, higher police cynicism, and increasing public dissatisfaction.[1]

What Community Crime Prevention Is Not

For a moment consider what this particular type of community crime prevention concept is *not*. First of all, it is not precisely the same theme used under a similar name by a task force of the National Advisory Commission on Criminal Justice Standards and Goals for the Criminal Justice System. To quote from their report, "Citizen involvement in crime prevention efforts is not merely desirable but necessary. The reports of the President's Commission on Law Enforcement and Administration of Justice emphasize the need for direct citizen action to improve law enforcement and for crime prevention to become the business of every American institution and of every American. Police and other specialists alone

---

[1] Anthony J. Schembri. "Crime Deterence." *Police Chief,* March, 1978, p. 60.

cannot control crime; they need all the help the community can give them."[2]

Similarly, a task force of the National Commission on the Causes and Prevention of Violence noted, "Government programs to control crime are unlikely to succeed alone. Informed private citizens, playing a variety of roles, can make a decisive difference in the prevention, detection and prosecution of crime, the fair administration of justice, and the restoration of offenders to the community."[3]

The Commission's report warns that "pleas for citizen action are heeded by too few. Most citizens agree that crime prevention is everybody's business, but too many fail to accept crime prevention as everybody's duty. There are simply too many important aspects of the private citizen's duty to expect local government to solve the crime problem by itself."[4]

Crime prevention as each citizen's duty is not a new idea. In the early history of law enforcement, well over 2,000 years ago, the peacekeeping system encouraged the concept of mutual responsibility. Each individual was responsible not only for his or her actions but also for the actions of neighbors. A citizen observing a crime had the duty to rouse his/her neighbors and pursue the criminal. Peace was kept, for the most part, not by officials but by the whole community.

With the rise of specialization, citizens began to delegate their personal law enforcement responsibilities by paying others to assume peacekeeping duties. Law enforcement evolved into a multifaceted speciality as citizens relinquished more of their crime prevention activities. The benefits of specialization are not unlimited. Criminal justice professionals readily and repeatedly admit

---

[2] National Advisory Commission on Criminal Justice Standards and Goals. *Task Force Report: Community Crime Prevention.* Washington, D.C., U.S. Government Printing Office, 1973, p. 7. *See* also President's Commission on Law Enforcement and Administration of Justice. *Task Force Report: The Police.* Washington, D.C., U.S. Government Printing Office, 1967, pp. 221-228, *and* President's Commission on Law Enforcement and Administration of Justice. *The Challenge of Crime in a Free Society.* Washington, D.C., U.S. Government Printing Office, 1967, p. 288.

[3] National Commission on the Causes and Prevention of Violence. *Staff Report: Law and Order Reconsidered.* Washington, D.C., U.S. Government Printing Office, 1969, p. 278.

[4] National Commission, *Law and Order Reconsidered*, p. 281.

that in the absence of citizen assistance, neither more manpower not additional financing can prevent rising crime rates.

Community crime prevention is not police-community relations in the traditional sense, although crime prevention has been the central theme of PCR for some time. The community crime prevention concept is also not just an anti-burglary program, as is explained in the following section.

What Community Crime Prevention Is

The concept of community crime prevention, insofar as a dominating characteristic, *is a pre-crime program*. In other words, this concept has *un-crime programs as a central theme;* it addresses what does not happen, in terms of crime.

Organized in late 1977, a statewide California Crime Resistance Task Force aims at three major objectives:

Statewide Publicity Campaign— The Task Force will develop and sponsor a statewide public awareness program to increase and maintain citizen involvement.

Crime Resistance Information Clearinghouse— The Task Force will oversee the development of an information center to serve local programs throughout the state. The center will provide background material and written program samples for agencies or citizens' groups interested in developing or improving community involvement programs. A toll-free number is being established for the center. This "800" number will provide agencies with information and assistance regarding community programs, and will permit would-be volunteers to be referred either to existing programs in their own communities or those in nearby areas where they could obtain practical help. The center will be a source of reproducible crime prevention brochures, and the like, including bilingual materials, that could be inexpensively adapted for a particular community's needs.

Technical Assistance for Local Programs— The Task Force will provide assistance in developing local citizen involvement programs through: (1) a "Host" program to help "sell" community involvement approaches; and, (2) an "on-Site" program to help to establish or upgrade crime prevention programs in communities requesting help.[5]

Federally funded, the success of this Crime Resistance Task Force could serve both as a national model and to bolster disenchantment, with specific use of funds to impact crime.

---

[5] Peace Officers Association of Los Angeles County: *Crime Resistance Task Force Formed,* 1977.

Success Criteria

How does one measure what happens if seeking an "un-happening"? Success is something to be dealt with in a number of ways. *Success in terms of this program has to be measured in terms of crime that does not occur, not just as a result of additional radio cars or a high police-to-population ratio, but rather crime that does not occur due to total citizen involvement* in the community. The involved factors then that must be dealt with are that crime is a vitally important factor in American life today; people are afraid; and people are concerned about what the *police* are going to do. However, *citizen involvement* is a major thesis of all "new looks" in crime prevention through community relations activities. The continental United States offers a variety of programs, but the author discovered an Anti-Crime Bus for citizen orientation on Guam that has no peer, plus a program in Hawaii which since 1975 has caused dramatic decreases in residential area crime. As reported in the *Honolulu Star Bulletin and Advertiser:*

> Tenant security patrols at two Oahu public-housing projects are an unqualified success, the Hawaii Housing Authority has reported.
>
> "The average number of selected criminal offenses has decreased 15 percent at Kalihi Valley Homes, and it has increased only 8 percent at Kuhio Park Terrace," said Elaine Ostrowski, head of the private management demonstration project.
>
> "Those figures compare with a 40 percent increase in crime at Mayor Wright Homes," she said.
>
> The figures also contrast with an over-all 26 percent increase in crime in Hawaii and a national increase of 16 percent. The figures compare 1974 with 1973.
>
> "I feel the project is a success because the concept is unique and effective," said Fred Wilson, manager of Tenant Security, Inc., which provides services at both housing projects.
>
> "We have an intimacy with the tenants that can't be duplicated. It's tenant-controlled, and tenants do the patrolling. They've hired only one outside professional — me."
>
> Tenant security patrols began in September 1973 as part of a demonstration project to upgrade living conditions at Kuhio Park Terrace.[6]

This approach is not new; it does show that crime is not a limited problem, but an all-pervasive stigma that requires concerted action. However, the crux of crime prevention in this text is better

---

[6] Tenant patrols cut crime rate. *Honolulu Star Bulletin and Advertiser,* June 29, 1975.

centered on specific crimes to be affected by community involvement.

Specific Crimes to Impact

The central issue of community crime prevention must eventually focus on such basics as whether narcotics trafficking and addiction, for example, can be controlled, or how to dissolve the clog in the felony court system — a clog so traumatic as to affect the whole system of criminal justice, in terms of bogging down all other aspects of dealing with criminal activity. Should we instead be focusing on something as mundane as bicycle thefts, for where else can a thief take an item such as a ten-speed bicycle that costs $150 and, for a few seconds work, sell it (no questions asked) for $100?

Perhaps attention should be given to that entire group of so-called "victimless crimes," including narcotics, pornography, abortion, and gambling? "Victimless crimes" are being talked about *after the fact*, yet it becomes increasingly apparent that continued failure to deal with them *before the fact* is rampant. Failure to change the approach can result in entropy and finally destroy social order.

Of course, we cannot ignore our so-called hard-core crimes — those the FBI designates as the *Crime Index* — burglary, rape, robbery, assault with a deadly weapon, grand theft, grand theft auto, and criminal homicide. *These are important, key crimes.* They are constantly brought up as the seven major offenses (the *Crime Index*) that have been recorded throughout the nation for well over four decades. We have more extensive data on these crimes than other offenses. While some people argue about the rate of reportability of certain of these offenses, there still exists massive data on them.

Past Passiveness—and Progress

What has really been done to deal in a before-the-fact sense with crime prevention, reduction, and elimination? Perhaps what little has been accomplished is immaterial, other than to ponder increasing crime rates and note that sincere but inadequate approaches are replete.

The most prevalent of the seven major offenses (excluding minor theft) is burglary. Disregarding petty theft, it accounts for over 40 percent of the *Crime Index*. Burglary is one crime where great progress has been and is being made. California leads the nation in developing types of "impact programs" that can, and do, work. The State's Attorney General and the Califonia Council on Criminal Justice (including the Office of Criminal Justice Planning) chose six major police areas in the State and allotted each a quarter of a million dollars to deal with burglary—Oakland, San Francisco, City of Los Angeles, County of Los Angeles, San Diego, and the Orange County Sheriff's Department. Each jurisdiction had something major and conceptually new to contribute. The theme generally was to see what different agencies could do to impact this particular crime. *The result was a dramatic reduction in crime and criminal activity*—thanks to this approach.

Various schemes were utilized. One jurisdiction offered every person in their target area an opportunity for a free home inspection, to see whether or not their particular area could be made safer. One program was committed to high racial disturbance areas, and another to a business area. The other programs took the theme that there was an area to impact, and that something could be done about burglary.

THE APPROACH

A sad but true reality is that it takes money to cause needed change.

A "second generation" approach that was used in California involved funding additional anti-burglary programs in other jurisdictions, letting smaller areas in the State try the same pre-crime thesis in limited jurisdictional areas. But this, as noted, costs money.

There must be input from the metropolitan areas, the small city, the rural area, and suburban sprawls—from all areas, so that not just one state but the entire nation can benefit from this and other aspects of the community crime prevention concept. This raises yet another vital issue which must be addressed: What other types of crime can be similarly impacted?

It is a question of where to best commit officers, and the real issue—the "conscience question"—that the police administrators of this nation should ask themselves, is whether they should allow themselves to be continuously lulled into the traditional, hard-core crime fighting approach, which follows the paths that have been followed in the past (paths that have admittedly failed), or whether to have a new commitment to new ways of doing things, a *National Community Crime Prevention Approach.*

A new national thrust has already begun to take place. The former Attorney General of the United States, Elliot L. Richardson, speaking in almost "heretical" fashion for the Department of Justice, asked, "Is the Department of Justice going to be an instrument for law enforcement, or for social improvement?"

Contrary to prior attorney generals, Richardson stated, in effect, that the two elements cannot be separated; law enforcement and social improvement are inexorably linked. This means that in the federal government the national approach is going to be one that does not separate the general idea of law enforcement from constant social improvement and involvement.

Causes of Social Unrest

Tracing the history of riots in this country, and reviewing the various reports that have been written on the subject, there emerge four major issues as the causes for social unrest: (1) education, (2) employment, (3) housing, and (4) police problems.

EDUCATION. The first is the constant issue of "under education" — not the fact that people are not going to school, but the idea that they are not vocationally prepared to do an available job. This situation is perhaps worse in a "ghetto."

Although there is disagreement on methodology, there is agreement on a general concept that people must be educated if they are going to do something productive. The point is that education germane to today's needs must truly be provided if people are to achieve goals that are going to be important for themselves, their families, and for their community.

EMPLOYMENT. One other critical issue is underemployment, which means underuse of resources that are there. For example, an ex-space engineer who developed concepts to place man on the moon now finds that he is a city parking meter enforcement clerk, earning $700 a month and writing tickets for illegally parked cars! His training and expertise are ignored, and that is a sad commentary on the use of our most vital resource — people.

In 1958, this nation became the first to reach a point where there were more people involved in the provision of services than in the production of goods. That means that we have extensive resources, and yet we have not learned how to use them.

HOUSING. Another critical situation is inadequate housing. Housing, however, is relative. It is not mandatory to have hot and cold running water, a stove or a refrigerator; yet, most people in the United States today expect and want to have these "necessities." A home without television is hard to find, and color television sets are commonplace.

Even if some of the populace do not have these items, most are still well above the standard of living of the majority of people in the entire world. However, the United States is the leader, and people who do not have these "necessities" are pitied and considered underprivileged. Our country spends billions to upgrade foreign lands and it seems that this generosity to underdeveloped abroad should also be mirrored in our approach at home.

POLICE PROBLEMS. The fourth area, and most disturbing in the context of this discussion, is the general idea that there continues to exist a need for improved rapport between the police of this country and the community—the people being served.

The Need for Focused Response

Four major, critical, identified problems have been facing our nation for almost a decade, and what has been done? The first three areas find massive efforts to try to overcome social inadequacy. The fourth area—poor police-community rapport—seems to be something of a stepchild.

The federal government is committing roughly one billion dollars a year to local law enforcement through the Law Enforcement Assistance Administration. Coupled with a national theme of comparatively low police salaries, inadequate budgets, and sometimes unsupportive elected and administrative personnel, one is faced with the lack of governmental commitment to *reducing* crime (or at least to slowing its rate of increase), the problem considered by most citizens to be a major problem facing this country.

Local leaders frequently address the problem of crime prevention in terms of "It's just another tax item!" The political rhetoric says "Hold the Line" on police salaries, but a closer look reveals a need for more people and adequate salaries. To obtain and retain personnel will require talent and creativity, as well as a law enforcement cultural revolution to bring about definite policies that will stop crime from systematically destroying this nation. Last year's reported crime increase was a record high. Past methods have failed. So, where do we go from here?

Dedication to a New Cause

Community crime prevention, involvement of the citizen to a greater degree than has ever been achieved, must become a *cause*. Essentially, it should be the central focus of the over 40,000 law enforcement agencies and the 500,000 officers in this nation. *There is urgent need for commitment to community involvement by police administrators.*

As a premise, consider this possibility: *For every five street police officers, one additional officer should be committed to the concept and function of community crime prevention* — a full-time commitment, to obtain the involvement of the community. Small departments necessarily have to deviate, but it should mean a 20 percent increase in every police agency in the United States.

The "one-to-five" commitment does not include police-community relations officers, or detectives, or supervisors, or anyone else. *Separate and distinct from all other involvements, the function and relative effectiveness of policing and community crime prevention as crime preventors need to be dealt with.*

LAW ENFORCEMENT: EVERYONE'S BUSINESS?

In the past, law enforcement has been regarded as "everybody's business." Everyone has a few words to say. It is as simple as the individual who gets a traffic ticket and immediately knows everything that should be done by the police, i.e. what the police should be doing instead of issuing traffic tickets. It is as complex as someone picking up the paper, seeing a report of a mass murder, and blurting out, "Why don't police go out and shoot the animal that did this?"

Displacing blame for disregard of the law onto the police is as basic as a sociocentric cult or a legislative body, for example, that refuses to recognize that propitious use of capital punishment may be a deterrent to crime.

Over the past several years, there has been a dramatic change in the nature of criminal homicide in this country. In the past, roughly 80 percent of all murders involved members of a family or close friends. This percentage was steady for many years, but it is now on a downward trend. In 1971, almost 30 percent of the homicides in this country were committed by persons unknown to the victims. This could indicate that restrictions on the use of capital punishment have caused an increase in indiscriminate, impersonal violence resulting in death.

Changing trends and other viable factors must be recognized and dealt with. Law enforcement must now *truly* become "everybody's business." This is an opinion shared by a great number of Americans, many of whom have researched the matter at length. Trojanowicz, Trojanowicz, and Moss capture the key considerations of community crime prevention:

1. Police officers must no longer be the only representatives of the community who consistently respond to social problems twenty-four hours a day. This situation places the police in an untenable position and convinces many citizens that the only "after-hours" community responsibility is a punitive one. Many social agencies do respond to emergencies, if notified, but this is a haphazard and uncoordinated effort.

2. A community response team, consisting of the police and representatives from various community organizations, (AA, crisis centers, drug centers, youth services, welfare, religious groups, neighborhood representatives, etc.), must be manned on an around-the-clock basis. Since the police have the greatest information-gathering resources and receive most citizen requests for aid, such a team might operate out of police facilities and respond to calls along with the police.

3. Representatives of all organized social welfare agencies must be convinced of the importance of the social problems that lead to criminal acts and must be fully integrated into the team effort. New local resources must be developed. Fraternal, business, and social organizations must be encouraged to lend their full support to a program of nonpunitive diversion, and team workers must be recruited from their memberships.

4. City management and every element within the formal criminal justice system must be made to see the rationale for such an approach and must provide moral and legal sanction for it. This will require great skill and effective diversion programs, so that the community continues to feel protected.

5. A system of case follow-up and review must be established and rigorously pursued, and a rigorous system of data collection must be initiated, so that the effectiveness of the program can be gauged and tech-

niques expanded or discarded. The opportunity for social research, especially relating to causation theories, must not be ignored.

6. The program must be organized so that the possibilities for favoritism or other abuse are minimized, information is collected for community feedback, research data are collected, and adequate, confidential case documents are maintained. At the same time, bureaucratic tendencies must be avoided, innovation encouraged, and new resources developed and integrated. Membership and employment must include all class, racial, religious, and ethnic groups.

7. Maximum effort must be expended to insure that the program remains person-oriented and does not become a platform for political activism.

8. Full and periodic disclosure of the results, problems, and needs of the program must be made to the public, in settings that guarantee the widest possible community participation. Legitimation for the program must be gained through the widest possible public participation.[7]

AWARENESS AND ACTION
Public Awareness—and Response

It is possible to stop a major portion of crime before it happens by making 200 million Americans aware of and capable of doing something for themselves. The key word to remember is "communicate."

In this regard, law enforcement has been dragging its feet. Although there is talk about personnel shortages, has any department in this nation required every officer to take a public speaking or communications course?

There has been little significant success in getting the message to the people on how they can keep themselves from becoming crime victims. The police are the only ones that can really inform citizens properly. Not a public relations man, not a journalist, nor a booklet, but only through a personal commitment by law enforcement dedicated to this cause can crime be dealt a blow of massive consequence.

Police Awareness—and Response

It is clearly up to the police administrators of the country to strive far more dramatically for adequate personnel, but this must be coupled with a personal commitment to a nonrote, nonroutine approach. Police administrators must get the attention of the

[7] Robert C. Trojanowicz, John M. Trojanowicz, and Forrest M. Moss: *Community Based Crime Prevention.* Santa Monica, California, Goodyear Publishing Co., 1975, pp. 162-163.

people who commit budgets, in fashions never before used; for example, they can be taken out in radio cars and shown the inadequacies of the programs that presently exist: officers can speak to them about people, homes, and businesses that are not safe.

Unionism notwithstanding, police officers and police administrators must stand together in convincing budget analysts, elected officials, and the public of the absolute necessity of both adequate personnel and appropriate salaries.

American society has usually been prompt throughout our history to protect our citizens from *outside* disturbances or threatening situations. However, if care is not taken soon for the safety of America from *within* — as we have tried to protect our shores from the outside — there will no longer be an America.

The Role of Tomorrow's Police

The issue of the role of police in future decades is very clear; *the choice is that of the police and the American people.* Yet, destiny is something to be faced, and it means that *police must cause needed change.*

This change cannot be allowed to just happen. Inertia has prevailed in the past. There is great hope, however, as certain pre-crime concepts already proven successful are a beginning, implementing the most "revolutionary" approach to crime control to be "redeveloped" — citizen involvement in the community crime prevention concept.

While anti-burglary programs are today the most discussed, other examples of high impact approaches include anti-rape campaigns, helping possible would-be victims protect themselves, and auto theft prevention, which has been tried, with *some* success. As Harter points out, "When the public is informed, aroused, and willing to assume its individual responsibility, the commission of crime will be dealt a severe setback."[5]

Every act that is a major crime still continues to be a plague and blight on the nation. We must involve citizens in the realization of what they can do to help themselves and thus help society. This implies an *educated police,* to communicate with the total com-

---

[5] From a personal interview with Donn Harter, Director, Security Barrier Institute, November, 1979.

munity on how to deal with all the ways in which the citizen can become less victimized by crime.

If we are to be a self-regulating society, a free and democratic entity, and one that believes in principles that plead against over-regulation, then the people of America must begin to depend on themselves to effect needed change. Still, it is up to the police of this nation to make it happen.

Discussion Questions

1. Is law enforcement in need of a new approach to crime prevention?
2. Can financial resources be diverted or increased to deal more effectively with crime?
3. Is total community involvement possible?
4. What crimes can best be "impacted" by community effort?
5. Can crime really be reduced?

. . . what can we do to help . . .

Chapter 14

POLICE-COMMUNITY RELATIONS PROGRAMMING

OBJECTIVE: To examine the philosophy, objectives, and reasons for formal on-going Police-Community Relations programming, and to illustrate how this programming can be activated in police departments.

- Traditional ideas of police being tested
- Recommendations for Community Service Officer
- J-Teams
- Personal public appearances
- Utilizing media
- "Adopt a cop" and "We TIP"
- Future Programming — "Blue Sky" Ideas

OSCAR WILDE once said, "The longer I live, the more keenly I feel that what was good enough for our fathers *is not* good enough for me." This epigram is applicable to contemporary law enforcement. The old order, the closed department, the "open in the name of the law" dynasty has passed away. In its place is a partnership between the police and the public, shaped by a growing awareness of their mutual responsibility for a decent and orderly society.

The one to take the lead in building and strengthening this partnership is not the community, with its multidimensional and everchanging configuration, but the police. Yet, exactly how can police encourage public awareness and action in the cause of law and order?

Many police agencies throughout the United States are engaged in a broad array of police-community relations programs. There is a rising interest on the part of the police and the public in fostering better relationships, and many, both in and out of law enforcement circles, have raised the question, "What can we do to help?"

WHERE ARE WE GOING

The fact that on-going programming is a reality is encouraging. However, more than a decade ago the most comprehensive study yet conducted on a national basis dealing with police-community relations policies and practices revealed a situation that is none too encouraging. In a synopsis, they reported the following:

1. Less than a third of the police departments studied have continuing, formalized community relations programs.
2. Two-thirds of the departments studied now have, are adapting, or are developing plans to cope with racial demonstrations and disturbances.
3. In cities with more than 5 percent nonwhite population, 70 percent of the studied departments reported that they are experiencing difficulties in recruiting nonwhite officers.
4. While more than 60 percent of the reporting departments indicated that they offer some training in police-minority group relations, there is wide diversity in the type and quality of training involved.
5. In only two regions did the responding departments report that they restrict the power of arrest of nonwhite officers — 10 percent of those in the South Atlantic and 14 percent of those in the West South Central. Assignments of officers either on a nonracial basis or to racially mixed teams is becoming increasingly general.
6. More than half of the departments studied are being charged by racial

groups with police brutality and/or differential treatment. Nearly two out of ten reporting departments indicate such complaints are increasing; about the same number report them to be decreasing.[1]

Existing Programs

Throughout the nation, programs for police-community relations do exist. In too many instances, they are sporadic, lack specific purpose, and operate on meager budgets, but they do exist. Although progress is far from ideal, one major achievement is that the dangers of an unsatisfactory relationship have been recognized, and police departments are striving to improve. Recent surveys by the Commission on Civil Disorders and the National League of Cities indicate that real improvement must be looked for in the long run rather than in the immediate future. The Commission reports, "Many police departments have established programs to deal specifically with Police-Community Relations. Although of great potential benefit, the results thus far have been disappointing. Many programs have little support of the rank and file officers; and at the command level, there is often little interest."[2]

These same findings are reflected in the nationwide survey of 284 police departments conducted by the National League of Cities. This survey revealed that only eighty-four agencies had established separate police-community relations units, and that direction of programs for the remaining departments was apparently handled by line or administrative officers assuming them as extra duties.[3] Unfortunately, many departments use financial crisis as an excuse for abandoning cost-effective PCR programs. Their "intelligence units" thrive, yet crime has reached an all-time high. Since tradition has failed, PCR offers hope, but only for the progressive police administrators.

This chapter describes a variety of possible programs. Much of the material was garnered from a select group of fifty-six profes-

---

[1] International Association of Chiefs of Police and the United Conference of Mayors: *Police-Community Relations Policies and Practices — A National Survey.* Washington, D.C., International Association of Chiefs of Police and United Conference of Mayors, 1965, p.ii.

[2] United States Riot Commission: *Report of the National Advisory Commission on Civil Disorders.* New York, Bantam Book Co., pp. 319-320.

[3] Raymond L. Bancroft: "Municipal Law Enforcement." *Nation's Cities,* February, 1966, p. 25.

sional law enforcement officers, representing sixteen states and including members of the state police, probation, parole, youth authority, seven sheriff's departments, and thirty-six police departments.

The programs reviewed here, both present and future, are for the consideration of any policing agency. They may or may not be applicable to a specific locale, as this can only be determined on a highly personalized, local basis. Programs must be considered in terms of expenditures — time and money, community participation and support, and local needs.

It is indeed doubtful that all areas dealt with herein could or should be a part of every police agency operation. However, all of them should be considered by knowledgeable police officials working in close cooperation with civic officials both in and out of official governmental circles to render a proper and profitable decision.

The real question needing an answer on utilization of police personnel centers around functions that have traditionally been considered "deified," as compared to the so-called peripheral operation, such as community awareness programs. One program receiving national acclaim (and criticism) regarding traditional utilization of personnel occurred in Kansas City, Missouri, and concentrated on the effectiveness of *police patrol*. Always before, this has been accepted as a major crime deterrent; experimental evidence in Kansas City raises serious questions. As reported in *The Hot Line;*

Does The Presence Of Police On Patrol Deter Crime?
Up to the present that has been a question too foolish even to ask. One of the cardinal principles of the American system of policing is that the visible presence of numbers of police on regular patrol discourages the commission of crime.

The results of a year-long study in Kansas City suggest that the surprising answer may be "NO!"

Fifteen beats covering an area of seventy-two square miles were divided a year ago into three groups of five beats each.

In one area, police procedures continued normally. Police cars on patrol responded to calls from the dispatcher, stopped if hailed by a citizen, or stopped and checked out anything the officer considered suspicious: Normal operating procedure.

In the second area, "reactive patrol" was instituted. Police did no patrolling, and responded only to orders from the dispatcher or to specific calls.

In the third area, "proactive patrol" was utilized. The police preventive patrol was greatly expanded and the number of patrol cars tripled.

When the one year experimental program was over, there was no statist- ically significant change in crime rates from prior years. In fact, area #2, which had "reactive patrol," showed a slight decrease, while the other two areas had minor increases.

Thomas Sweeney, an administrative specialist who served as liaison with the Police Foundation in this study-project, cautions that you can't gen- eralize for the whole country on the basis of the Kansas City experience, and suggests that this data needs to be tested elsewhere.

Col. James Newman, acting chief at the time the study was completed, says: "The liberal cliché is correct — Crime is caused by social conditions which very frequently are beyond the control of the police."[4]

Significant use of police personnel may well need re-evaluation in many areas, not the least of which is the effective crime-reducing impact of the "routine of tradition" versus on-going programs for interinvolvement of police with the community in personal, nonen- forcement contacts.

ON-GOING PROGRAMS

Civil rights, civil liberties, civil disobedience, and race relations are subjects that may dismay many persons who believe an already too wide rift exists between law enforcement and the community. On-going programs designed to offset this situation and foster better understanding are in existence in many areas. In a day when people are demanding action in every conceivable area of human activity, the police must stop the traditional practice of pointing the finger of guilt at "offending" groups and individuals, when this is done without also providing a possible solution.

This does not preclude the obvious — some groups do not want solutions — but it does mean that the overwhelming majority of responsible Americans must be provided with tangible proof by the police that their law enforcement officers do wish to improve police- community relationships.

No magical formula exists for improved conditions: "What does count in human relationships, as shown by a flood of reports from surveys and experiments, is the human atmosphere, or human climate. It is not tricks, or 'sizzles,' which hypnotize others. It is the

---

[4] Donald W. McEvoy: "Community Relations and the Administration of Justice." *The Hot Line,* 6 (1), January, 1974.

way we change the human atmosphere so that people feel friendly rather than hostile, so they come to us rather than avoid us." [5]

The existing programs that follow require hard work and are the subject of occasional setbacks, but to re-emphasize, each area should be carefully considered by the police administrator desirous of improving police-community relations.

Community Service Officer

The recent recommendation by the President's Crime Commission to create a new position of "community service officer" has received considerable attention and applause by persons interested in promoting better police-minority group communication and understanding. The Commission visualized that the community service officer would "Be a young man, between the ages of 17 and 21, with the aptitude, integrity, and stability to perform police work. He would, in effect, be an apprentice policeman — an entirely new type of police cadet working on the street under close supervision and in close cooperation with regular policemen. He would not have full law enforcement powers or carry arms, neither would he perform clerical duties as many police cadets do today."[6]

The Commission defined five major reasons for this recommendation: (1) to improve police service in high crime areas; (2) to enable police to hire persons who understand minority group problems; (3) to relieve police officers of lesser police duties; (4) to increase the opportunity for minority group members to serve in law enforcement; and (5) to tap a new reservoir of manpower by helping talented young men and women who have not been able to as yet complete their education to qualify for police work.[7]

The Commission stressed that the standards of selection for community service officer should ensure that the majority of young blacks are eligible to participate in the program. They cautioned that selection should not be based on inflexible educational requirement, but instead "should be made on individual basis with priority

---

[5] Donald A. Laird and Eleanor Laird: *The Technique of Handling People.* New York, McGraw-Hill, 1954, p.3.

[6] President's Commission on Law Enforcement and Administration of Justice: *Task Force Report: The Police.* Washington, D.C., U.S. Government Printing Office, 1967, p. 123.

[7] President's Commission, *The Police*, p. 123.

being given to applicants with promising aspirations and an understanding of the neighborhood and its problems."[8]

The United States Riot Commission, reporting on civil disorders, has fully endorsed the President's Commission's proposal: "The community service officer program should be adopted. Use of this program to increase the number of Negroes in police departments will help to establish needed channels of communication with the Negro community; will permit the police to perform better their community service functions, especially in the minority group neighborhoods; and will also create a number of badly needed jobs for Negro youths."[9]

J-Teams

One of the most unusual units ever devised to improve police community relations *and* reduce crime is one that was developed in New Zealand. The function of these units is to reduce crime through techniques that are, to say the least, unconventional. Known as "J-Teams," each is typically composed of a police officer (male or female), a social worker, and a minister. Instances of crime in areas in which they were working in 1975 show major crime down by as much as 30 percent!

The *Auckland Star* describes the program briefly but cogently:

The J-teams which have specialized in youth aid work in Auckland for the past three years or so have done a splendid job.

Each of the three teams is made up of a policeman, a Maori Welfare officer and a social worker. Their role in the community has been vital.

So vital, in fact, that the Government should long since have ensured they were given all the facilities they needed to keep up the good work.

Minister of Maori Affairs, Mr. Rata, certainly has no doubts about their value. He has noted how violent crime in South Auckland dropped by 20% in one year because of the teams. And he would like six to eight teams in action in Auckland.

He has been quick to order an inquiry into the reasons behind the Anglican Church decision to ask the South Auckland J-team to leave its offices in Selwyn Church, Mangere.

Whatever the circumstances that led to this setback for the team, though, one factor is dominant — its work mustn't be impeded.

Mr. Rata is right to stress that the J-team needs the help of the whole

---

[8] President's Commission, *The Police*, p. 124.

[9] United States Riot Commission, *Report on Civil Disorders*, p. 317.

community in this work. But it shouldn't be forced to mark time until
arguing groups resolve their differences.

The Government should see that the team gets the accommodation—and
other facilities—it requires. The social work it does deserves positive encouragement.[10]

It may not be applicable for the United States, but then again,
some police visionary may want to see if it can work.

A number of departments are either developing novel procedures
to adopt this theme or have already implemented them. In January,
1969, the New York Police Department appointed thirty-two
trainees between the ages of seventeen and nineteen to a six-week
training course to prepare them for the department's newly created
position of Precinct Service Officer. Upon graduation, the new
officers were to work with a community relations patrol officer and
specialize in youth problems. Former Police Commissioner Howard
R. Leary, in commenting on appointments, stated, "The Department believes that the young men will be familiar with both the role
and problems of the police and, also, the aspirations and problems
of young people . . . the program is similar to the one proposed by
the President's Commission on Law Enforcement and Administration of Justice and can be considered a major broadening of the
Police Department's Community Relations program."[11]

Personal Public Appearances

"Personal appearances," as defined in this text, refers to a peace
officer addressing a group on a subject germane to law enforcement, with the officer officially representing his/her police agency.
The practice of maintaining a program of personal appearances is
perhaps the most universal police-community relations activity of a
tangible, programmed nature in which police agencies engage. In
smaller departments, the principal participant is the chief law
enforcement officer of the agency. As departments become larger,
there are two courses of action: The first is the use of a public
information officer—a person who is specifically trained and
designated as a public information officer and who speaks on a

---

[10] J-teams role. *The Auckland Star*, July 18, 1975.

[11] *Crime Control Digest*. Washington, D.C., Industry Reports, Inc., January 28, 1969,
p.9.

broad variety of subjects in the general area of law enforcement. As a departmental speaking program grows, this person may be assisted by another officer, or the policing agency may consider the second type of organizational structure—a speaker's bureau. This concept involves organizing key members of departmental units into a functional working relationship, for the part-time participation in a program for public appearances. If this is to be done in a professional manner, those selected must be proficient both in their police role and public speaking.

The key to success in all police public appearance programs lies in training the top peace officers to be top speakers, and there is no shortcut. To the group he or she addresses, each speaker personifies the policing agency, and demeanor will be the subject of astute scrutiny.

TRAINING AIDS. Personal appearances may be enhanced through the use of enlarged photographs, professionally drawn designs, slides projected on a screen, etc. The precise visual aid utilized for a specific presentation is often a matter of what is available, frequently subject to the discretion of the speaker, and sometimes it may be an aid tailored to a specific group.

The type of aid is not as important as (1) anticipating areas where visual aids can assist, (2) developing these aids, and (3) making appropriate use of them. Many otherwise dull topics can be enlivened and enhanced and a receptive audience created through use of these devices.

Another form of training aid technique involves the actual use of demonstrations, in programs such as gun safety, hunter safety, car clubs, canine corps demonstrations, and motorcycle teams. In any case, it is essential that both speakers and training aids be well prepared in advance, for a faulty presentation can render the police image a severe blow.

RECORD OF PERSONAL APPEARANCES. Each police agency should maintain a record of personal appearances. Information that is mandatory includes the date of the address, the speaker, the group, and other information relating to the mechanics of the presentation.

Use of News Media

It is important to re-emphasize the establishment and maintenance of contact with all the news media. Regular news releases can include such topics as safe driving and current photographs of crime scenes, while "as needed" information on street and weather conditions typifies a type of useful public service and police image enhancement the police may provide.

In addition, a police agency may consider contributing a regular article in local papers or a scheduled radio or television broadcast. Discussions with appropriate members of the news media can usually elicit public service time or space and should definitely be considered. One department carries this concept a more restrictive but focused step further through utilizing closed circuit television to present a one-half hour broadcast to every school classroom on a once-a-week basis.

The point is that the time and space are usually available for the asking, but in many instances the police administrator must take the initiative, then be willing to follow through on a regular and continuing basis, if the function is to be useful.

Motion Pictures

Police agencies have made extensive use of training films in recent years. Production costs have been reduced to a point where this same vehicle may be produced as a motion picture suitable for use as a public service device. Many agencies take subjects of greatest public interest, produce a ten-to-twenty minute film, and are thus able to present a story to the public in an appealing, interesting manner.

The use of professional assistance is often available without cost, and some departments have a photographic reserve unit composed of experts in the field.

One word of caution is that films automatically date themselves. Do not be guilty of showing a motion picture that has some of the good and all of the inglorious aspects of certain "late late shows" on television!

Crime Prevention and Youth Programs

Various crime prevention and youth programs are in existence and take many forms. For example, special events for children, such as bicycle safety programs, Christmas parties, vehicle safety checks for vintage cars (and teenage drivers)—each of these can provide a practical and positive contact when conducted professionally. Junior police and deputy programs have many possible advantageous features. Once again, it creates an involvement type of situation between police and this all-important segment of the public, and this involvement is of a positive nature.

Youth bands have a similar effect, as do police-sponsored boys and girls clubs, summer camps, and car clubs. A major area of concern to nearly every American police department in the police community relations field is contact that is appropriate with all levels of young people. Every effort should be made to present the police to our youth in a positive light, as soon and as continuously as is possible.

A new and imaginative approach in this area is the "adopt a deputy" or "adopt a cop" program. In this program a deputy sheriff or a city police officer is "adopted" by a school as their law enforcement representative and advisor.

The purpose of the program is to generate feelings of understanding, friendship, and rapport between school children and sheriff's deputies and city police officers, based on informal, friendly relationships with an individual "adopted" peace officer. One of its main objectives is to enable youngsters to talk to men and women in uniforms without fear.

Duties include visiting classrooms and participating in and originating special all-school assemblies where various aspects of safety, citizenship, and the administration of justice are explained. In both the classroom and assemblies, questions are solicited and open discussion is encouraged.

Although the program was originally designed to accommodate the elementary and junior high schools, because of its warm reception it now encompasses such preschool projects as Head Start. The eventual objective is the "adoption" of a peace officer by *every* elementary and junior high school.

The prime directive for all crime prevention and youth programs is that they be planned well in advance and presented according to a well-defined plan. There is no room for the "play it by ear" disasters that have too often been termed "on-going programs" in the past. Crime prevention and youth programs are an integral part of community crime prevention (*see* Chapter 13).

BIRTH OF A CITIZEN ACTION PROGRAM

In January of 1970, a special task force met in Tampa, Florida, to explore in detail all aspects of drug abuse. It was found that education and rehabilitation were being adequately handled by a variety of community programs. The greatest area of need was found to be that of *enforcement*—catching and stopping the pushers. Information that was developed revealed a growing cancer of pushers working in all urban centers of the country. The pushers were dealing in hard drugs, and taking their wares to schools, including the lower grades. Heartbroken parents testified to the task force of their complete hopelessness in dealing with their children, lost to the world of addiction. Citizens expressed great concern at the increase in crimes interrelated with the addict's need for large cash sums in order to support his/her habit.

The task force established a "TIP" project in Tampa as a positive method to combat the drug problem, which was immediately successful, and directly assisted law enforcement in keeping a tighter control over drugs in the area.

In November of 1971, Bill Brownell, a retired law enforcement officer, backed by the Ontario, California, Merchants Association, sparked the first citizen participation project to fight drug pushers in California—"We TIP." The original plan for the "We TIP" program limited the operation and service to the Pomona Valley and adjoining cities, but the rising tide of crime throughout California quickly forced statewide service.

Service clubs and citizen groups provided the backbone of support for the program, raising for the first year's budget a total of $14,300. The program's growth has catapulted forward at a rapid pace, and the budget for 1977 was $113,000, with the key word being *economy*. A recent audit disclosed We TIP to have more volunteer man hours (197,500) in relation to budget than any other program in California.

How does We TIP work? A telephone operator at a secret location is available at a toll-free statewide line (800)472-7785. The line is open Monday through Friday, 9 A.M. to 9 P.M. and Saturday, 9 A.M. to 5 P.M. The operator's first words are, "This is a Tip Line, please do not give your name!" She will ask twenty-five questions designed to obtain the maximum of information that would assist law enforcement agencies in making an arrest, while also screening out crank calls. After the information is taken, a code name and number is assigned to the informant. The caller always remains absolutely anonymous.

We TIP then forwards the information to the closest narcotics division of the suspect's local police and sheriff's departments, U.S. Customs, Drug Enforcement Administration, and the Internal Revenue Service. Arrests are never made on the basis of a telephone call alone but are made as a result of intense law enforcement investigation.

Rewards up to $500 are given in cash to those informants desiring this incentive; however, 61 percent of the citizens calling do not seek a reward. Rewards are only given after official reports have been received from law enforcement agencies verifying that the "TIP" resulted in an arrest and conviction or the seizure of a large cache of drugs.

Since its inception in 1971, the We TIP program has provided law enforcement with information which has directly affected 1,394 arrests, 864 convictions, and the seizure of $19,454,027 worth of narcotics and illegal dangerous drugs. We TIP reflects true total community involvement through the dedicated efforts of volunteers, municipal leaders, news media, and law enforcement.

As of November 3, 1977, We TIP entered into a major expansion program at the request of law enforcement based on the program's high rate of success. Information is now solicited on all major crimes, such as arson, burglary, robbery, murder, and child abuse.

An intensive on-going public relations campaign has brought 123 California cities into the We TIP committed circle of citizen crime fighters, with the prospect of many more joining.

We TIP's annual convention for 1978 was held April 28 through April 30, at the Newporter Inn in Newport Beach, California. At this time, founder Bill Brownell, law enforcement personnel, service club representatives, We TIP staff, and board members gathered to evaluate, educate, exchange information, and select goals for their continued united efforts in the fight against crime.

Any interested citizen can join the We TIP organization by sending three dollars (yearly) to We TIP, P.O. Box 858, Glendora, California 91740. In return they will be placed on the mailing list for all publications including a bi-monthly newspaper. For further information, call (213) 686-2621.

Adult Group Contacts of a Generic Nature

Without attempting to list the various councils, boards, lodges, and community social organizations that warrant a police agency's participation there appears to be something of a pattern forming across the nation. Departments are, more than ever before, encouraging officers to participate in key organization activities. From a formalized standpoint, police may provide merchants with bad check warnings as well as information on shoplifting, short-change artists, counterfeiting, and alarm systems.

Regular checks on the homes of vacationing residents of an area is another common practice, and many departments have an officer call on each new resident of the area to personally welcome the newcomers and provide them with appropriate printed matter about their police department.

The inspection tour of the police facility offers yet another vehicle for group contacts. A neat and orderly facility, available at a specified time weekly or monthly or on a request basis, can enhance the police image if presented appropriately.

Exhibits and Displays

The outdoor advertising agencies are often more than willing to provide billboard space for some appropriate police message. This type of "advertising" can place the police in a position to present a message such as "school's out, drive carefully," "lock your car," or some message of a similar nature.

Police equipment may be the subject of displays in store windows. National Police Week—a name the author feels should be changed to National Criminal Justice Week—provides a logical opportunity to hold a station open house, have billboard displays, place signs or displays in shops, bumper strips on cars, and to place or encourage feature articles by the press.

All of these programs should be considered for continuous, year-round presentation.

Race-Religious-Ethnic Considerations

Many departments find the public composed of sufficiently large and identifiable racial, religious, and/or ethnic groups to warrant formal programming of contact and participation. One department has provided a sizeable racial grouping with regular, continuous association since 1935.[12]

Gangs

The term "gang" has both good and bad connotations. They exist for good and evil, yet many times it is impossible for the police to play a role in determining the course a gang ultimately chooses.

AN EXAMPLE. Since the Zoot Suit Riots of World War II, the Los Angeles Sheriff's Department has had a unit of its juvenile bureau assigned to the investigation and control of gangs. In a metropolitan area, gangs are not unique to minority groups but are commonly associated with areas of high density population. The memberships of gangs are not confined to juveniles, but often include young adults. Some gangs develop as a result of or spring from special interests, e.g. motorcycle clubs, surfers, etc. Some people would type both the Boy Scouts of America and the Symbionese Liberation Army as "gangs"!

Because there is a high rate of all types of criminal activity within certain gangs, and in more recent times a relationship with community tensions, police must be concerned with all of these groups—both adult and juvenile. The main concern is with the gathering of information and maintenance of records of the memberships, locale, and activities of these gangs. Liaison should be maintained with all concerned agencies for the gathering and dissemination of intelligence. Also, contact should be maintained with the gangs themselves. Specialized knowledge is of great assistance in spotting potential dangers.

The Los Angeles Sheriff's gang detail assists in the investigation of slayings, assaults, party crashings, etc., stemming from gang activity. Racial unrest is causing an increase in gang activity, in that it is an additional excuse for precipitating unlawful acts. This police detail often performs the valuable service of preventing retaliatory action by one group against another.

Finally, these officers lecture at the training academy and in-service training sessions and are available for informing and advising the community and schools, with the objective of diverting or eliminating problems of a gang nature.

[12] Los Angeles County Sheriff's Department: *International Liaison Bureau.* Los Angeles, County Sheriff's Department, 1976.

Conclusion

The areas dealt with in the general realm of operational programs are those which appear to have received the greatest amount of attention by policing agencies thus far. The following section will consider another aspect—a dreamer's approach to police-community relations.

BLUE-SKY POLICE-COMMUNITY RELATIONS

Imagine for a moment that you are a police administrator in charge of a relatively large policing agency. You have just been informed by your budget-providing body that you have been given unlimited funding to be utilized for the improvement of police-community relations. The obvious question then becomes, "What should I do?"

The answer, in each instance, lies with a thorough review first of the basic programs, formal or informal, in which the department is currently engaged. For example, with rare exception, personal appearances are being made; but should this be done on a haphazard and relatively informal basis? The police administrator may wish to organize the function and/or solicit speaking engagements. Then, too, with unlimited funds, training aids of a wide variety should be considered.

The Blue-Sky Survey

The National League of Cities Survey group mentioned previously was presented this general situation: You are the chief of your agency; you have unlimited funds for police-community relations activities; what do you consider primary areas in which to increase or commence programs in your own department?

Specific contributions of the survey groups were, in this instance, confidential. However, the material gathered was then synthesized into a brief synopsis of the areas they felt (1) warranted greater consideration and (2) were mentioned most often. It should be emphasized before reviewing them that most of the factors dealt with offer no new or startling development in the area of what may be done in police-community relations programming. The summary of their findings is included, however, as it indicates some additional, specific "fringe police-community relations programs" that offer a wide range of thought for those interested in suggestions. They are presented in no particular order, but include the following:

1. Allocate funds for *more intensified training*, consequently raising the standards of police officers.
2. Have a *public information bureau with full-time personnel assigned.*
3. *Develop stories*, human interest and factual, *for the news media.*
4. *Produce or solicit production of a television series*, either fictional or factual, *depicting life* of an *average police officer.*
5. *Develop a tour guide system* staffed by well-informed personnel.
6. *Raise basic standards* of applicants from high school graduate *to a minimum requirement of a bachelor's degree.*
7. Have *government assume school tuition costs*, permitting those already on the roles to attend college.
8. *Assign* well-educated *officers to high school social studies type classes* for teaching purposes.
9. Hire a *professional public relations firm* to coordinate news media contacts and to develop an intensive and continual "propaganda" or *professional "advertising" program* such as "Radio Free Europe" or advertising campaigns such as large manufacturers use for their products.
10. *Have only ranking personnel assigned to general public relations,* since rank denotes knowledge and intelligence.
11. *Utilize* space in the *police facility for a display of police equipment,* with each item of equipment *accompanied* by a *short* written explanation of its use.
12. Inaugurate an *intensive public relations in-service training program.*
13. *Purchase the very latest and best equipment* available to law enforcement to enable the completion of a more efficient job.
14. *Utilize the news media plus billboards to their fullest.*
15. *Develop a weekly fifteen-minute television program* designed to apprise the public of police operations.
16. *Have a "Policeman of the Month" and "Policemen of the Year"* ceremony, the annual winner to receive a sizeable monetary bonus and an extra length of time for vacation.
17. Have each police *agency assume costs of uniforms.* Furnish each officer with sufficient supply to enable him or her to have a *clean freshly pressed uniform each tour of duty.* Enforce appearance through daily inspections.
18. Establish a special recording unit, with *movie equipment to be on the scene of each major incident* recording the operation. These movies would be shown to the officers for the purpose of improving appearance.

19. Develop a "campership" or *similar summer program*, controlled by the juvenile unit, for elementary and junior high level underprivileged children. Extreme care is to be applied to remove the "charity" stigma from the program.
20. *Form a police band*, staffed by policemen, for use in parades and civil activities. *Form a junior police band* for the same activities, staffed by children.
21. Form one or more *motorcycle drill teams*.
22. Establish *better communication lines between administration and the working policeman*.
23. Establish a *liaison board*, to work *full time between the probation department and police agencies*.
24. Establish *citizen "clinics" in high tension minority areas* to serve and advise the public.
25. *Assign an officer to work* at least one day a week *at each of the junior and senior high schools*. Provide for specific days and office hours, and decorate his/her office to be as warm, friendly, and interesting as possible.
26. Set up a program with the schools to *solicit and encourage teachers and students to ride in a radio car* as an observer during a full eight-hour shift.
27. *Set up a series of boys' clubs* staffed by full-time police officers to be open until 10 P.M. Operate the clubs with emphasis on *recreation, athletics, hobbies, and social activities*.
28. Conduct monthly *community relations meetings* in the various districts. Involve the commanding officer of the district and responsible citizens and businessmen.
29. Provide a *5.5 percent pay raise to all officers with an associate of arts degree* and a *10 percent pay raise for a bachelor's degree*.

THE IMPORTANCE OF CONTINUITY

The need exists for organized and additional police-community relations programs; equally important is the continuance of existing functions that are successful. New ideas to improve existing programs, as well as the adoption of new and innovative techniques, are desirable and in many instances mandatory.

The future police-community relations programming in any police agency involves a process of choice, as it is doubtful whether police budgets will ever approach the utopian proportions mentioned in the preceding section of this chapter. It still behooves the police administrator to view activities of an on-going nature with an eye to their future, based on their past and present results.

A Modern Phenomenon

Scientists tell us that the world has progressed further during the past fifty years than in all the previous years of mankind on earth. However, law enforcement has remained traditionally conservative in its approach to change. It is indeed remarkable how nearly every new idea presented to many traditionally minded peace officers can be offered such a variety of reasons why "It won't work!" However, as the eminent Doctor Johnson pointed out, "Nothing will ever be attempted if all possible objections must be first overcome."[13] This statement, proclaimed two centuries ago, is applicable to the police of modern times, especially in the realm of police-community relations programs.

This text emphasizes the vital role of the individual officer in creating an appropriate police image to the public. Too often, however, law enforcement stops here and does not program and plan additional concentrated activities. The fostering of community support is a responsibility of each peace officer, but nowhere are we afforded an opportunity to concentrate and provide additional centered impetus to gain a better rapport with the public than in the area of on-going, continuous police-community relations programs.

Discussion Question

1. What can police do to encourage further public involvement in police-community relations?
2. Is the public responding to the community relations programs enacted by the police?
3. Offer some ideas of your own on programs that might be used to bring the police and the community closer together.
4. Discuss some objectives of police-community relations programming not mentioned in this chapter.

---

[13] Dr. Samuel Johnson (1704-84); English author and Lexicographer.

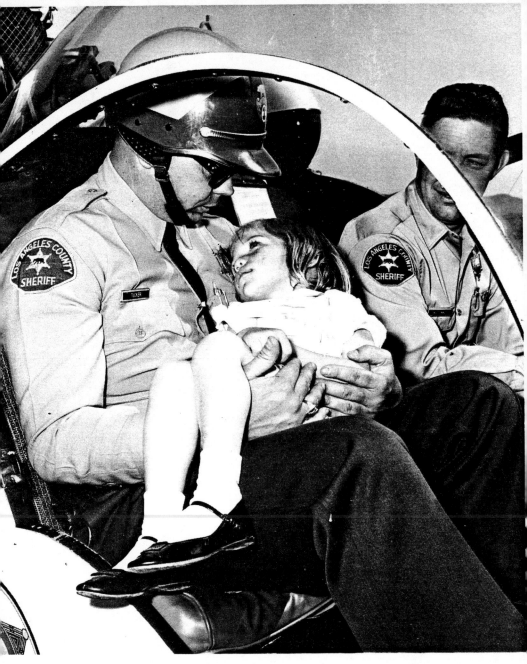

. . . the humanitarian role of the most hardened law enforcement officer . . .

Chapter 15

ROLE OF THE INDIVIDUAL OFFICER

Objective: To analyze the role and importance of the individual officer to the task of upgrading the police image and professionalization of performance.

- Personal responsibility of each officer
- Specialization versus generalization
- Above and beyond the call of duty
- Spirit of the law

IT HAS BECOME almost a truism that the individual officer is the foundation of excellency in law enforcement. Too often this assessment is awarded with little thought of its meaning.

Why is each officer so important? Without the backing of the individual officers, progressive police-community relations is lost. He or she is the most important component to any program. The officer's daily contacts can weld a police-people relationship in the direction of understanding, confidence, and loyalty, or suspicion, hostility, and hate.

LAWMAN MEETS LAYMAN

Throughout the course of this text, great emphasis has been placed on the collective departmental responsibility of law enforcement agencies to deal with police-community relationships. This collectivization — organizationally or philosophically — is an important aspect of overall accomplishment of the police mission. However, it is the individual, person-to-person, day-to-day contact of the law officer in the field, with people, that in the final analysis is responsible for a great portion of the police image discussed earlier.

Quinney emphasizes the point that "most people have little idea about the extent of discretionary decisions in law enforcement and little knowledge of the ways in which discretion operates."[1] To many citizens, the officer is the law; his/her performance constitutes the law in all its majesty, or lack of majesty. Thus, an officer's daily actions are of considerable significance, since faulty enforcement can spoil the best laws that can be conceived. Even if every law were so carefully thought out and written that it was sociably acceptable and applicable, it is the men and women who act on a violation that spells the law's success or failure: "The police officer's role is a crucial one in an era of rapid and complex social change — in other words, the best law is only as good as the man who enforces it."[2]

The most sophisticated plan for police-community relations cannot be effective without the support of each officer. Each bears a

---

[1] Richard Quinney: *Criminology: Analysis and Critique of Crime in America.* Boston, Little, Brown & Company, 1975, p. 173.

[2] William F. Fitzgerald. Address given at Institute on Police-Community Relations, Los Angeles Police Department, University of Southern California, February 1, 1961.

grave responsibility, and improper execution of this role can result in public demands for changes in police procedures and personnel.

Often, such demands are regarded as the result of overall difficulties between police and public, but as Center explains, "If any one public relations problem can be said to hit almost every American community, it might well be the one where citizens demand a change in police tactics and personnel. Yet, strangely, the change usually is sought not because of particularly inefficient law enforcement by the department as a whole, but because of poor public relations on the part of the individual officer."[3]

Thus, the personal touch, whether administered by the sheriff or chief or the newest patrol officer, has an impact that is hard to overemphasize. Peace officers who ignore this important part of their personal responsibility for the good of the service are at best incompetent, at worst misguided, engines of distruction.

Respect for the Law: Whose Responsibility?

It is important for law enforcement agencies to recognize that responsibility for creating an atmosphere of respect for peace officers in the mind of the public has as a base individual police-public contacts. The facelessness of the modern American police officer appears to be increased by the donning of the uniform; with the addition of helmets as standard equipment in many police organizations, it becomes difficult for even peace officers to recognize a fellow officer with whom they are rather well acquainted!

When a citizen is stopped for a traffic violation, or talks to this faceless personification of the law, the impression he or she gathers is affected by this lack of personal identity. Many departments have added name tags to uniforms of their officers to try and offset this collective approach people take toward officers. In any event, here once again it must be emphasized how the actions of the individual officer thus become the expected actions of the entire department. The citizen remembers how he or she is treated, though not necessarily the person who rendered the service — or disservice.

A high percentage of lawman-layman contacts are nonpunitive. Herein lies an area where the police can take positive, effective action to improve their lot. Respect for the law is a shared responsi-

---

[3] Allen H. Center: *Public Relations Ideas in Action.* New York, McGraw-Hill 1957, p. 273.

bility of the public and the police, but the police must never fail if they are to collectively and individually merit respectful treatment by the citizens they contact daily. This can go far to foster positive attitudes when the "chips are down." If some aspect of law enforcement has been attacked by an identifiable segment of the public, only through this long-range personal acceptance of police responsibility can the appropriate attitude be permanently and forcefully demonstrated to the American people: "The first step is to elevate police discretion from the *sub-rosa* position it now occupies; the role of police as decision-makers must be expressly recognized. Then, as has been found possible with respect to other administrative agencies, the areas in which discretion properly may be exercised must be delimited, principles to govern its exercise must be established, and effective means of control must be discovered."[4]

The Challenge

Too many peace officers place police-community relations in the same category as budget preparation, twenty-year planning, and other relatively abstract and somewhat unexciting elements of what is loosely termed "Police Administration." The need to recognize the importance of this relatively new and rapidly developing field of police work has long existed, probably in acute status since the formation of the first policing agency.

This unfortunate disregard for police-community relations programming and its relative position of low esteem are dispelled almost instantaneously when a major riot erupts or social unrest develops. Police and citizens alike cry out for greater community contact and support. Unquestionably, few policing agencies of this nation have a sufficiently well-organized and functioning overall police-community relations program. Budgetary considerations have been blamed. Personnel shortages are offered as an excuse. These and other reasons all have merit, but the fact remains the programs' existence might well discourage the development of chaos within any given community; and most assuredly, they could provide contact with leaders in a certain locale when crisis of any nature strikes.

The challenge presented here centers around the need for police administrators to imbue each officer, just as they themselves must

---

[4] Wayne R. LaFave: "The Police and Non-enforcement of the Law." *Wisconsin Law Review*, January-March, 1962, p. 239.

be inculcated, with a personal challenge to foster a truly personal attitude of cooperation with the public he or she has sworn to protect and serve. If this is to be accomplished on a continuous basis, it means more than training programs and lip service; it means each officer must willingly accept a personal challenge for professional exhibition of the attitude and qualities that spell good law enforcement to the layman. The lawman contacts "the public," but the public is highly individualistic and should not be the subject of overgeneralization. Only a sincerity of attitude on the part of officers can make for truly successful lay contact.

The police agency requires formal programs in police-community relations, just as it requires a formal policy to insure that each officer knows what is expected of him or her. It is of great importance to consider more than simply the major disciplinary factors; such ordinary matters as proper wearing of the uniform, being well informed, personal hygiene, and similar aspects of a somewhat common and mundane nature have their effect.

Good PCR is more than having regulations. It is the acceptance by all law enforcement officers of their own responsibilities to see that they willingly exert every effort to conform to all of these highly important requirements, while exhibiting an attiude that shows that they are not just "doing a job" but are engaging in the professional execution of their police responsibilities.

POLICEMANSHIP: SPECIALIZATION VERSUS GENERALIZATION

While training was dealt with at some length in Chapter 7 the point for reemphasis in this area centers around a rising controversy over the general area of just what a police officer should know. The controversy is seen in newspaper print and raises the issue of a liberal arts educational background, i.e. training in the social sciences, human relations, even music appreciation, versus the hard-core police subject matter to which our new cadets are exposed and to which many police college curricula conform. There is a need for the individual officer to have a broad generic educational background, coupled with specific police training; the infusion of the two into an individual mode of conduct in the performance of duty enables him or her to be, at once, a trained peace officer while at the same time escaping the dismal, undesirable role of the automaton mechanically doing a tour of duty. Holcomb commented on this, noting that "One of the earmarks of a good officer is his interest in improving himself and his interest in learning more about police work."[5]

Through broadening horizons provided by educational achievement, which go well beyond the laws of arrest and other equally necessary but ingrain courses, the police officer is rendered capable of contact with the widest possible range of people in a manner that indicates he or she is not only a success in the science of policemanship but is also a blend of human and social practices, which make his/her performance of duty acceptable to the public and thus successful from long-range policing point of view.

It is indeed ironic that in the author's study of the police agencies of twenty-seven other countries, nowhere is training and education given such little emphasis from the police agencies themselves as in the United States (our universities and colleges feel otherwise). Obviously, our country's crime rate—the highest in the so-called Western world—needs to be attacked by all agencies of criminal justice, and indeed by society as a whole.

The police in the interim need *more* mental input—not less, as some agencies have tragically devised—to equip them for a role that has expanded explosively in the last two decades. It is "administrative amnesia" to forget the lessons of history, requiring a riot and social unrest to cause a reluctant admission (again!) that our law enforcement excellence is to a major degree a reflection of our selection, training, and educational commitments, from the outset of the officer's career.

A PHILOSOPHY FOR THE INDIVIDUAL OFFICER

Peace officers are required to meet and deal with a continuously changing set of circumstances, with a calmness and ability not present or required in many occupations. The officer is not a god, yet many professional police agencies have selection standards that place the accepted police recruit in somewhat the same category as the wearer of the Congressional Medal of Honor. Prideful wearers of this most distinguished award engage in highly individualistic duty accomplishment and offer a basic lesson law enforcement might review, that their collective reputation is a product of personal endeavor; they all served "above and beyond."

[5] Richard L. Holcomb: *Police Patrol.* Springfield, Thomas, 1948, p. 50.

The challenge for each peace officer then is to accept a role—above and beyond—in both the development of and adherence to a philosophy of professionalization being called upon to carry out a broad array of duties. A police officer is not an ordained minister, a medical doctor, a marriage counselor, a professional athlete, nor a lawyer, a judge, or a legislator. Yet, in the course of field assignments, an officer may deliver babies or arbitrate marital disturbances and is required to pursue an escaping criminal over backyard fences—even engage in a form of "curb-stone justice." By today's standard, this latter refers to the fact that the law officer many times is placed in a position where an arrest is possible under the letter of the law, but a warning may more appropriately adhere to the spirit of the law.

The Spirit of the Law

It is in this category, as compared to the letter of the law, that the correct philosophy of each officer is so intricately entwined with police-community relationships. Tamm captured the essence of this subject: "The greatest responsibility and obligation of a law enforcement officer is that of enforcing the law, not solely in a skillful and effective manner but in accordance with the rule of law and the spirit of the law enshrined in our Constitution."[6]

Traditional law enforcement responsibilities include protection of life and property, apprehension of offenders, recovery of stolen property, maintenance of public order, and regulation of non-criminal conduct. Peace officers have a responsibility and a duty to every member of the community to perform these minimum functions. This has traditionally been the letter of the law. We must now, as never before, be cognizant of the other area of enforcement—the spirit of the law, or the method and attitude of enforcement.

Disregard for the spirit of the law, either intentionally or inadvertently, opens a chasm between the citizens and the police and loses the support so essential to police efficiency.

The true spirit of professional law enforcement means a great deal more than simply having a code of ethics. It also extends

---

[6] Quinn Tamm, former Assistant Director of the FBI: "Constitutional Law Enforcement." Address delivered to the International Association of Chiefs of Police.

beyond the mere receipt of a degree of police science or public administration. It involves each man and woman knowing that these are important tools of the trade and then applying these principles in combination with the other vital factors with which he or she is equipped. The officer then must exhibit them in action each time he or she has a contact in the field.

Police officers will find it difficult to restrain from personal involvement when the drunk spews vomit on their clean uniforms, or when they must make a death notification or arrest a child molester. The point is that law enforcement today requires a professional approach to each and every such incident.

Discussion Questions

1. Discuss what you believe should be the role of the individual officer in police-community relations.
2. How close are the police to attaining their goal of professionalization? Is this goal attainable?

. . . in the course of his assignments he may deliver babies . . . arbitrate marital disturbances . . . pursue an escaping criminal . . .

Chapter 16

ROLE OF THE FIRST-LINE
PEACE OFFICER

Objective: To review the major problems plaguing the cop-on-the-beat today and state some suggestions for improving the situation.

- Reasons for becoming a police officer
- Communication with the public
- Progress through education
- Citizen complaints
- Effecting needed change
- Social problems and the police
- Role definition

Author's note: This chapter has appeared in similar form as an article in *Police* (September-October, 1969, pp. 23-28) and was reprinted as one of several readings in *Police-Community Relationships* (1972), a Thomas publication edited by William J. Bopp. Because of numerous requests and its uniquely special approach to street policing police-community relations problems, a revision of the original chapter is included as part of this new edition.

INTRODUCTION

POLICE-COMMUNITY relations is a field as rife with social dissension as any endeavor in history. Whether they know it or not—or like it or not—peace officers spend much more time engaged in police-community relations activities than they suppose.

At this point, an additional definition should be helpful. Radelet writes that "it is the sum total of the many and varied ways in which it may be emphasized that the police are a part of, not apart from, the communities they serve."[1]

Yet, definitions of PCR present a long-range point of view, almost ethereal in some ways because they are so broad. This text's conceptual definition posits that police-community relations is an art, and thus the problems that are most germane to PCR cannot be approached in automaton fashion.

Cromwell and Keefer surveyed 500 peace officers with varying backgrounds and experience. The results have basic implications for community relations:

> Knowing the dangers which lie ahead: the probable lack of applause, the possible violent reception—why does a young man aspire to play the part? What motivates a police officer to stay on stage in spite of the eggs and tomatoes thrown by an unappreciative audience?
>
> In an effort to discover an answer to these questions a form entitled "I am a policeman because . . ." and containing forty reasons was given to approximately five hundred officers, ranging from recruits to experienced men. Each was asked to choose the ten reasons which were the most impelling in the selection of his career.
>
> The reasons receiving the greatest number of votes are listed here in the order of their popularity:
> I want to improve the community.
> I want to improve the police work.
> I am part of a team effort.
> I feel civic responsibility.
> My imagination is stimulated.
> I have loyalty to the Country.
> I can be "in the know."
> I have good fellow workers.
> I enjoy prestige in my neighborhood.[2]

---

[1] Louis A. Radelet: "Police and Community Relations." *Police Chief*, September 1964, p. 841.

[2] Paul F. Cromwell, Jr., and George Keefer: *Police-Community Relations: Selected Readings*. 2nd ed., St. Paul, Minnesota, West Publishing Co., 1978, p. 5.

Communications Dilemma

Police-community relations is not new. In a letter to the Corinthians, St. Paul wrote that "evil communications corrupt good manners." He went on to relate how government officials can be responsible for creating their own problems with the public. John Milton related almost the same idea, but in a different manner: "Good, the more communicated — the more abundant grows." In modern times, the sentiment concerning many police-community relations programming is, at best, one of apathy — "I don't give a damn."

Before the Watts riot, police-community relations could not have been sold to many peace officers at the point of a shotgun! They might concede that it was needed but felt there was too much talk about all the things police had to do and not enough thought and action about stopping the crime problem. After the Watts riot, an amazing transformation started across this country. People everywhere — citizen and law officers alike — began asking themselves, in retrospect, "What happened to that great city that couldn't have a riot? It just couldn't happen in Los Angeles!" But it did, and the tragic consequences of it, in terms of social trauma and problems we live with today, are awesome indeed. The Watts riot did have one beneficial result, if such a thing is possible: Law enforcement began looking at itself more intensely than ever before, in terms of "How can we perform our functions better?"

Role Definition Explored

Peace officers perform a complex type of activity, which some people have called the "most difficult job in the world today." The work is viewed and reviewed by thousands of people, but law officers should not expect to be clothed in love or universally wanted and liked. All we can hope to do is to improve the level of acceptance through good police-community relations, so that law enforcement can accomplish its purpose.

It is the author's opinion that until recently, efforts to improve the level of acceptance for PCR have been inadequate. One reason for this is being overly concerned with what was "*not* our job" and what was "*not* our role," thus eliminating a vast array of activities that constituted positive public contact. Police tried to get out of juvenile activities, going into the schools, and giving speeches; and when some holocaust occurred, many sat back and said, "Why doesn't anybody understand the role of the police?" Who is going to tell the public about the role of the police if it isn't the police? No one else is going to go out and tell it the way it is! This means that all peace officers have more at stake than they realize.

To view another example, consider the various consequences to the first-line officer of the establishment of police-review boards. Few officers are in favor of them, but if police-review boards are thrust upon police, it will be the fault of no one but the police. We have not bothered to tell the public what excellent procedures are available for dealing with the problem of citizen complaints. They are not really aware that police would rather "clean their own house," and that they do, in fact, clean house. In the words of one line officer, "If we fail ourselves, let us not turn around and talk about a public that fails to understand what our function is and what our role is. If anybody is to tell our story, we have to do it."

California is often referred to as a leader in progressive police methods, and rightfully so. Yet it was only in 1959 that California finally adopted a formalized minimum recommended training program for its peace officers. Before that date, many agencies failed to provide even token training for a job that had already become highly sophisticated and extremely sensitive.

The current time is labeled as the most educationally oriented and sophisticated era of mankind. Peace officers should remember the words of Henry Baron Brougham: "Education makes a people easy to lead but difficult to drive; easy to govern but impossible to enslave." The truth of this statement is being etched in our consciousness by daily events, and law enforcement has no alternative but to involve itself in this age of scholasticism, although some traditionalists meet this fact with the fiction of deemphasis of education.

Law enforcement must upgrade itself both internally and externally. For example, we have all worked for someone who unquestioningly adhered to the status quo, where "don't make waves" was the watchword. Take the case of a patrolman asking the sergeant, "Why have we been making up this form in four copies? The secretary types them up and she brings them in to you, and you sign them, and then she takes them back, tears off the three copies underneath and throws them away." And the sergeant replies testily, "We've always done it that way. Now why don't you get on with doing your job?" This kind of attitude is prevalent in law enforcement.

To upgrade by educational involvement means something more than textbooks and training sessions. It also means a broadening of professional perspectives and operational procedures to include better communication with, and understanding of, the public served.

Watson captures certain key factors that line officers must necessarily consider, and supervisory personnel should require, reinforce at briefings, and believe in themselves:

1. Don't be trapped into unprofessional conduct by a threat or challenge.
2. Make sure everything you do is calculated to enhance your reputation as a good officer — one who is firm, but fair and just.
3. When you are faced with a threat and can't tell how serious it is, try to "buy time" in which to size up the situation by engaging the person in conversation. Make a comment or ask a question to divert his attention, if possible.
4. Don't show hostility even if the other fellow does. Many times a quiet, calm, and reasonable manner will cause his hostility to evaporate or at least to simmer down. An important point is that the next time he will not be so hostile because he doesn't think you are.
5. Reduce your "threat" potential. Avoid a grim or expressionless continence. Be an approachable human being. Too many officers habitually appear gruff and forbidding.
6. Cultivate a pleasant, friendly manner when making nonadversary contacts. Be ready with a smile, a pleasant word, a humorous comment, when appropriate.
7. Let your general demeanor and especially your facial expression and tone of voice indicate that you respect the other person as a human being.
8. Let the other fellow know by your reception of him that you don't expect trouble from him and that you don't consider him a nuisance. (Maybe you do, but don't let it show.)
9. Show an interest in the other fellow's problem. Maybe you can't do anything about it, but often it is a great help just to be a good listener. Most people will respond in kind.
10. Go out of your way to contact people in the interest of improving police-community cooperation. No group of specialists can establish or build readily effective police-community relations without you. More important, however, is the *fact* that effective police-community relations means more to you than to anyone else. This means that you, more than anyone else, should be actively working toward the establishment or the improvement of police-community relations. The

essence of good working relations between the people and the police is to be found in the way you handle yourself. You and your fellow officers on the street can do more to improve (and to destroy) police-community relations in one day than your specialized unit and your command staff can ever do.

11. There is an old show-business maxim that runs, "Always leave them laughing." Let us paraphrase that and say, "Always leave them satisfied." There are people who react to an arrest or a traffic ticket by feeling the officer was fair, was just doing his job, and they had it coming. They don't like it, but they have to admit that the officer did his job properly. When you render a service or react to a request, show some interest and give some explanation. This will promote good feelings which, if carried on consistently by the entire force, will have a cumulative effect, resulting in vastly improved human relations.

12. Try in every way you can to encourage people to work with the police for their own protection. Let the average citizen know that far from being a threat you are interested in being a help. Drive home the point that he is threatened by crime and disorder, not by the police.[3]

Communication

Perhaps the biggest social problem faced today is communication: We talk *at* each other rather than *with* each other. To communicate involves the concept that we have a two-way problem, and its solution can only be found through a two-way exchange of ideas. This is what many of the minority groups are saying today. They are talking. They are not just talking at police; they want police to listen. They want police to hear what they have to say.

Another vital question is, "Do police know what their communities think?" Even more important, does law enforcement understand the reasons they think that way? There is a pressing need for greater contact with people. For example, should there be in-depth meetings with militant groups? (Consider this in terms of knowing what these groups are thinking. Many times peace officers could deal with them more appropriately if they knew what was, in fact, their motivating force.)

Dealing with the Public

Groups, militant and otherwise, frequently do not grasp the various facets of police problems, and this is not usually matched by a sincere effort on the part of the police to explain the law enforce-

---

[3] Watson, Jeanne: "Issues in Human Relations, Threats and Challenges", Rand McNally College Publishing Company, Chicago, Illinois, 1978, pp. 21-22.

ment position. There is communication—but *at* them, and they *at* the police. This is not communicating, but rather "verbal hand-cuffing." The point is that more thought must be given to this idea of "dealing with groups," because whatever their opinions or back-grounds, they represent a part of the community.

There is an urgent need to deal with attitudes that *actually exist* rather than those we think should exist. All too often when com-municating with groups, there is a tendency to listen for awhile and then "tune them out" because their views conflict with our own. It really does not matter whether we like their views, or whether we agree; if members of the public are thinking a certain way, police must listen.

A Fable

A great king once ruled the entire world. The king had seven sons, and as each of the sons became of age he was sent out to rule one-seventh of the earth. In a very private conference with each son, the father asked each, as the son was to leave the family home, what was the one possession of the father that the son wished to have when the father passed on. Each of the seven sons indicated pri-vately that the one possession he wanted more than anything else was the ring the father wore. Finally the father died. Shortly there-after, messengers came seeking the seven sons—now located in seven corners of the earth—and delivered the rings. Obviously, six of them had to be fraudulent. But they were enough like the real thing so they appeared to be real. What does this mean in terms of communication patterns and systems of response? We have to understand that what looks like a cold hard case of right or wrong to us may also look like the precise opposite to someone else. There are many different people, and they have different viewpoints. We must tune them in, just as we would expect them to tune us in, because if we all tune out on one another, one thing is guaranteed: Police-community relations is lost.

Complaints Against Police

Some estimate that as much as 90 percent of a peace officer's time is spent in nonpunitive activities. In other words, for 90 per-cent of their time, they can be "good guys." Yet, to recall the survey conducted by the National League of Cities, revealing basic complaints that the public has against peace officers, surprisingly, the number one complaint was discourtesy—the "ten-pound lip" and the "twenty-pound badge!" The other three complaints were equally surprising: Number two was traffic-citation issuance. (Note that there is a subtle difference between just receiving the citation and the manner in which it is issued.) Third was police brutality; and the fourth was response time—getting to the location where there is some kind of trouble.

The main theme of this survey that must concern the first-line officer is not so much whether these problems do in fact exist, but that *the public believes the problems exist.* The task must now be to correct, in the eyes of the public, this belief system. If their beliefs are not in tune with the way things are, police must bring them into tune. They must search continually for answers and for better ways to deal with problems. A person cannot mold the world to fit his or her dreams as to the way it should be; it is going to be the way it is. Law enforcement is going to have to live with the real world or help change it for the better, but to hope for a changing world with no overt action on the part of law enforcement is ridiculous. The role of the police is changing, and the police must be the leading engineers in designing a future role.

Change

In 1929, the two-way police radio car was put into operation, and, with rare exception, street patrolling patterns and techniques have not changed since that time. The sirens are louder, the lights are brighter and redder, the cars go faster, and the tires are safer, but the basic procedures have not changed. This resistance to change or, perhaps, satisfaction with the *status quo* obstructs progressive police work. Computerization and aerial assistance cost considerably, but these are changes and advances that must be instituted if line policing is to have the necessary tools for its role. Other advances, ranging from nonlethal weaponry to use of police dogs, are still controversial. Field research can be of great assistance to see if these and other approaches can assist.

However, some improvements have been implemented. In 1926, a book was written on police interrogation. The fourth paragraph of the first chapter contained a classic statement: "The judicious use of corporal punishment will elicit an admission from even the most hardened of criminals." In other words, beat someone long enough and he or she will say something! How times have changed! Today, we fire and prosecute peace officers for such criminal conduct.

While the great majority of complaints against police are unfounded, circumstances do occur where all of us must realize that brutality, for example, still happens, and if it happens at all, it is wrong. What must be done is to firm up policies, procedures, and supervision so derelictions happen as rarely as possible.

This is especially true of overreaction. Today, as never before, the police just cannot afford to overreact. It is all too easy and normal to meet aggression with aggression: When a part of the public acts aggressively toward the police, the natural tendency for the police is to respond in like manner. Such overreaction has been talked about and dealt with extensively; the consensus is that police must react and perform in a manner they can live with afterward.

Achieving Change

Another deplorable activity is for police to strike or "pseudo-strike." The shame and sham of so-called mass sickness in certain areas of our country is something law enforcement can do without, and the actual strike may mean more money, but how does one explain it in terms of professionalism?

Law enforcement needs help, but jeopardizing public safety to gain this help is—at the very least—open to the most severe questioning. There are better ways with more benefits in the long run, such as selling and educating the public to our needs.

Stereotyping

Along with educating the public, law enforcement might be able to resolve another two-way problem which hampers police-community relations—"generalizations" or "role defamation," as it is currently called. Examples of role defamation would include sweeping statements such as "All students are liberal," or "All policemen are conservative." Also included would be statements where a particular group, usually a minority, is generalized into one restricted category.

Peace officers frequently complain that people stereotype them in a specific category, and that all policemen do certain predictable acts. Yet, the ones most guilty of stereotyping, says the taxpayer, are police officers! For example, while on duty, someone is stopped by a peace officer and a first impression is formed. Psychologists and most sociologists warn that first impressions are usually false — and lasting. Yet we frequently judge the goodness or evil of a person with no more evidence than an impression that is likely false. As Oliver Wendell Holmes said, "Generalizations aren't worth a damn," and he quickly added, "and that's generalization."

Peace officers have been "typed" as a very conservative group. Indeed, quite a few people believe that police comprise one of the few groups that would classify the John Birch Society as left-wing radicals. This may or may not be true, but one truth is that there is greater social pressure today for change than ever existed before; for better or for worse, police are going to participate in this process of change.

Confusion from Change and Stereotyping

Change happens so fast that today's roles and occupations cannot be well defined because they are in a constant state of alteration. In fact, some authors have suggested striking the word "change" from our language and substituting the word "changing" in its place. Bennis quotes J. Robert Oppenheimer characterizing the essence of the modern world: "One thing that is new is the prevalence of newness, the changing scale and scope of change itself, so that the world alters as we walk on it . . . not some small growth or rearrangement or moderation . . . but great upheaval."[4]

How do these changing, confusing times affect police-community relations? The McCone Commission, the National Commission on Civil Disorders, the President's Commission on Law Enforcement and the Administration of Justice, and the National Commission on Standards and Goals for the Criminal Justice System all point to major sociological problems with which police have to be concerned, because they are the root causes of civil disobedience: unemployment, undereducation, and substandard housing. These three can be considered "causal" as compared to the fourth problem: police-community relations.

---

[4] Warren G. Bennis: *Changing Operations.* New York, McGraw-Hill, 1966, p. 19.

Social Problems and the Line Officer

Police-community relations is perhaps the most visible adjunct of government because it is "out front." Because it is so publicly visible, police receive the brunt of all the social evils created by unemployment, poor housing, and undereducation that have built up for years. Police cannot say that these problems are not their concern. They are not for law enforcement to solve, but they are major sociological problems that every working police officer should be aware of during the performance of his/her job. Also, an informed public recognizes that these problems affect law enforcement in a manner that cannot be corrected by police officers simply being "good guys."

An example of these sociological problems is seen in the recent commodity riots of Washington, D.C. People formed bands for the purpose of breaking store windows and stealing merchandise. This was their way of obtaining goods they could not have otherwise. This is a sad commentary on our society today, and heir to this dilemma is the police.

Anomie

The term *anomie* was utilized many years ago in France; it means "normlessness." All of us at one time have been either homesick or felt that the world was against us. Anyone who has not had this feeling is rare indeed. How does *anomie* apply to police-community relations as they affect the first-line officer?

Think about a person as a child who is educated and instilled with the concept that he is going to have a respectable job (role expectation) and prepares to obtain all sorts of good things — and then it does not happen. Look at him as a teenager (since the peak age of criminality in this country is now fifteen) when what he probably wants most is a car. He sees one he cannot afford, and he begins to wonder why he fails to fit in that part of an "in group." Then he thinks about the parents he seldom sees, and begins to be attracted to an "in group" that says burglaries are viewed as socially acceptable within that group. He goes from normlessness to a norm contrary to the norms of society. He becomes a criminal by our standards when he becomes a member of this "in group," and their standards become his new standards.

How do the police deal with these subcultures of criminal structure? Cultures spawned by the squalor and hopelessness of the ghetto proliferate police problems. What is the line officer's role in this sociological morass in society today? Is it to maintain social order and to protect life and property? What does the word "service" imply, which today has a broader connotation than ever before?

Identification of Role/Duty/Goal

Perhaps we expect too much if we want a complete definition of the line officer's role. The concept of changing certainly applies here, and a narrowing of parameters of police definition—if it could be done—may not be beneficial. It is safe to assume that the changing role of the past reflects the future, and thus we must be committed to a philosophy of greater and greater openmindedness. Perhaps even more important is to learn from past mistakes.

We all know of thousands of instances of good police action, and we know of too many instances of poor police action. One recent instance involved an officer eating a snack at a drive-in restaurant. A young student of police science ran up to him and said, "Officer, there is a woman over in the vacant lot across the street and she's screaming and laying on the ground." The officer looked back and said, "Let her scream. I'm eating a sandwich."

This instance illustrates an important concept about the police role. It is all well and good for police administrators to talk about police-community relations programs, and often, the working police officers say of it, "Well, here comes another PCR program and a lot of chit-chat about what we have to do!"

If the individual officer does a good job in first-line police work, this so-called need for redefining the role can become a minimal thing. The public will not need definitions because good police officers do not put his/her peers in a position to receive public criticism. As an illustration: a bad arrest occurs, and the case goes through the court system and a *Miranda* comes down to haunt us. It should not be forgotten that we are living with problems created by a few officers who did not really believe in police-community relations. It takes something as terrible as a riot to convince most parties concerned that there is a problem.

Jerome Skolnick[5] visualizes the peace officer, just a few years from now, as being more qualified than the police agent recommended by the President's Commission, possibly a kind of "street-corner ombudsman." If the officer sees a health problem, it is reported to the proper people in the health field; he or she makes sure the problem is being solved. A fire hazard, a water hazard, food hazard, any type of hazard — the officer is still there to handle the police role. Skolnick is implying that even though we have already expanded the concept of what we do, it is expanding and changing even more drastically and thus is requiring much more expertise and ability on the part of *each individual officer.*

A New Era

We shall eventually progress to a stage in this country when we will hire people for police work right out of high school; they will not see police work per se as regulars until they have spent perhaps four years in a program that (hopefully) will be as prestigious as the military in terms of West Point and Annapolis and as educationally sound as any criminal justice, criminology, police science, or public administration program existing today. If peace officers are going to have to be more qualified in the future, we must upgrade their abilities to cope with the problems with which they must deal.

Peace officers today are not in the same role as yesterday; yet many agencies still provide precious few weeks of training. In other agencies they receive eight or ten or twelve or sixteen or twenty weeks of training — all of which is totally *inadequate* to adapt to the new role being pressed on the police.

Line Problems and Solutions

People *outside* police work declare that police have more responsibilities and more problems than ever before. This may be true. If it is, then law enforcement must demand that the public accept, along with this philosophy of requiring more of a peace officer, the philosophy that they, the public, must be responsible for assisting in preparing *their* officers before they are sent out to handle "the most difficult job in the world today."

This is exactly what must be done in terms of police role defini-

---

[5] Jerome Skolnick, noted author and lecturer, has voiced this position in numerous articles and public statements.

tion. If individual officers think about it and are willing to try to do something, then police-community relations will progress. But we must define our role in our own minds, individually, if we are going to accept it, and then go out and obtain public acceptance of it through both demeanor and education. But each officer must participate.

In the final analysis, is it not the individual officer who gets us into trouble, and is it not individual officers who can get us out of all this trouble?

Discussion Questions

1. Is the first-line officer today *really* in a different position from his/her counterpart of a decade ago?
2. Can an "open communications" approach really *compel* an "open-mindedness?"
3. What subjects of an instructional nature can be considered "training?" What can be typed as "education?" Which is more important?
4. What do we mean by stereotyping?

Chapter 17

THE Z-COP: EMERGING MODEL FOR
THE YEAR 2000

*Objective: To attempt the impossible: to predict what
the peace officer of the year 2000 may be like.*

- Continuing change
- Theory X and Theory Y
- Society's demands on police
- Abraham Maslow and Theory Z
- Profile of the Z-Cop

Author's note: The Z-Cop has been emerging and has been presented to a number of groups for review and comment. The image is vague and distorted, much as that of the officer is of today. Through the superior work of a group dedicated to progress in the face of entropy—and the belief that traditionalism has not successfully coped with crime—futurism and the prediction of what the cop of the future may be are linked with the writings of perhaps the greatest visionary of them all—Abraham Maslow.

← . . . cop of the year 2000 . . . how will he change . . .

INTRODUCTION

FROM THE BEGINNING of human kind's uncertain and stumbling journey across the endless stretches of space-time, the "Ship of Humankind" has housed two main types of people: the immobilists and the activists.

The immobilists, vowing to defend the sacred established order, declare that nothing changes or can change. Armed with common sense, pessimism, apathy, and, to some extent, morality and religion, they forbid the Earth to move, and the ship drifts purposelessly on a shoreless sea.

The activists, restless with entrenched traditions, look out at the stars, study the lapping of water against the hull, and breathe the scents on the breeze. As they begin to question the "eternal verities," a strange transformation occurs and they acquire a new sense: *Change is normal;* the fixed and static universe is seen to move!

Throughout the millennia, the immobilists have waged a losing battle. As the Ship of Humankind moves toward the year 2000, the one condition that stands out with startling prominence is the unprecedented pace of fundamental social changes. Time-honored philosophies and values such as the Protestant Ethic, economy of scarcity, and logical positivism are being challenged as inadequate for many aspects of human experience. As the "Establishment" struggles to adjust to the unrelenting momentum and magnitude of political, social, ideological, and technological changes, new processes and philosophies emerge as so many new patches on an old suit — Adhocracy (the temporary society), politics by confrontation, existentialism, strikes by public employees (police included), self-actualization centers, alternative organizational forms, and community living patterns.

But social systems can assimilate, stretch, and adapt just so much — and time is needed to do so. As profound changes leapfrog across a shortening timespan, one wonders when they will cluster into the critical mass that will transfigure society and, in the process, the role of police.

An Unorthodox Precept

A curious phenomenon is emerging amid the flood tide of change — a phenomenon that could revolutionize the psychology and dynamics of interpersonal relations, especially for the peace officer.

We are witnessing the birth of a different theory of interpersonal communication — one different in dimension rather than degree, a dimension more commensurate with the complex, knowledgeable individuals that people today's pluralistic postindustrial society.

This theory is emerging in much of the current literature, and the recurring theme conceptualizes a nobler model of man and his future: *Homo humanus* rather than *homo rationalist* or *homo economicus.*

The desire to comprehend this theory at a level of realism permeates society; it frequently surfaces as social unrest. Protest groups and social reconstructionists demonstrate their disenchantment with an ethos that measures life's meaning around professional accomplishments and status symbols. Many of the "counter-cultures" rebel against the hyper-rational technocracy that threatens the kind of development they value; what they seek is increased openness to experience, emotional honesty, and authentic personal interaction.

Echos of this view are rampant in the none-too-gentle criticisms of the flaws in our institutions, the hypocrisy in our dealings with one another, and the discrepancy between national goals and government in action. Watergate will still be a factor in the year 2000!

In Eric Fromm's denunciation of the type of person he saw dominating our personality landscape, he noted: *"The marketing automaton conformist* — The person who sees himself and others as commodities whose worth is judged by their exchange value in the marketplace."

This theory expressed in young people's demand for *quality in life for all human beings,* centers around the forces of truth, love, and trust, i.e. Theory Z — the next logical step in Douglas McGregor's Theory X and Theory Y.

Theory X and Theory Y

In 1960, Douglas McGregor, a behavioral scientist, authored a text called *The Human Side of Enterprise* (McGraw-Hill) that marked a turning point in organization and management theory. Using the intriguing framework entitled Theory X versus Theory Y,

McGregor compared traditional, authoritarian management (Theory X) to the participative and democratic style (Theory Y).

Theory X

In his book, McGregor proceeded to relentlessly demonstrate how the rigid, hyper-rational, hierarchical requirements and perceptions of Theory X are actually counterproductive to organizational development and effectiveness. Founded on a rational-economic model of man, Theory X views employees as primarily motivated by money; they will accept authoritarian management in return for economic rewards. Their irrational emotions and motives interfere with organizational goals, and they must be watched closely and controlled through explicit and strict procedures. Lastly, Theory X sees people as disinclined to work, uncreative, and, when given a chance, as loafers on the job.

Theory Y

In contraposition, Theory Y agrees that money is important, but that there are other facets of the human enterprise. People want a feeling of belonging; they need friendly and supportive relationships. They also need opportunities to self-actualize to fulfill their needs for involvement, recognition, and achievement—in short, to expand their potential. Numerous research findings indicate that when organizations meet these higher-order needs, people will align their personal goals with those of the organization.

Some Thoughts on X and Y Relative to Law Enforcement

McGregor's theories apply not only to organizations but to most social interactions, and they are of vital importance to effective, goal-achieving policing. A vital question is, What is the general philosophy of many officers toward the people they serve? If an officer is Theory X oriented—commonly expressed as "People are no damn good"—his or her callous indifference can taint every contact and tarnish the entire department.

The role of the police is so critical to the country's future that there is little sane choice but to opt for the participative Theory Y in all possible contacts.

Since the early 1960s the flood tide of radical social change has so recast what police do—and the public's interest in what they do—

that the process of policing has catapulted into a pivotal position in national planning and policy making.

Before the 1960s, the police were looked on as just part of the background of daily life. This anonymity began to fade rapidly in the wake of increasing crime, increasing social unrest, and increasing public sensitivity to both. By 1970 awareness of the impact of police functions on the multidimensional and systematic networks of social order ignited what amounts to a wildfire of interest in what police do and how they do it. The police are hard pressed to help alleviate the turmoil; they cannot work too effectively with other agencies to put the country back in the black ink; they cannot alone adapt and cope and change and renew and revitalize.

In other words, *the police are expected to help put the country back in the black ink!* Yet they are sorely limited as to what they can contribute to molding the future; they cannot alleviate the crime and violence and turmoil; they cannot as a lone entity adapt and change and renew and develop. Succinctly, they cannot do their jobs authoritatively.

Interaction with the public and other organizations must spring from Theory Y convictions — the participative collaborative method of transacting with people, for only then can the police realize a viable people-police partnership.

This may be just the beginning. The model performance of today's effective officer portrays a Theory Y orientation; but what will the officer of the future, of the year 2000, be like?

First, it is mandatory to note the work of the author upon which the "Future-Cop" is predicated. Abraham Maslow has been a significant predictor of human achievement, one of the great prognosticators of our time. His untimely passing prevented him from full conceptualization of his "Theory Z," which first appeared publicly in 1969 in the *Journal of Transpersonal Psychology*.

A brief review of this presentation is necessary for an understanding of the cop of the future. In a highly condensed format, Maslow looked at the "big picture" in this fashion:

A differentiation is made between two types or degrees of self-actualized people.
1. Healthy self-actualizers — but no transcendence.
2. Those in whom transcendent experiencing is important and even central.

Note: The author admits he is reporting his impressions from the most preliminary of explorations, prescientific.

In essence the transcenders are what he refers to as "peakers" versus the others who do not "peak." They (the former) tend to be yes-sayers, life-positive, eager for life, rather than nauseated by it. The transcenders have fulfilled and surpassed Theory Y. They live at a different level on a continuum.

The transcenders have the following characteristics or have more of them than do the nontranscenders:

1. Peak experiences, the validators of life — the most precious aspect of life.
2. The transcenders speak easily, normally, naturally, and unconsciously the language of being, the language of poets, mystics, of men who live at the Platonic-idea level, under the aspect of eternity.
3. They perceive the sacred within the secular, or they see the sacredness in all things at the same time they also see them at the practical everyday level.
4. Their most important motivations are the values of being, or being itself seen both as fact and value, e.g. perfection, truth, goodness.
5. They seem to be able to recognize each other and to come to almost instant intimacy and mutual understanding even upon first meeting.
6. They are more responsive to beauty or to see as beautiful that what is not officially or conventionally beautiful.
7. Mankind is one and the cosmos is one, and such concepts as the "national interest" or the "religion of my father" either cease to exist or are easily transcended.
8. They have a natural tendency to synergy — intrapsychic, interpersonal, intraculturally, and internationally. They transcend competitiveness, of zero-sum or win-lose gamemanship.
9. They often produce the thought in other people that "this is a great man."
10. They are apt to be innovators, discoverers of the new. Transcendent experiences bring clearer vision of the ideal, of the perfect, of what ought to be, what exists in potential, and therefore of what might be brought to pass.
11. Transcenders are less happy than healthy self-actualizers. They are prone to a cosmic sadness over the stupidity of people, their self-defeat, their blindness. *Perhaps this comes from the contrast between what actually is and the ideal world that transcenders can see so easily and which is in principle so easily attainable.* [Emphasis added.]
12. The sacredness of every person and even of every living thing, even of nonliving things that are beautiful, is so easily and directly perceived in its reality by every transcender that he can hardly forget it for a moment.

13. Mystery is attractive and challenging; it is a reward rather than a punishment.
14. The more they know the more apt they are to go into ecstacy before the tremendousness of the universe, or the stunningness of a hummingbird.
15. They are less afraid of "nuts" and "kooks" and thus are more likely to be good selectors of creators.
16. They are more reconciled with evil. They can compassionately strike down the evil man if this is necessary.
17. Transcenders should be somewhat Taoistic. There should be more of an impulse simply to stare at a phenomenon and examine it than to do anything about it or with it.

Mystics and transcenders have throughout history seemed spontaneously to prefer simplicity and to avoid luxury, privilege, honors, and possessions. *

Based on Maslow's Theory Z, what follows is a criminologically oriented impression of tomorrow's policeman.

THE Z-COP

By the year 2000, or sooner perhaps, the Z-Cop (possibly called Assistance Officer) will be performing tasks of which we cannot be sure, in a world difficult to describe, but we can postulate some of the Z-Cop's characteristics.

A Really New Breed

The Z-Cop will be a radically new breed of officer. This officer's attributes will embrace a broad spectrum of education, training, experience, empathy, and capabilities, and he or she will be able to see unity within disunity, harmony within dissonance. The Z-Cop will view life as a continual unfolding process where means are not allowed to become ends and will see fellow humans as the complex phenomena that they are and will respect the strengths and weaknesses and uniqueness of that complexity. The Z-Cop will be a free-thinking citizen of the world and will recognize his/her world as a limited part of the greater totality. He or she will be a searching

---

* For further readings on this subject refer to the following:

Teilhard de Chardin: *The Future of Man.* New York, Harper & Row, 1964.
John Platt: *The Step to Man.* New York, John Wiley & Sons, 1966.
J. Samuel Bois: *Breeds of Men.* New York, Harper & Row, 1969.
Pitrim Sorokin: *The Ways and Powers of Love.* Boston, Beacon Press, 1954.

person, without neat answers, and will be willing to live with uncertainty, relativity, and ambiguity.

The Z-Cop will feel the "rhythm of life" permeating all things and manifesting between flow and stability, process and structure. This officer will recognize the Z-Cop's role as one of guardianship of the laws and mores of a particular culture at a particular time and in a particular place and will appreciate the relativity of all "reality."

Concern for People

The Z-Cop will be more concerned with ideas and people — movement, change, becoming, growth, learning, understanding — than with fixed and static *things*. He or she will be able to strike down fellow human beings when necessary but is apt to weep afterwards, for he or she will recognize the temporal necessity but be dismayed by the ultimate futility in any society where people are pitted against people.

Any attempt to describe a Theory Z-Cop involves much latitude, for even a Theory Z person (as distinguished from a police officer) portrays paradoxes that make definitive descriptions suspect. A Theory Z person, as a lay person or police officer, displays certain characteristics that distinguish him/her from others. The main difference embraces an expanded mental outlook. The Theory Z person has experienced a vision of *what can be* rather than *what is* and thinks in terms of *possibilities,* and these possibilities enter a realm where few people tread for fear of being labeled dreamers or idealists. But the Theory Z person ventures there often, dreaming "The Impossible Dream" and seeing Utopia as an attainable goal if we would but *look.*

THEORY Z AND CONTEMPORARY POLICING

There may be Z-Cops working today, but it is difficult to picture them in a radio car. To begin with, contemporary society is turbulent and mortally dangerous for police officers — not a setting conducive to developing Theory Z. Additionally, an effective police officer must be gregarious, curious, and suspicious, with an attitude of maintaining control in all situations. The Theory Z person is unconcerned about control per se; his or her attitude is one of observation, appreciation, and noninterference unless he/she senses that trouble is imminent.

Lastly, police officers must be courageous and fearless because they safeguard the lives of others. A Theory Z person possesses these traits but considers them of secondary utility and deplores the circumstances where they must be foremost — violence, war, and natural disasters. The Theory Z person can undoubtedly function in this tumultuous milieu, but it can be dissonant to his/her continuing development.

These few reasons illustrate why one seldom observes a Theory Z patrol officer in today's society. By shifting our environment to a less turbulent surrounding, the emergence of a Z-Cop is possible, and thus raises the question, What behavioral patterns might be expected of a Z-Cop, the future social scientist who maintains law and order in the community?

Meaning in Policing

The Z-Cop will find great meaning in police work. He or she will not be too concerned about salary or retirement or other details such as overtime, for these are not relevant issues as long as he/she is (within reason) financially secure.

Rank Unconsciousness

The Z-Cop will tend to overlook rank, especially his/her own, considering this a condition incompatible with a world-view that all men and women are equal — some just fulfill different missions.

Having transcended egotistic demands for status and prestige, the Z-Cop will feel indifference toward climbing the hierarchical ladder, but will likely do so because of his/her ability and dedication.

Loneliness

As most transcenders, the Z-Cop will experience great happiness and despair, contrasting what is with what can be. He or she will also experience great loneliness induced partly by fellow officers' inability to comprehend many of the metagoals he or she lives by.

Dignity

To the Z-Cop, every person is sacred and he or she will abhor gross generalizations, stereotypes, and other appellations that negate the innate dignity of people. Indeed, if all police officers were Theory Z oriented, there might be little need for such books as *Police-Community Relations: crisis in our time.*

He Stands Out, Yet Stands Alone

Because of differing goals and life-style, the Z-Cop may not be popular socially, his/her ways and ideas will be questioned, and he/she will often stand alone. But, also because of this officer's charismatic quality, love of life, and demonstrated ability, he/she will compel attention, respect, and credence.

The Z-Cop will seek those people and officers who can envision other domains of doing and being, having learned the value of hypothetical thinking, and questioning the status quo to his/her own development and that of the department.

This officer's knowledge and understanding of law enforcement will be immense, and yet — realizing how little he/she knows — he or she will be humble; this lack will be inspiring rather than frustrating.

A Concern for Reality

The Z-Cop will interact with the "long hairs" and "weirdos," realizing that creativity is no respecter of persons, and he or she will be able to separate the creative person from the imitator.

This officer will consider the pragmatic but will be equally concerned with the possible, the untried, the Galilean leap in thinking. Realizing the significance of "common sense," this officer will also know that this credo may house more commonality than sense.

A Concern for the Past and the Future

How can one best generalize about this "New Breed" to gain some footing about the right way and how to get there? This is most uncertain, yet great men of all beliefs and times and countries have sounded forth the same guiding principle, from Lao-tzu in 500 BC to Gautama Buddha in 400 BC, to Jesus Christ in 30 AD, to Spinoza in 1600 AD, to Mahatma Gandhi in 1948 AD, to the dream of countless people in the 1970s — that is, for Truth-Love-Trust to permeate the interpersonal relations in the human family.

A FINAL THOUGHT

The Z-Cop is coming, and although he or she may differ substantially from our projected description, the Z-Cop *is* the future and is going to be!

Discussion Questions

1. Is today's law enforcement officer of Theory X, Theory Y, or Theory Z?
2. How would you compare the police officer of today as opposed to what he can be?
3. How are police-community relations and the Z-Cop related?

law enforcement . . . required mechanization today includes the depersonalization
of society from the police . . . a fact to overcome . . .

Chapter 18

POLICE-COMMUNITY RELATIONS IN AMERICAN SOCIETY TOMORROW

Objective: To explore and understand some of the more urgent problems of police-community relations as they relate to maintaining the social order.

- Social workers with guns or gunmen in social work?
- Social order as a goal
- PCR as an art
- Internal leadership and organization
- Checklist for police agencies
- Facing the challenge

ANY TEXT dealing with a law enforcement prospectus of past, present, and future borders on what aviators term "high-speed stall-out." Predicting the future from the lessons of history was sane and appropriate until expotential change overpowered many time-honored theories, thus the conclusion that "the future isn't what it used to be!"

Just as the Z-Cop is emerging, so is the role of law enforcement generally, and police-community relations in particular. Certain questions emerge, as noted by Radelet:

> Are the police to be concerned mainly with peacekeeping or with crime fighting?
> Are the police to be blind enforcers of the law or the discretionary agency of a benevolent government?
> Are the police to be social workers with guns or gunmen in social work?
> Are the police to be facilitators of social change or "defenders of the faith"?
> Are the police to be enforcers of the criminal law or society's legal trashbin?
> Are the police to be a social agency of last resort after 5:00 PM, or more watchmen for business and industry?[1]

The renowned American philosopher, Alfred North Whitehead, once said, "Social order is the groundwork of civilization. Without a society in which life and property are secure, existence can continue only at the lowest levels." Social order is the starting point and the essential condition for all human endeavors.

The turbulent history of mankind is replete with war and civil strife. Attempts — internationally, nationally, and locally — to curb this unwanted, despicable curse still seem blessed with only mild success.

Today the United States faces social upheaval and unrest internally and on an international plane. Modern America is a curiously apathetic-affluent society composed of urbanization and depersonalization factors which mold or at least affect every aspect of national endeavor. Productivity in terms of physical products is gigantic, but in certain aspects of man's role, this becomes, ironically, a sociologically consumptive productiveness!

To illustrate this in another way, ask the man on the street what generally he knows about his neighbors; too often he does not even know their names!

---

[1] Louis A. Radelet: *The Police and the Community: Studies.* Beverly Hills, California, Glencoe Press, 1973, p. 288.

This, then, typifies a modern dilemma that further compounds the problems of those who seek greater communion and understanding between fellow human beings.

Law enforcement is, of course, only one factor in this plight of the modern American. Still, it has a tremendous bearing on what the future holds for the police, and we must look to the future today, lest the police function fall further into a gray-shaded enigma tomorrow.

SOCIETY IN TURMOIL

In recent times, the immortality of God was questioned, with various theologians and a whole host of others making a variety of comments pro and con relative to His purported death. Yet, law enforcement has joined many others during the past several years in watching God and many statutes of great importance to law enforcement being legislated out of existence! Thus, the issue of whether or not God is dead might be viewed from either the technical or legalistic point of view. The point is that the social and moral fiber of the nation has much to do with the behavior of its individual citizenry. Even while we lay waste to much that is strong in our American heritage, crime has continued to spiral upward out of all proportion to population growth. Though many persons blame the indicated rise on more accurate statistical reports, there still appears to be a concrete upward trend accelerated, and perhaps stimulated, by increasing restrictiveness on the actions of the police.

That moral decay lies at the root of destruction of many empires is fact, evidenced by countless rhetorical and historical reviews of fallen societies.

Most law enforcement officers view with alarm the losing battle against a decline in morality, as they see it expressed through disregard for laws that, though not founded on moral principles, are also ignored by various social structures' membership met by police. "Victimless Crimes" terminology may be in vogue, but what about the social chaos that erupts when the "nonvictims" consequences create massive peripheral problems, such as Charles Manson?

When young persons seek a career in law enforcement, they view higher crime rates, riots, and revelations that over 10 percent of all peace officers fall victim to a serious assault in a given year, and thus learn something of court decisions that are restrictive to law enforcement; they often turn to other occupational areas. A basic contention of this text is that police-community relations programs can instill greater respect for law and order and perhaps restore order from chaos. If social upheaval and misunderstanding between the police and the people they serve cannot be eliminated, they can be reduced through proper police-community contacts. These same contacts can give the American public a graphic view of their social system and thereby allow them to decide for themselves what is the next appropriate course of action. Team policing offers a path of opportunity, yet only the interaction of the people and the police can cause it to work.

The admonition of Wasserman, Gardner, and Cohen is worthy of note, as it speaks to the issue of police-community relations programs and their lack of *impact without considerable assistance:*

Experience has demonstrated that a community relations program, by itself, will have a minor impact on the police-community relationship. Experience further suggests that the departments with good police-community relationships are those which have instituted a number of basic reforms, the effect of which has been an improvement in the delivery of police services. For example, when a department adopts a training program that improves the skill displayed by its officers when they respond to citizen calls, then respect for the department generally increases. Similarly, when a department adopts forthright policies on such issues as firearms use, citizens' rights, and stop-and-search, then police action generally becomes more acceptable to the community.

There is little hard data to support these observations. In fact, some observers insist that police performance is like a haircut, that nobody notices them unless they are badly done. Even so, a better police department — like a better haircut — is likely to meet with a more favorable reception, despite the fact that the public is unaware of the change.

The question now arises of how a department can implement reforms that will have a positive effect on police/community relations. . . No formula or model program will be presented, because widely differing community compositions result in equally varied problems, expectations, and responses. However, the improvement process in all cases must go through three specific stages:

• The police administrator makes an objective assessment of police/community relations in his city.

• The administrator provides for the coordination of the necessary improvement program — frequently accomplished through the formation of a specialized Community Relations Unit.

• Under the guidance of this central unit, the department adopts methods of police operation that have been proven to be effective and constructive.[2]

The people, through their legislative bodies, make the laws which the police enforce. Law enforcement, as an arm of the executive branch of government, is not in a position to legislate; however, it is remiss when it fails to concretely and forcefully tell the public where a weakening court decision or legislative action is placing the honest and law-abiding citizen in jeopardy.

Social order requires something more than individual freedom. If the police state is undesirable — and it is — so then is a government emasculated of its ability to protect the law-abiding members of its citizenry.

POLICE-COMMUNITY RELATIONS:
AN ART PRACTICED AND REVIEWED

Much remains to be accomplished in the field of police-community relations, and this text has belabored this fact from beginning to end. Yet it is important to re-emphasize that much is being done throughout the nation. If accomplishments are too often disjointed, lacking organization and continuity, and in need of funds and love from a still unsold host of officers; if all this is true, then it still offers hope for tremendous advancement in the immediate future.

The police must accept the concept of police-community relations if they are to create an atmosphere for a more friendly and appreciative public. In defining police-community relations, Radelet noted an important aspect of this concept which is worth repeating: "Generally defined, it means that sum total of the many and varied ways in which it may be emphasized that the police are part of, and not apart from, the communities which they serve."[3]

Infusion with the Community

For law enforcement to become a part of the community stands

---

[2] Robert Wasserman, Michael Paul Gardner, and Alana S. Cohen: *Improving Police/Community Relations.* Washington, D.C., United States Department of Justice, 1973, p. 7.

[3] Louis A. Radelet: "Police Community Programs: Nature and purpose." *Police Chief,* March, 1965, p. 38.

as a vital goal in need of fulfillment. Participation in many community activities is a necessity, but it is "expensive." The monetary costs are tangible and can be determined with great precision; the intrinsic expenses—the time spent to truly convince police and public alike that police-community relations is necessary and desirable—are difficult to assess, yet vital for effectiveness.

Professional Outside Assistance

Many business agencies utilize professional assistance to sell their products. These same "selling" techniques have been applied to law enforcement activities by some policing agencies, with remarkable success. The need to formalize and regularize this type of activity and to have full-time police-community relations units in larger departments received considerable attention recently in the *PR Reporter*: "Basic to public regard, as any PCR professional knows, is a set of plus factors which can be translated effectively to the public through various techniques in such a way that in time public understanding, then acceptance, then enthusiasm result. The plus factors are abundant in big-city police departments, and the need to translate them to the communities involved has never been more obvious, more important, or more understood by police and public than now. Yet barely a handful of America's larger cities maintain PR divisions."[4]

Crisis Revisited

The lessons we have learned from riots and other forms of social turmoil are evidence of the impact with which the twentieth century has descended upon this nation. The important point for law enforcement is that the police must live with the problems of today while they work for certain basic changes they consider desirable and perhaps mandatory.

Crisis areas are more than small problems growing into trauma, then crisis; they involve opinions and factors that exist and lie dormant beneath the surface. The police must recognize the generic aspects of both large and small segments of the problem,

---

[4] "Value of Public Respect for Police Stressed in Special CBS Program, But Citizen Understanding Lags; PR Needed." *PR Reporter,* The Weekly Public Relations Letter, Meriden, New Hampshire, April 4, 1966, p. 2.

then do something to correct the small inequities, as well as deal with overall situations such as certain inglorious aspects of the police heritage along with the need "to be everywhere," when the latter is impossible.

Police Must Organize

The police must organize for an effective program to create a favorable public image and reaction to law enforcement. For example, bifurcation and disassociation of various fraternal and confederation-type adjuncts of law enforcement — internally — can only weaken existing unity. It can lead the resident of any area to wonder, "Just who or what organization speaks for law enforcement?"

The same basic management principles that apply to organizing for any activity apply to law enforcement, but there is a specific need to systematically review the police-community relations function and act accordingly. It has been too often and too long ignored that this "tooling-up" technique has applicability in police-community relations, just as it does elsewhere.

Group Contact

The size and population of a given policing jurisdiction will in large measure determine how many group contacts are to be made. Collectively meeting with group leaders can serve as a starting point for areas without regular group contact. The decision on precisely how to proceed in any given area is subject to the needs of each specific jurisdiction.

Professionalization

The professionalization of law enforcement requires leadership from inside the police agencies of this country. The arguments for and against a particular type of training to assist in this, coupled with the need for adherence to a code of ethics, point to the need for further advancement in these two vital areas of concern.

From a generic point of view, Reiss contributes to an understanding of the dilemma:

> Most attempts to make a profession of police work have led to a professionalization of the police department, to a lesser extent a professionalization of those in staff positions, and only to a relatively minor extent to pro-

fessionalization of the rank and file officer in the line. In stating the
evidence for this conclusion, two arguments [follow]: . . . First, that the
nature of changes within police departments work against the professionalization of the line officer; rather the department is professionalized through
bureaucratization and the line officer becomes, at most, a technician, at the
least a person who is commanded. Second, that changes in the Great Society
work against professionalization of the line, primarily through redefinition
and monitoring of the police role and work . . . the nature of police work
coerces discretionary decision-making in social situations, and . . . both the
ends and means valued by our society require that in the long run at least
part of the line must be "professional".[5]

There are professionals in police work, but police work is not yet
a profession. Police-community relations activities demand that
police work as a profession be a goal of the immediate future, and
this will require assistance and support from the outside, to raise
status and concomitant standards and benefits; most of all, it must
be believed in and accepted as a goal by the great majority of
present-day American police officers.

What Future for Police-Community Relations?

From the standpoint of police-community relations, implementation of various aspects of such programming as has been discussed
throughout this text is considered a way of partially solving the
problems of social disorder created by poor police-community relations. There will continue, however, to be strife, and some will be
caused by outside forces, both identifiable and intangible, inten-
tional and unwitting.

Judge George Edwards presented a veritable "checklist" of seven
areas which offer a course for consideration and, "if the shoe fits,"
adoption by police agencies:

POLICE PROFESSIONALIZATION:
- Forbid use of racial slurs and other "trigger words" by policemen.
- Replace rudeness with good manners, starting with the giving of
  traffic tickets.
- End investigative arrests.
- Ban the use of police dogs in core areas of cities.
- End "alley court" (police punishment).
- Identify troublemakers on the police force and transfer them to non-
  critical jobs.

---

[5] A. F. Brandstatter and Louis A. Radelet: *Police and Community Relations: A Sourcebook.* Beverly Hills, California, Glencoe Press, 1974, p. 215-216.

THE DISCIPLINED USE OF FORCE:
- Set clear standards for the proper use of force.
- Promote the development of more effective, less destructive weapons.
- Press for national and state regulation (including registration) of firearms.
- Train police to deal properly with disturbed persons.

MORE — AND MORE EFFECTIVE — LAW ENFORCEMENT:
- Increase law enforcement in high-crime precincts.
- Devise methods for faster police response.
- Drive out organized crime, paying particular attention to core areas.

EFFECTIVE RACE RIOT CONTROL:
- Maintain steady communications between blacks and the police to insure citizen cooperation in times of trouble.
- Provide for rapid mobilization and deployment of anti-riot forces.
- Meet racial disturbances with well-trained, disciplined, integrated forces in adequate numbers.
- Keep curiosity seekers and known inciters of riots out of trouble areas.
- Set up stand-by arrangements with state and national military forces.

CHANNELS OF COMMUNICATION:
- Organize for day-to-day contact with all sections of the community.
- Deal courteously and cooperatively with potentially hostile organizations.
- Provide for direct staff investigation of complaints from the public, and for final decisions on such complaints by the highest civilian authority in the police department.

ORGANIZING CITIZEN SUPPORT:
Police Initiatives
- Actively seek the cooperation of all citizens for law enforcement, particularly in high-crime areas.
- Make it understood that improved crime control will produce an increase in the number of crimes reported, independent of actual incidence.

Community Initiatives
- Step up community involvement with law enforcement.
- Help police obtain needed financing, manpower, equipment.
- Support programs to overcome young people's hostility against police, and to interest them in police careers.
- Help dispel distorted images of police in the community.
- Seek business backing for programs to counter community tensions.[6]

---

[6] Judge George Edwards: *The Police on the Urban Frontier.* New York, Institute of Human Relations Press, 1968, pp. 39-40.

The police administrator cannot ignore formal police-community relations programming to improve the department and its image with the community. Neither can the individual officer afford to neglect his or her duty to further the profession. This means that police agencies in toto have a vital role to play in improving police-community relations; but it also presents a highly personalized challenge to every working law officer. The eight-hour day may be desirable, but no thinking peace officer, regarding this chosen field of endeavor as something more than a job, can honestly do his/her share unless a considerable amount of "off-duty" time is spent on personal improvement and that of the profession.

Bopp notes the essential elements of an important aspect of yesterday and today:

> The dilemma that historically aware police administrators find themselves facing is this: How do you on the one hand *professionalize* your police department, and on the other improve its relationship with the community, in light of almost overpowering historical data which clearly indicates that as law enforcement has become more professional, the social distance between police and the public has increased, though not necessarily in direct proportion.
>
> A century ago, American law enforcement was characterized by corruption, collusive involvement with criminals, brutality, and political domination. However, policing in the "old days" was characterized by something else, an element that may aptly be termed *social consciousness*, for aside from their traditional enforcement duties, police forces functioned as a kind of social service agency, performing charitable and humanitarian services which would otherwise have gone undischarged. Drunks and indigents were lodged in jail in lieu of arrest. Hundreds of gallons of soup and tons of bread were dispensed to the needy, who twice daily lined up in the rear of the station houses. Christmas food baskets were given to deprived families. Policemen served as parole officers, social workers and youth counselors.[7]

The words of the late President John F. Kennedy offer a course of action to every American: "A man does what he must, in spite of personal consequences, in spite of obstacles and dangers and pressures — and that is the basis of all human morality."[8]

In the final analysis, is this not the choice faced by every present-day and would-be peace officer? To say "yes" is one thing; to believe

---

[7] William J. Bopp, *Police-Community Relationships; An Introductory Under-Graduate Reader*. Thomas, Springfield, 1972. p. ix–x.

[8] John F. Kennedy, Thirty-Fifth President of the United States.

and do something about it is another. Police-community relations cries for the same type of devotee attracted to medicine, or teaching, or to dedicated involvement in high public office.

The challenge is there. The American peace officer of the future can answer this challenge positively and forcefully, but only if each of them worthy of the name "police officer" believes in doing something concrete, and then does it!

Discussion Questions

1. It has been said that mankind's most precious possessions are individual freedom and order in society. Discuss how these two can be maintained concurrently.
2. Why are police-community relations necessary for the maintenance of individual freedom and social order?
3. Discuss the suggestion that police employ professional outside assistance to improve public relations.
4. Many other problems not covered in this chapter will tax police resources and capabilities in the future. Discuss some of the problems you consider of pressing importance.

BIBLIOGRAPHY

Adlow, Elijah: *Policemen and People.* Boston, Massachusetts, William J. Rockfort, 1947.

Ashenhust, Paul H. *Police and the People.* Springfield, Thomas, 1956.

Aubry, Arthur S., Jr.: *The Officer in the Small Department.* Springfield, Thomas, 1961.

Bent, Alan Edward: *The Politics of Law Enforcement.* Lexington, Massachusetts, Lexington Books, Division of D. C. Heath & Co., 1974.

Blake, Eugene Carson: "Should the Code of Ethics in Public Life be Absolute or Relative?" *The Annals of the American Academy of Political and Social Science,* Vol. 363, January 1966.

Bloch, Herbert A. and Frank T. Flynn: *Delinquency.* New York, Random House, 1956.

Bloch, Herbert A. and Gilbert Geis: *Man, Crime & Society,* 2nd ed., New York, Random House, 1970.

Boles, Edmond D.: *The Secret of Public Relations.* Fresno, California, Edmond D. Boles & Associates, 1961.

Bopp, William J., (Ed.): *Police-Community Relationships: An Introductory Undergraduate Reader.* Springfield, Thomas, 1972.

Brown, William P.: *The Police and Community Conflict.* New York, National Conference of Christians and Jews, 1962. Presented at the Eighth Annual National Institute on Police and Community Relations, Michigan State University, May 1962.

Caddell, Walter A.: *Law Enforcement and Police Work.* New York, Record Press Inc., 1957.

Cahill, Thomas J.: "Special Unit Revives Police-Community Relations." *American City,* June 1965.

California Advisory Committee to the United States Commission on Civil Rights, Report on California: *Police-Minority Group Relations,* August 1963.

California Department of Justice, Division of Criminal Law and Enforcement: *Guide to Community Relations for Peace Officers.* Sacramento, California, E. G. Brown, 1958.

California Department of Justice: *Police Training Bulletin.* Sacramento, California, State Printing Office.

Center, Allen H.: *Public Relations Ideas in Action.* New York, McGraw-Hill, 1957.

Clift, Raymond E.: *A Guide to Modern Police Thinking.* Cincinnati, Ohio, Anderson Publishing Co., 1965.

Coffey, Alan R., Edward Eldefonso, and Walter Hartinger: *Police-Community Relations.* Englewood Cliffs, New Jersey, Prentice-Hall, 1971.

Cohn, Alvin W. and Emilio C. Viano: *Police Community Relations: Images, Roles, Realities.* Philadelphia, Pennsylvania, J. B. Lippincott, 1976.

Cromwell, Paul F., Jr., and George Keefer: *Police-Community Relations,* 2nd ed. St. Paul, Minnesota, West Publishing Co., 1978.

Curry, J. E. and Glen D. King: *Race Tensions and the Police.* Springfield, Thomas, 1962.

Cutlip, Scott M. and Allen H. Center: *Effective Public Relations.* Englewood Cliffs, New Jersey, Prentice-Hall, 1962.

Empey, La Mar T.: *Alternatives to Incarceration.* Washington D.C., United States Department of Health, Education and Welfare, Welfare Administration, Office of Juvenile Delinquency and Youth Development, 1967.

Epstein, Charlotte: *Intergroup Relations for Police Officers.* Baltimore, Maryland, Williams & Wilkins, 1962.

Giallombardo, Rose: *Juvenile Delinquency: A Book of Readings.* New York, John Wiley & Sons, 1972.

Gittler, Joseph B.: *Understanding Minority Groups.* New York, John Wiley & Sons, 1956.

Gourley, G. Douglas: *Public Relations and the Police.* Springfield, Thomas, 1963.

Governor's Commission on the Los Angeles Riot: *Violence in the City — An End or a Beginning?* Los Angeles, California, Jeffries Banknote Company, December 2, 1965.

Holcomb, Richard L.: *The Police and the Public.* Springfield, Thomas, 1964.

Holcomb, Richard L.: *Police Patrol.* Springfield, Thomas, 1948.

Hollingsworth, Dan: *Rocks in the Roadway.* Chicago, Illinois, Stromberg Allen & Company, 1954.

Holmgren, R. Bruce: *Primary Police Functions.* New York, William C. Copp and Associates, 1962.

International Association of Chiefs of Police: "The Police and the Community." *Police Chief,* March 1965.

International Association of Chiefs of Police: *Police Community Relations: Policies & Practices.* A National Survey, 1965.

International City Managers Association: *Municipal Police Administration.* Chicago, International City Managers Association, 1961.

Irwin, John: *The Felon.* Englewood Cliffs, New Jersey, Prentice-Hall, 1970.

Jandt, Fred E.: *Conflict Resolution Through Communication.* New York, Harper & Row, 1973.

Jenssen, Ward W.: "Preliminary Image Assessment, Los Angeles County." Special Report, April 24, 1961.

Kenney, John P.: *Police Management Planning.* Springfield, Thomas, 1954.

King, Everett M.: *The Auxiliary Police Unit.* Springfield, Thomas, 1960.

Ladd, Walter D.: *Organizing for Traffic Safety in Your Community.* Springfield, Thomas, 1959.

Laird, Donald A. and Eleanor Laird: *The Technique of Handling People.* New York, McGraw-Hill, 1954.

Lawler, Irvin D.: *A Training Program in Human Relations.* Detroit, Michigan, Detroit Police Department, 1952.

Lemert, Edwon M.: *Instead of Court: Diversion in Juvenile Justice.* Chevy Chase, Maryland, National Institute of Mental Health, Center for Studies of Crime and Delinquency, 1971.

Leonard, V. A.: *The Police of the 20th Century.* Brooklyn, New York, The Foundation Press, 1964.

Lincoln, C. Eric: *The Black Muslims in America.* Boston, Massachusetts, Beacon Press, 1961.

Lohman, Joseph D.: *The Police and Minority Groups.* Chicago, Illinois, Chicago Park District, 1947.

Los Angeles County: *Conference on Community Relations.* Police Relations Committee B'nai B'rith, Anti-Defamation League, Southern California Office. Los Angeles, California, 1950.

Los Angeles Police: *Daily Training Bulletin.* Springfield, Thomas, 1954.

Los Angeles Police: *Institute on Police-Community Relations Race Problems Annual Institute.* National Conference of Christians and Jews, 1957.

Los Angeles Police: *Public Relations Survey.* Los Angeles, LAPD, 1949.

McEntire, Davis and Robert B. Powers: "A Guide to Race Relations for Police Officers." Department of Justice, State of California, 1946.

Merchants and Manufacturer's Association: "Employers Press Relations Manual and Directory." Los Angeles, California, Merchants and Manufacturers Association, January 1960.

Miller, Robert W.: *Profitable Community Relations for Small Business Administration,* 1961.

Milwaukee Police Department: *A Guide to Understanding Race and Human Relations.* Milwaukee, Wisconsin, Police Department, 1951.

National District Attorneys Association: *A Prosecutor's Manual on Screening and Diversionary Programs.* Chicago, Illinois, National District Attorneys Association, 1974.

National Advisory Commission on Criminal Justice Standards and Goals: *Report on Community Crime Prevention.* Washington, D.C., U.S. Government Printing Office, 1973.

National Advisory Commission on Criminal Justice Standards and Goals: *Report on Police.* Washington, D.C., U.S. Government Printing Office, 1973.

Nettler, Gwynn: *Explaining Crime.* New York, McGraw-Hill, 1974.

Newman, Donald J.: *Introduction to Criminal Justice.* Philadelphia, Pennsylvania, J. B. Lippincott Company, 1975.

Nimmer, Raymond T.: *Diversion, the Search for Alternative Forms of Prosecution.* American Bar Foundation, 1974.

Office of the County Counsel: "Joint Report and Review of the Sheriff, District Attorney, County Counsel and Probation Officer of Existing Legislative Program Relating to Amendments to the State Narcotics Law." Los Angeles, California, Office of the County Counsel, December 29, 1960.

Parker, William H., Chief of Police, Los Angeles Police Department. Quoted in *Los Angeles Mirror,* December 22, 1960.

Parker, William H.: *Parker on Police.* Springfield, Thomas, 1957.

Pope, John K.: *A Handbook of Police-Press Relations*. Fresno, California, Academy Library Guild, 1954.

Pope, John K.: *Police-Press Relations*. Fresno, California, Academy Library Guild, 1954.

Public Relations Advisory Group: "Report of the Communications Committee." Los Angeles, California, Los Angeles County Sheriff's Department, September, 1960.

Sacks, David M., Vice-President and General Manager, KGO-TV (San Francisco): "Layman Looks at Lawmen." Address presented to the 67th Annual Conference of the League of California Cities, Police Chiefs Section, San Francisco, California, October 11, 1965.

Scott, Sir Harold: *Scotland Yard*. Tonbridge, Kent, Tonbridge Printers, 1954.

Shaffer, Helen B.: *Negroes and the Police*, Editorial Research Reports.

Siegel, Arthur I. and Roy C. Baker: "Police-Human Relations Training." Prepared for Commission on Human Relations, and the Police Department, City of Philadelphia, by Applied Psychological Services, Wayne, Pennsylvania. Philadelphia, Commission on Human Relations, January 1960.

Siegel, Arthur I., Philip J. Federman, and Douglas G. Schultz: *Professional Police-Human Relations Training*. Springfield, Thomas, 1963.

Skehan, James J.: *Modern Police Work*. New York, Francis M. Basuino Company, 1951.

Smith, Bruce: *Police Systems in the United States*. New York, Harper & Row, 1960.

Stahl, Oscar Glen: *Public Personnel Administration*. New York, Harper & Row, 1962.

Tenth Institute on Police and Community Relations. East Lansing, Michigan, Kellogg Center for Continuing Education, Michigan State University, 1964.

Towler, Juby E.: *The Police Role in Racial Conflicts*. Springfield, Thomas, 1964.

Tunley, Roul: *Kids, Crime and Chaos*. New York, Dell Publishing Company, 1964.

United States Commission on Civil Rights: *Civil Rights U.S.A., Housing in Washington, D.C.*, 1962.

"Value of Public Respect for Police Stressed in Special CBS Program, But Citizen Understanding Lags; PR Needed." *PR Reporter, The Weekly Public Relations Newsletter*, Meriden, New Hampshire, Vol. 9, No. 14, April 4, 1966.

Whisenand, Paul M.: *Crime Prevention*. Boston, Holbrook Press, 1977.

Wilson, O. W.: *Police Administration*. New York, McGraw-Hill, 1950.

Wilson, O. W.: *Police Planning*. Springfield, Thomas, 1952.

Winters, John E.: *Crime and Kids*. Springfield, Thomas, 1959.

Wolfle, Joan L. and Heaphy, John R.: *Readings on Productivity in Policing*. Police Foundation, 1970.

Zeichner, Irving B.: "Human Relations and the Police." *Law and Order*, April, 1956.

Zeichner, Irving B.: "The Police Image." *Law and Order*, August, 1963.

INDEX

A

Activists, 256
"Adhocracy," 256
Administration of law enforcement "blue sky survey" of, 224-26
community crime prevention efforts of, 199-200, 204-205
contact responsibilities of, 92-93
flexibility of, to police community relations, 58, 61-63
and formal juvenile programs, 85
news notification duties of, 98-99
specific police-community relations functions of, 63-69
training for, 118
"Adopt-a-cop," 219
Aerial assistance, 246
Aesthetic appreciation, 260
Affiliation instinct, 136-37
Age groups, in crime surveys, 25-27
"Age of the Riot," 167
Allport, Gordon, 159
Anomie, 146, 249
Anti-crime buses, 197-98
Appearance, 45, 113
Aristotle, 38
Arrest technique training, 114
Atlantic City, 150
Attitude change, 122-23, 125-26
Automobiles. See Traffic citations

B

Bail Reform Act of 1966, 144
Baton usage, 114
Belief systems, 12
Benedict, Ruth, 160
Bennis, Warren, 248
Bent, Alan E., 20
Bilingual programs, 139-40
Balck, Hugo, 157
Balck-Americans. See Minority groups
Blake, Eugene, 33-34
Bloch, Herbert, 32, 109-10
Bopp, William, 276

Brandeis, Louis, 144
Brenner, Harvey, 138, 144
Brougham, Henry Baron, 242
Brownell, Bill, 220-21
Brown v. Board of Education, Topeka, Kansas, 144B
Buddha, Gautama, 264
Burglary prevention, 198-99

C

Cadet training, 111-16
California
burglary prevention programs in, 199
Commission on Peace Officer Standards and Training (POST), 171-72
Crime Resistance Task Force, 196
progressive policing in, 242
State College at Los Angeles, 129.
See also Los Angeles; Ontario, California; Temple City, California
Captial punishment, 202-203
Carzo, Rocco, 136
Center, Allen, 231
Channeling. See Diversion
Chase, Stuart, 137
Chicago, 149
Christ, Jesus, 157-58, 264
Cincinnati, Ohio, 128
Citizen Advisory Committees, 82-83
"Citizen and the Law," 79-80, 126-30
Citizen complaint procedures, 47-48, 90-91, 176-77, 245-46
Citizen-Police Review Boards, 48
Civic Liaison. See Group contacting
Civil disobedience, 15, 50-51, 76, 154-62
Civil disorders. See Demonstrations and protests; Riots
Civil Law Enforcement training, 114
Civil rights, 15, 108. See also Minority groups
Class structure. See Social stratification
Coffeey, Alan, 58-59
Cohen, Alana, 270-71
Cohn, Alvin, 38-39

Colleges and universities, 110-11, 118, 162.
See also names of specific institutions
Common Law, 29
Communication
  between law enforcement and educators, 123-24
  in community crime prevention programs (*see* Community Crime Prevention).
  for conflict resolution, 53
  with minorities and militants, 244
  N.C.C.J. conference proceedings on, 89-90
  role of citizen advisory committees in, 82-83
  stereotyping and generalizations in, 247-48
  technological advances in, 108
  of transcendent personalities, 260.
  See also Public relations; Public speaking
Community Crime Prevention
  basic tenets of, 203-204
  to control burglary and rape, 205
  future of, 205-206
  introduction to, 194-99
  personnel requirements for, 202
  resource allocations for, 199-200
  See also "We Tip"
Community services. *See* Police-Community Relations
Community size, 25-27
Computerization, 246
Conflict resolution, 53
Conformity, 142, 145-46
Conspiracy, 76
Constitution of the United States, 111-12, 156
Corliss, C.P. ("Spud"), 96
Corporal punishment, 246-47
Corrections agencies, 182
Cost effectiveness
  of diversion programs, 189
  of patrol policing, disproved, 212-13
  of police community relations and community crime control, 41, 69-72, 189, 197.
  See also Productivity
Counterculture, 257
Courtroom demeanor, 112
Courts, criticized, 182

Courts of the Star Chamber, 30
CPR. *See* Police-Community Relations
Cressey, Donald, 143
Crime
  "acceptable level" of, 8
  causal approaches to, 145-46
  community control of, 194-99
  fear of, 24, 26-28
  hard-core, 9-11, 198
  impact of unemployment on, 138
  increases in, 108
  police as scapegoats for, 137
  public awareness of, 154, 55
  public surveys of, 22-28
  sociological basis of (*see* Sociology)
Crime prevention and reduction
  in diversion programs, 188-90
  ineffectiveness of police patrols for, 212-13
  and law enforcement cost effectiveness, 7
  through police-community relations, 13-14, 61-63, 218-19
  public's duty in, 194-95 (*see also* "We Tip")
Crime reporting, 22, 38, 71-72, 174-75
Criminals
  childhood behavior of, 122
  "hard-core," 9-11, 198
  labelling of, 189-90
  subcultures of, 145-46, 249-50
Cromwell, Paul, 60, 240
Crowd control training, 114-15

D

Data banks, 173-74
Demonstrations and protests, 14-15, 50-51, 88.
  See also Civil disobedience; Riots
Determinism, 145
Dignity, 263-64
Disaster reporting, 174
Disorderly conduct management, 115
Displays and exhibits, 67, 222
Dissidents, 59-60, 161-62
Diversion programs, 183, 186-91
Domestic complaint management, 115
Drummond, William, 138
Durkheim, Emile, 146

E

Education and training

continuity in, 118-19
as a factor in crime surveys, 25-27
as a factor in riots, 163, 168, 200, 248
and the humanization of the justice
   system, 109
of police, 81, 109-19, 139-40, 233-34.
   See also Colleges and universities; Role
   playing
Edwards, George, 274
Efficiency, 31-32
Eldefonso, Edward, 58-59
Enlightened self-interest, 11
Epstein, Charlotte, 61
Exhibits. *See* Displays and exhibits

F

Family, 142, 186
Feature stories 97-98
Federal government, 41-42, 125, 167-68,
   201-202.
   See also names of specific agencies and
      anti-crime commissions
Ferguson, R. Fred, 139
Field-press relations, 112
Films, training, 218
Folkways, 143
Freedoms Foundation, 80
Free will, 145
Fringe-area youth, 84
Fromm, Eric, 257
Frye, Marquette, 12

G

Gallup, George, polls, 22-28, 154-55
Gambling laws, 51
Gandhi, Mohandas K., 157-58, 264
Gangs, 84, 223
Gardner, Michael, 270-71
Geis, Gilbert, 32, 109-10
God, man's alienation from, 269
Gourley, G. Douglas, 72, 129-30
Grace, Richard, 58-59
Gray, Thomas, 84
Groups
   development of prejudice among, 159-60
   dynamics of, 49-50, 76
   norms of, 142
   and social affiliation, 136-37
   sociology of, 141-42.
   See also Minority groups

Group contacting, 40-41, 64-65, 273, 275
   with adult groups, 77-79
   area-specific training in, 112
   with juvenile groups, 79-80
   through leadership conferences, 85-86,
      exemplified, 86-92
   with minorities, 222-23

H

Harris, Louis, 21
Harrisburg, Pennsylvania, 128
Harter, Donn, 205
Hawaii, community crime control in,
   197-98
Holcomb, Richard, 233-34
Holmes, Oliver Wendell, 248
Home, insecurity in, 24, 27
Homicide prevention, 202-203
Hoover, J. Edgar, 161
Housewives, 129-30
Housing, as a factor in riots, 163, 168,
   201, 248
Human relations, 112-13
Human Side of Enterprise, The
   (McGregor), 257
Humphrey-Hawkins Bill of 1977-1978, 144

I

Image, 20, 28. *See also* Police image
Immobilists, 256
Income, as a factor in crime surveys, 25-27
Indian (subcontinent) independence, 157-
   58
Individual line officers
   discretionary powers of, 230, 232, 235-36
   personal press contacts of, 100
   police-community relations commitment
      needed from, 9, 11-12, 43-47, 52-53,
      169, 243-44, 250-52, Chap. 15
      passim
Industrial relations disputes, 113
Integrity, 263-64
International City Managers Association,
   8-9, 40
Interpersonal relations, utopian revolution
   in, 256-57
Interrogation techniques, 30, 47, 246-47
Irwin, John, 189-90
Isom, James, 122

J

Jandt, Fred, 53
Jesuit Society, 123
Johns Hopkins University, 129
Johnson, Lyndon B., 138, 167-68
Johnson, Samuel, 227
Journal of Transpersonal Psychology, 259
J-teams, 215-16
Juveniles
  delinquent socialization of, 83, 223, 249
  diversion programs for, 185
  police liaison with, 83-85, 218-19
  training for work with, 115

K

Kansas City, Missouri, 212-13
Keefer, George, 60, 240
Kennedy, John, 276
Kenney, John, 110
King, Martin Luther, Jr., 158

L

Labor disputes and slowdowns, 113, 247
Ladd, Walter, 44
Lao-Tzu, 157, 264
Law enforcement
  basic mission of, 15-16, 59
  criticisms of, 182
  data standardization by, 173-74
  emasculation of, 11, 108, 271
  federal grants to, 42
  image of (*see* Police Image)
  future academies for, 251
  historical perspective on, 276
Law enforcement (continued)
  linked to social improvement, 200
  management styles in, 258-59 (*see also*
    Administration of law enforcement)
  organizational unity needed in, 273
  oversight of, 242
  professional ethics of (*see*
    Professionalism)
  public trust in, 6, 20-28 (*See also* Police
    image)
  rapport of, with educators, 123-24
  specialization of, 195-96
  and "the spirit of the law," 235-36
  technological changes in, 246-47
  traditional vs. modernizing approaches
    to, 13-14, 242-43

Law Enforcement Assistance
  Administration, 201
Laws
  inconsistencies in, 51
  sociology of, 143-45
Leadership conferences, 85-86
  example of, 86-92
Leary, Howard, 216
Leavitt, Harold, 76
Legalization, 166
Legal realism, 145
Lenin, Vladimir, 123
Lett, Harold, 161
Levi, Edward, 8
"Liberty under the law," 15-16, 91-92
Lohman, Joseph, 52
London police, 177
Loneliness, 263
Los Angeles
  "Citizen and the Law" in, 79-80, 126-27
  City News Service, 98
  civil service qualifications, 172-73
  gang detail in, 223
  "Law Enforcement Explorer Program"
    of, 83
  McCone Commission in, 12, 168, 248
  Police-Community Relations Institute in,
    81
  police recruitment policies in, 171-72
  public knowledge about police in, 32
  riots in, 12, 166 (*see also* Watts Riot)
  Rumor control Clinic in, 175
  sociological approaches to crime in, 148-
    49
Luther, Martin, 157

M

Mala in se crimes, 13, 59
Mala prohibita crimes, 13, 59. *See also*
  Victimless crimes
Management theory
  authoritarian vs. participative forms of,
    257-58
  in law enforcement, 258-59 (*see also*
    Administration of law enforcement)
  theory Z of, 259-61
Manpower shortages, 48-49
Manson, Charles, 269
Maslow, Abraham, 259
Mass communications media

equal treatment of, 97, 99
official policy toward, 102-104
and the police image, 99
press passes issued to, 101-102
regualr contact with, 67-68, 100-101, 217-18
releases to, 65-66, 97-98
scoops for, 99.
See also entries beginning with "Press"
Mayo, Elton, 136
McCone Commission, 12, 168, 248
McGregor, Douglas, 257-58
Michigan State University, 124
Military deployment for riot control, 168-69
Milton, John, 241
Minority groups
communication and contact with, 60-61, 112, 222-23, 244-45
criticisms of police by, 46, 182
fear of crime among, 24-27
and police image, 21, 60-61
recruitment of police from, 171-73, 214-15
sterotyping and defamation of, 158-62, 247-48
Mobility
of populations, 143
through social classes, 147-48
Momboisse, Raymond, 9
Monism, 260
Moral decadence, 269
Mores, 143
Moss, Forrest, 203-204
"Most esteemed officer" program, 117-18
Motion pictures, 218
Municipal Police Administration ((ICMA), 30

N

Narcotics offenders
citizen action programs against, 220-21
diversion programs for, 186-87
trafficking and addiction of, 198
National Advisory Commission on Civil Disorders, 11, 38, 41-42, 46, 150, 167-68, 211, 248
National Advisory Commission on Criminal Justice Standards and Goals for the Criminal Justice System, 184, 194, 248

National Commission on the Causes and Prevention of Vilence, 168, 195
National Conference of Christians and Jews (NCCJ), 85
Seventh Annual Institute on Police and Community Relations, 86-92
The Hotline, 103
National Institute of Law Enforcement and Criminal Justice, 168
National Institute on Police-Community Relations, 41-42
National League of Cities, Department of Urban Studies, 13, 211, 224-26, 245-46
National Opinion Research Center (NORC), 21
National Police Week, 222
Nettler, Gwynn, 71
New Left Movement, 161
Newman, Donald, 188
News clipping service, 66
Newspaper industry, 96. *See also* Mass communications media
New York City Police Department
established, 30
precinct service officers in, 216
School liaison programs of, 124
sociological crime control in, 148
New Zealand, 215-16
Nichols, John, 108-109
Nimmer, Raymond, 184
Nonconformists, 61. *See also* Dissidents
Nonlethal weaponry, 246
Nonviolent protest. *See* Civil disobedience
Norman Conquests, 29

O

Occupation, as a factor in crime surveys, 25-27
Office of Law Enforcement Assistance, 42
Ombudsman, 251
Ontario, California Citizen Action Program, 220-21
Oppenheimer, J. Robert, 248
Organizations. *See* Groups
Ostrow, Ronald, 8
Outdoor advertising, 222
Overcriminalization, 190

P

Parker, William, 31-33

Parole, 183
Passive resistance. *See* Civil disobedience
Patrols, 47, 212-213
Peace officers. *See* Police
Peak experiences, 260
Personality, transcendent vs.
  nontranscendent forms of, 259-61
Personal appearance, 45, 113
Personnel (staffing) shortages, 48-49, 108,
  125, 202. *See also* Resource shortages
Pfiffner, John, 140
Photography, 66-67
Physical control, 46-47, 275. *See also*
  Police brutality
Plea bargaining, 183
Police
  advisory groups to, 81-83
  apprentices and cadets, 111-16, 214
  attitudes of, 30, 43 (*see also* Z-cop
    subentry below)
  courtesy, 44-45, 246
  education and training of, 81, 109-19,
    139-40, 233-34
  etymology of, 29
  isolation of, 49-50, 139-41
  job actions by, 247
  job satisfaction among, 240
  as middlemen, 88, 140
  patrol procedures for, 47, 212-13
  power maintenance function of, 60
  public speaking by (*see* Public speaking)
  public trust in, 6, 20-28 (*see also* Police
    image)
  recruitment of, 171-73, 214-15, 269-70
  reserve groups of, 80-81
  support services of, 39, 61
  as symbols, 61, 169-70
  violent attacks on, 38
  Z-cop vision of, 261-63
  See also Group contacting; Individual
    line officers
Police brutality, 29-31, 46-47, 109-10, 176-
  77, 246
Police chiefs. *See* Administration of law
  enforcement
Police-community relation 5, 7-9, 271
  after working hours, 276
  and the causes of riots, 163, 168, 201
  contemporary problems in, 210-11
  cost effectiveness of, 41-69-72, 189, 197,

212-13
  education and training for, 68, 110-19
  escalation of antagonisms in, 38-39
  future of, 16, 274-77
  headquarters function of, 63-64
  and the "human climate," 213-14
  importance of continuity in, 68, 226-27
  with juveniles, 83-85, 185, 218-19
  need for, 6-7, 241-42, 270-72
  preventive powers of, 72-169-77, 232-33,
    272-73
  specific programs in, 214-26
  ultimate role of, 63
  Watson's code of, 243-44.
  See also Public relations
Police Community Relations Institute, 81
Police Image, 20
  depersonalization of, 31-32, 231
  determinants of, 28-29
  obstacles to the improvement of, 33
  and the press, 65-66, 99, 103
  racial differences in, 32
  and the socioeconomic background of
    officers, 32
Police Foundation, 71-72
Policemanship. *See* Professionalism
Political parties, as a factor in crime
  surves, 25-27
Police-review boards, 242
Population mobility, 109
Powell, Leonard, 148-50
Power maintenance function, 60
Pre-crime program, 196
President's Commission on Law
  Enforcement and Administration of
  Justice, 9, 14, 38, 42, 43-44, 46, 51,
  62, 124, 137, 175, 183, 248
Press boards, conferences, passes, policy,
  and rooms, 100-104. *See also* Mass
  communications media
Prejudice, 158-62
Prevention
  of riots, 167, 169-78 passim, 232-33,
    272-73.
  See also Crime prevention
Prisoner interviews, 103
Probation, 183
Productivity. *See* Cost effectiveness
Professionalism, 273-74
  in attitudes, training and experience, 44-

47, 113, 233-34
conflict of, with community relations,
    276
philosophy of, 234-36
Watson's police-community relations
    code of, 243-44
of the Z-cop, 263-64
Public
    belief modification among, 246
    community crime control duties of, 33-
        34, 194-99
    complaints against pplice by, 47-48, 90-
        91, 176-77, 245-46
    confidence and trust of, in police, 6, 20-
        28 (*see also* Police image)
    incidence of criminality in, 9-11
    inculcation of law enforcement
        ' philosophy in, 251-52, 275-76
    need for civic vigilance by, 38
    survey of urban issues among, 28, 154-55
    traffic violations of, 33, 44, 114, 231,
        246
Public Law 89-465, 144
Public relations, 216-17, 230-32, 272.
    See also Police image
Public Relations and the Police (Gourley),
    32
Public speaking, 43-44, 68, 101, 112-13,
    216-17

Q

Quinney, Richard, 39, 177, 230

R

Race. *See* Minority groups
Radelet, Louis, 240, 268, 271
Rank unconsciousness, 263
Reagan, Ronald, 162
Recruitment, 171-73, 214-15, 269-70
Regional differentiation, in crime surveys,
    25-27
Reiss, 273
Religious differentiation, in crime surveys,
    25-27
Resources
    allocated for community crime control,
        199-200
    for diversion programs, 187-89
    shortages of, 125 (*see also* Personnel
        shortages)

Response time, 48-49, 246
Richardson, Elliot, 200
Riots
    causes of, 11-12, 39-40, 51, 163, 168,
        200-201, 248
    control of, 168-69, 173-74, 275
    historical perspective on, 166
    incident reporting during, 174
    investigatory commissions on, 167-68 (*see
        also* names of specific commissions)
    prevention of, 167, 169-78 passim, 232-
        33, 272-73
    rumor control in, 175-76
Role-playing, 115-16

S

Sacred appreciation, 260-61
Safe Streets and Crime Control Act of
    1968, 42
St. Paul, 241
Schoepenhauer, Arthur, 123
Schools
    lack of law enforcement programs in,
        122-24
    police contact with, 84, 124-25, 219.
    See also "Citizen and the Law"
Scott, Harold, 66
Scout groups, 83-84
Service functions, 61
Sexual differentiation, in crime surveys,
    25-27
Skolnick, Jerome, 84, 251
Smith, Bruce, 33
Social change, 160
    and the changing role of law
        enforcement,
        108-10, 248
    inevitability of, 256
    in the 1960s, 259
Social control, 142-43, 147-48
Social jurisprudence, 145
Social order, 15-16, 59, 91-92, 268
Social stratification, 32, 146-48, 160
Social turmoil, 269-70
    conference on, 86-92
    utopian psychology of, 256.
    See also Demonstrations and protests;
        Riots
Sociologgy, 141
    in crime prevention, 52, 148-50, 173-74

and forces beyond police control, 58-59
  of small groups, 141-42
Solomon, 123
Suburban crime, 22
Subversion and sabotage, 59-60, 161-62
Success criteria. *See* Cost effectiveness
Supreme Court, U.S.A., 11, 108
Surveys
  of police administrators' utopias, 224-26
  of police image, 20-22
  of police-school liaisons, 124
  of public attitudes toward police, 30,
    129-30
  of public knowledge of police duties, 32
  of urban issues, 28, 154-55.
  See also Crime reporting
Sutherland, Edwin, 143

T

Tamm, Quinn, 16, 235
Tampa, Florida Citizen Action Program,
  220-21
Tannenbaum, Frank, 190
Taoism, 261. *See also* Lao-Tzu
Taylor, Steve, 139
Teachers
  attitudes toward police of, 129-30
  leadership role of, 125-26, 129
Technological advances
  in mass communications, 96, 108
  in police work, 246-47
Telephone demeanor, 45-46
Temple City, California, 79-80
"Third degree" interrogations, 30
Thoreau, Henry David, 157-58
"TIP" project, Tampa, Florida, 220
Torture, 246-47
"Total Immersion Spanish Language
  Program," 139
Tours, 68-69
Towler, Juby, 15
Traffic citations issuance, 33, 44, 114, 231,
  246
Training. *See* Education and Training
Travis, Edmunds, 96

Trojanowicz, John, 203-204
Trojanowicz, Robert, 203-204
Turk, Austin, 166
Twain, Mark, 96

U

Un-crime programs, 196
Unemployment
  and crime, 138
  and riots, 163, 168, 200-201, 248
United States of America
  apathy and depersonalization in, 268
  sociology of law in, 143-45.
  *See also names of specific American
    institutions*
University of California at Davis, 139
University of Southern California, 87
Urban crime, 22

V

Verbal abuse and harassment, 43-44
Viano, Emilio, 38-39
Victimless crimes, 13, 115, 198, 269. *See
  also Mala prohibita* crimes

W

Washington, D. C., 149-50, 249
Wasserman, Robert, 270-71
Watson,   , 243-44
Watts riot, 39-40, 167, 175, 241
Weapons, 48, 246
"We TIP," 220-21
Whisenand, Paul, 69-70
Whitehead, Alfred North, 268
Wilde, Oscar, 96, 210

Y

Yanouzas, John, 136

Z

Z-cop
  professionalism of, 263-64
  as a transcendent breed, 261-62
Zoot Suit Riots of W.W. II, 223